RIVER OF CONFLICT, RIVER OF DREAMS

A gift from the
SAINT PAUL RIVERFRONT CORPORATION

Made possible by
Pat & Christee Donovan.

GRAND EXCURSION 2004™

RIVER OF CONFLICT, RIVER OF DREAMS

Three Hundred Years on the Upper Mississippi

by Biloine Whiting Young

ISBN 1-880654-30-x

Book design and typesetting by Percolator.

Cover design by Mighty Media.

PHOTOGRAPHIC AND OTHER CREDITS

Floyd Risvold, for the front cover photograph and the images at pages 5, 150, 155, 163, 167 and 223

Frank Harris, for the photograph at page 261

Minnesota Historical Society for the photographs at pages 49, 133, 140, 151, 153, 159, 186, 251 and 268

St. Paul Riverfront Corporation, for the image at page 190

Grand Excursion, Inc. for the map at page 2

Pogo Press, Incorporated, for the title page illustration and the images at pages 16, 30, 33, 125 and 173

James L. Stokes for the photograph at page 115

Gregory Page for the images at pages 82, 83, 137, 138, 250 and 265

Minneapolis Institute of Arts for the photograph at page 202

Title page illustration of St. Paul is from Laurence Oliphant, *Minnesota and the Far West* (1855).

Cover is based on a photograph of a steamboat race in 1896.

Printed in Canada

CONTENTS

PREFACE

The Mississippi River has been a source of inspiration for poets, artists, scholars, capitalists and politicians. It has also recently inspired cities seeking to regenerate themselves. Once separated from their riverfronts, cities are, quite literally, turning back to the water. Like living organisms growing roots to a source of nourishment, cities along the entire stretch of the upper Mississippi River are finding new ways of reconnecting to the Father of Waters.

Saint Paul has been on the leading edge of this movement. In the early 1990s, with the strong advocacy of its then new, young, and energetic mayor, Norm Coleman, Saint Paul's leadership declared a new vision. Saint Paul would be a city of vitality, prosperity and optimism. And the center of that vision would be a revitalized Mississippi River.

Long abandoned, oft polluted, and ever ignored, the Mississippi River was suddenly offered celebrity status. Once thought of as the neighborhood troublemaker, the Mississippi has become a Hollywood star. In its name, town hall meetings were held, the *Saint Paul Pioneer Press* and the *Star Tribune* editorialized, leading community foundations endowed, corporate executives rallied, and elected officials campaigned. And the investment community invested.

It was decided that the river would no longer be a detriment to city life. Once fouled by pollution, it would become home to competitive fishing events. Once flood prone, new parks, green space, and trails would be built with the difficulties caused by high water in mind. No longer a divider of neighborhoods, its bridges would be designed as extensions of neighborhood streets.

And the Mississippi River, at the core of Saint Paul's proud past, would become central to its future. Mayor Coleman clearly understood the long-term commitment necessary to ensure such a transformation. He and other leading thinkers such as Dick Broeker, former Saint Paul deputy mayor; Mike O'Keefe of the McKnight Foundation; Paul Verret of The Saint Paul Foundation, and others, established an organization to

1

steward, advance, and promote this vision. In this way the Saint Paul Riverfront Corporation was born. It would become the conduit through which the community's energy would be channeled.

Together with such partner organizations as the Saint Paul Port Authority, the City of Saint Paul, the Capital City Partnership, and the West Side Citizens Organization, the *Saint Paul on the Mississippi Development Framework* was created. The community's passion for the Mississippi River was codified. At the same time a ten-year time horizon was dedicated. A decade of commitment, it was said, would be necessary to begin the change. By 2004 we would see a difference.

Next, a tongue-in-cheek idea emerged. Why not use the 150th anniversary of obscure President Millard Fillmore's even more obscure

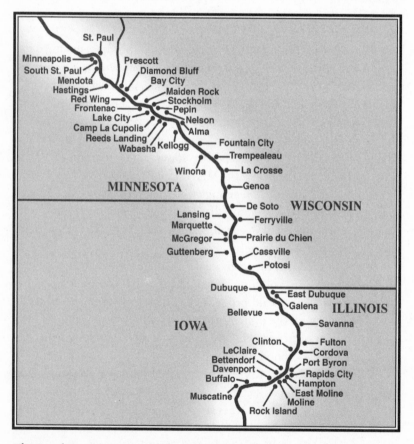

The Grand Excursion 2004 map shows towns in the four states bordering the Upper Mississippi River. Courtesy of Grand Excursion, Inc.

1854 visit to Saint Paul as an occasion to celebrate riverfront progress? A re-creation of President Fillmore's Grand Excursion, barely a footnote in American history, could be the rallying cry for Saint Paul. We thought this would be our opportunity. Let us focus the community's attention and energy on restoring Saint Paul's relationship to the Mississippi River, use 2004 as a deadline, and celebrate successes. Let us properly welcome people to our riverfront, whether they come on land or arrive by water as they did in 1854.

The Saint Paul Riverfront Corporation's annual dinner would also carry President Fillmore's name. Soon the Millard Fillmore Dinner, began in a small way in 1995, grew to become *the* annual town dinner. Now each May a sell-out crowd of 1,600 gathers to learn about progress on and the promise of the Mississippi River. They leave each year energized for the year ahead.

The story of Saint Paul's riverfront revitalization effort is unfinished. However the plot is set, the earliest scenes are written, and many characters have already played a role. The story is unfolding. And the star is the Mississippi River itself.

Patrick Seeb, President,
Saint Paul Riverfront Corporation

INTRODUCTION

Mark Twain forever planted the Mississippi River in the national consciousness. Along with the Rocky Mountains, the Mississippi is the geological feature that defines North America. Thanks to Twain, generations of Americans have dreamed of sailing down the great river and a surprising number of them have actually done it. Writers who take the river as their topic find themselves unwittingly imitating Twain—whose accounts are still the "last word" on the Mississippi. The Mississippi described by Twain was largely the middle and lower river, that portion of the steam than flows past his Hannibal, Missouri, home and on down to the Gulf.

There is another, more robust section of the river called the Upper Mississippi. This section flows between bluffs that early visitors likened to castles on the Rhine or the palisades of the Hudson. Here the river tumbles over the only waterfall on its entire twenty-five hundred mile length and, flowing south, widens into Lake Pepin like an aneurysm on a massive artery.

Carte de visite photograph of Falls of St. Anthony. Large building in distance is Winslow House, built 1856–7. Courtesy of Floyd Risvold.

I have spent most of my life on the watershed of this section of the river. Our family album has a photograph of me as a ten-year-old tip-toeing over the rocks that span the stream at the headwaters. Performing such a feat in the late 1930's conferred significant bragging rights in the elementary schools of the Midwest.

From the beginning of human settlement, the Upper Mississippi River has been the defining fact in the lives of those who lived near it. Pioneer communities conducted love affairs with the river. How a town related to the river determined if it would thrive or soon fade away.

The river belonged to everyone, and everyone used it. Lumbermen floated logs to the mills, steamboats opened up the Northwest Territory, settlers selected river town-sites, the founders of Minneapolis used the river to power their lumber and flour mills.

Other uses of the river were more problematic. Clammers dredged the river for clams until there were no more. Every town on the Mississippi used the river to dispose of its untreated, raw sewage. Shippers dredged the channel and then dredged it again. When a still deeper channel was called for, the Corps of Engineers built the dams that transformed the Upper Mississippi from a flowing stream into a series of twenty-seven pools connected by locks. Wing dams narrowed the river. A narrowed river flows faster and floods more often. Destructive floods came every few years.

When the river changed, so did attitudes toward it. When people thought of the river at all, it was as an enemy, a threat, a troublesome obstacle to be overcome. The river lost its commanding position at the heart of community life. One by one towns turned their backs to the stream that had been the reason for their founding. Residents who once studied the flowing water of the river with the concentration Minnesotans devote to the weather, let the memory of the river slip away from them.

Now a new story is unfolding as communities have learned that the route to civic renewal leads back to the banks of the river. The return to the Mississippi resurrects old unanswered questions. How can we best use this great river? How do we reconcile the conflicting demands on its waters? And whose river is it anyway?

The shipping industry needs a deep channel for its barges but high water destroys the plants the waterfowl depend on. Recreational boaters crowd the river with powerful cruisers that erode the river banks and make it difficult for commercial fishermen to set their nets. Pollutants still flow into the river from sewers and these are sickening fish and killing the remaining mussels. Fertilizers used by farmers seep into the river and cause algae to bloom, depleting the oxygen in the river. Environmentalists, concerned for the waterfowl and migratory birds, want a river returned to an approximation of its natural state while commercial interests want a twelve-foot channel and longer locks. Biologists warn of an ecosystem collapse.

Questions about the use of the river hover like morning fog over the water. The questions matter because the Upper Mississippi flows through more than the four states of Minnesota, Wisconsin, Iowa and Illinois. It flows through our imaginations, through our songs, our art, our stories, our history—through our ambitions for the future of the Upper Midwest. Our lives are as entangled with the Mississippi as are the roots of the trees on the river's banks.

This is the story of much that has happened on the waterway of the Upper Mississippi. The story has not ended and the big questions remain to be answered.

Books are not created by authors alone. The following are among the many who provided information and assistance: Kathy Wine, of River Action, Inc., Davenport; William Meissner and Don Wiederaenders, archivist-historians at the Mississippi River Museum, Dubuque; Mark Peterson and Walt Bennick, director and archivist at the Museum of Winona; Char Mason, Riverfront Corporation; Jean Schmidt, librarian for the Corp of Engineers; John Anfinson, National Park Service; Captain William Bowell, Padelford Packet Boat Company, Harriet Island; Mary Anne Collins-Svoboda, Stockholm; Mary Flicek, Wabasha Area Chamber of Commerce; Teri Goodman, Mississippi River Museum, Dubuque; Robert Taunt, of La Crosse, who gave me a private tour of the artifacts remaining from the *War Eagle;* Eunice Schlichting, Putnam Museum of History, Davenport; Amy Groskop, Davenport Public Library; Mary Dejulio, Prairie du Chien historian; Dallas Valley, Mike Valley and Ted Sheckler, of Prairie du Chien; Wayne Hammer of Hammer Lumber; Anita Doering, archivist, La Crosse Historical Society; Sheila Bosworth, Princeton; Dorothy Hill, Deer Island; Mary Beth Garrigan, director of the National Eagle Center, Wabasha, who introduced me to James L. Stokes of Eau Claire and Curt Campbell of Welsh; Lee Nelson, Upper River Services, St. Paul; Krista Grueninger of Heartland Boating; Robin Young who bought his mother a laptop so she could better take notes in libraries; Marcia Aubineau who gave editing advice; Charlie Maguire, formerly the singing ranger of the National Park Service; Merve Hough and Leaetta Hough-Dunette for their rapid-response creative team, and Tom Trow for the final wording of the title.

My special thanks go, also, to the Minnesota Humanities Commission for their grant in support of my research.

Finally, special recognition is due the Riverfront Corporation of St. Paul, originator of the Millard Fillmore dinner and the re-creation of the Grand Excursion. The Corporation, through its Board of Directors and Executive Director Patrick Seeb, promoted the idea that the entire Upper Mississippi region should jointly participate in forging new relationships with the waterway. Encouraged by the Corporation, all of the communities of the Upper Mississippi have developed connections of their own with the river, undertaken ambitious projects and forged new partnerships with each other—united by the great river that runs through them all.

Biloine Whiting Young
St. Paul, Minnesota
January 15, 2004

CHAPTER 1

The River

Down the Yellowstone, the Milk, the White and Cheyenne;
The Cannonball, the Musselshell, the James and the Sioux;
Down the Judith, the Grand, the Osage, and the Platte,
The Skunk, the Salt, the Black and Minnesota;
Down the Rock, the Illinois, and the Kankakee
The Allegheny, the Monongahela, Kanawha, and Muskingum;
Down the Miami, the Wabash, the Red and Yazoo—
Down the Missouri, three thousand miles from the Rockies;
> *Down the Ohio, a thousand miles from the Alleghenies;*
Down the Arkansas, fifteen hundred miles from the Great Divide;
> *Down the Red, a thousand miles from Texas;*
Down the great Valley, twenty-five hundred miles from Minnesota,
> *Carrying every rivulet and brook, creek and rill,*
Carrying all the rivers that run down two-thirds the continent—
> *The Mississippi runs to the Gulf.*

> –Pare Lorentz, from the film *The River*, produced
> in 1937 for the Federal Resettlement Administration,
> as part of the second phase of the New Deal.

The Mississippi River is so small, at its beginning. Seeping out of a marsh of sumac and tamarack—a trickle of water flows over sand and grasses that dip and bend in the flow as if to show the hesitant water which way to go. Only inches deep, too shallow for fish, the stream looks like any other in this north country of bogs and brooks. Water is everywhere—in the lakes and swamps—and this gently moving stream with watercress growing on its banks looks no different from a thousand others. But it is. This straggly creek is the unprepossessing beginning of one of the fabled rivers of the world.

Rivers have a logic-defying aura about them. Lakes are easier to understand. Water in a lake comes from streams and underground springs. But where does all of the water in a great river come from? Why does it not eventually run out? Tens of millions of gallons of water rush past a point of land hour after hour, day after day, century after century—in a global recycling process that circulates water from oceans to sky to land over and over again in a colossal, cosmic connection. If great rivers are natural wonders of the world—the Mississippi is foremost among them.

The headwaters of the Mississippi are enshrined in a park, called Itasca, after the lake from which it flows. A wood signpost marks the starting point of the river's long journey to the sea. On that signpost is the statement, "Here 1475 ft. above the ocean the mighty Mississippi begins to flow on its winding way 2552 miles to the Gulf of Mexico." Water from Itasca will take 60 days to reach the Gulf. Generations of visitors have had their pictures taken at this spot, posing with a hand on the marker or balancing on the rocks that span the stream. Some take off their shoes and wade into the water as if to enter into a personal relationship with this rivulet—the benign beginning of a river that has sunk a thousand boats, inspired artists and poets and, for two hundred years, was the storied highway into America's frontier.

Once it leaves Lake Itasca, the infant Mississippi runs through forests of Norway pine, sugar maples, birch and poplar toward the north and east for 100 miles before turning south, as if unsure which direction it is destined to go. The stream does not remain unassertive for long. By the time it has coursed the thirty miles to Bemidji it is flowing at a rate of one hundred cubic feet a second. At Grand Rapids, the pace picks up to a thousand cubic feet every second. Yet it is still a wilderness stream, flowing past only two towns in its first two hundred miles.

Charles Lanman, a painter and journalist, wrote of the Mississippi in 1847, "When it leaves this lake [Itasca] it is only about 20 feet wide but after passing through a number of lakes it spreads itself out to the width of 150 feet. This portion of the Great River might well be likened to the infant Hercules, for it is the master of everything around it and rambles onward as if conscious of its dawning power."

Flowing through Lake Bemidji the Mississippi continues east, entering first Cass Lake and then Lake Winnibigoshish where the river reaches its northernmost point—only 87 miles from Canada. Here its bed is a broad savanna, from 1,000 to 5,000 feet wide, filled with reeds and fields of wild rice and iris through which the channel wanders leisurely from bank to bank. Finally the river circles south, blocked from emptying into Lake Superior by the Mesabi Iron Range. By the time the river reaches Crow Wing it has meandered 375 miles, yet is only 75 miles—as a bird flies—from its beginnings in Lake Itasca.

From Aitkin the adolescent Mississippi flows purposefully south, no longer the docile stream finding its way through basswood forests and sedge marshes. The bluffs bordering the river are from 20 to 60 feet high. The current runs swiftly, passing over a succession of rapids and ripples as if in anticipation of its plunge—now more like a tumble— over the cataract of St. Anthony. Here the river widens from 675 feet above to over a thousand feet wide below the falls. Once in the 80-mile loop through the Twin Cities of Minneapolis and St. Paul the mature river flows at more than seven thousand cubic feet of water per second. The river has dropped almost 900 feet in its 600-mile journey from its Itasca source.

Visitors to the headwaters see a stream far different from the one described by Henry Schoolcraft when he reached the source of the Mississippi on July 13, 1832. Schoolcraft described the stream running out of the lake as "perhaps ten to twelve feet broad with an apparent depth of 12 to 18 inches." The present stream is a domesticated one, its wildness gone, its waters blocked by a concrete dam faced with a pathway of rocks.

Nature did not change the stream, man did. In the early 1930's Itasca's park management decided that the modest trickle seeping out of the swampy marsh at the end of the lake was an unworthy beginning for the mythic Mississippi. How, they wondered, could visitors be enticed to visit the park to look at *that* paltry flow? Was not the Mississippi worthy of something more impressive than this humble beginning?

Park authorities determined to improve upon nature. In the 1930's, working with technical support from the National Park Service, the Civilian Conservation Corps began to change the river. First they brought in soil to fill in the surrounding swamps and confine the river to a narrow, well-defined channel. Then they built a concrete dam to control the flow out of Lake Itasca and covered the dam with boulders to give visitors a natural-looking path on which to walk across the Mississippi. To complete the scene they planted trees, grouping them to produce a visually pleasing effect along the riverbank.

The Ojibwe called the lake that was the source of the Mississippi "Omushkos Sagaeigun" meaning Elk Lake because the branches of the lake resembled the horns of an elk. The French translated it into Lac La Biche. Schoolcraft had other ideas. As he was canoeing with the Rev. William T. Boutwell, his companion on the search for the river's source, he turned to him and remarked," I would like to give a name to Elk Lake that will be significant or expressive, as the head or true source of the Mississippi. Can you give me any word in Latin or Greek that will convey the idea?"

The nearest Boutwell could come were the Latin words, "Veritas Caput—true head." A few minutes later Schoolcraft exclaimed, " I have got the thing." He handed Boutwell a piece of paper on which he had written the word "Itasca." As Schoolcraft later described it, "This lake is about 7 miles long, having somewhat the shape of the letter Y. It has clear water and pleasant woody shores."

For fifty years following Schoolcraft's discovery few visited the headwaters. Schoolcraft, himself, did not linger but departed the same day downriver for Fort Snelling. Then, in 1888, the Minnesota Historical Society sent historian Jacob V. Brower to Itasca to map the headwaters area. He camped there for five months and conceived the idea of making Itasca a state park. At his own expense, Brower kept the idea alive until the legislature, in 1901, passed a bill authorizing the park but not before lumber interests, which opposed it, succeeded in tacking on an amendment stating that the salary of the new park commissioner would run out in 60 days.

Undaunted, Brower took the job anyway and worked to create the land for the park, eventually acquiring 10,870 acres, one third of its eventual size. In 1895 authorities replaced Brower with a political appointee and Brower spent the rest of his life trying to stop lumbering in the park. Minnesota's attorney general expressed the prevailing attitude when he said that purchasing standing pine in Itasca to preserve it "would be an idle waste of money." Brower lost his fight. Over his objections, roads were built in Itasca and a logging dam, called a boom, was constructed, flooding the trees on the shores of the lake. Brower never was paid for his four years of service at the park.

The new park commissioner was Jonathan Puckett Gibbs. When he died in 1903 Minnesota governor Samuel R. Van Sant appointed Gibbs' 24-year-old daughter, Mary, to take her father's place, making her the first female park commissioner in the United States. Not many public officials were clamoring for a post in the mosquito-ridden north woods. Mary soon faced the test of her career. Lumbermen were cutting logs at Itasca and their dam on the Mississippi, located a quarter mile below the river's outlet, was flooding water into the park.

When spring came to Itasca that first year of Mary's tenure, water rose higher and higher behind the boom. By early April loggers had cut and floated nine million board feet of lumber to the dam. Water was backing up and, according to Mary, it was "flooding the shorelines of Itasca and Elk Lake to the great damage of growing trees, tamarack forests, meadows, creeks and camping resorts."

As park commissioner Mary believed she had to act. On April 12, taking Itasca neighbor Theodore Wagmann with her, Mary went to the lumber camp and asked M.A.Woods, the company foreman, to open the dam gates to prevent the water "from criminally damaging park property." Woods refused. Mary left but returned on April 15 to repeat her request. Again Woods turned her away.

On April 16, this time accompanied by more neighbors and with Constable Heinzelman to serve a warrant, Mary came back and for the third time confronted the foreman, demanding that he lower the water level behind the dam. When Woods refused, she asked the constable to serve the warrant. Heinzelman stepped forward, warrant in hand, but stopped when Woods pulled a pistol out of his pocket and aimed it at Heinzelman's chest. The two men stared at each other for a long moment. Then the constable stepped back and handed the warrant to Mary.

If she were to protect Itasca Mary would have to act. Stepping past Heinzelman she reached the mechanism that opened the sluiceway. " I'll shoot anyone who puts a hand on those levers," shouted the lumber company foreman. Ignoring Woods, Mary firmly grasped the sluiceway lever. "I will put my hand there and you will not shoot it off either," she declared. She was right. Woods did not fire. Gibbs was not sure how long she stood there on the muddy dam, grasping the lever. She did know that her action was purely symbolic. "I could not raise the gates," she later confessed, "as it took six men to do that."

When the lumber company found it could not intimidate Mary at gunpoint it went to court. Though flooding the park "forcibly violated" the law in "a criminal manner," the timber men's lawyers obtained a court order keeping Mary Gibbs away from the dam site. She appealed to Minnesota's attorney general and a week later he lifted the injunction

—as well as the gates to the dam. "The sheriff arrived . . . and lowered the water from 3 feet down to 18 inches, " Mary wrote with satisfaction.

The conflict between Mary Gibbs and the lumber foreman revealed in a single isolated incident opposing visions for the use of the Mississippi River—a schism that persists to the present day. Though they may not have realized it at the time, both Mary Gibbs and Woods were in agreement on one point—that the river should be put to use. Mary held that the river should be used primarily for recreation. The lumber foreman maintained that the river was there to serve the timber industry. Both, however, accepted what to them was as inevitable and natural as sunlight—the Biblical injunction to subdue the earth and put it to use. The Mississippi was to be subdued and its waters used. Manifest Destiny was in the air they breathed.

GEOLOGY OF THE RIVER

The Mississippi River was born over a period of time so vast the mind grows numb contemplating it. The parents of the great river are the two ranges of mountains that flank it. The older parent is the Appalachians, the eastern range of mountains that sends waters flowing west. The other parent is the younger range, the Rockies. When—millions of years ago—the Rockies began their thrust skyward water raining down on the slopes cascaded to the east. As a result the land between the ranges, the great midsection of the continent, tilts inward toward its middle down which the river flows along some geologic centerline.

Water dripping from a leaf in Western Pennsylvania, rain pelting down from cloudbursts in Colorado and water bubbling up from underground Ozark springs—all flow inexorably toward the valley of the Mississippi. The tributaries of the great river extend to within 250 miles of the Atlantic on the east and 500 miles from the Pacific on the west. Where flowing water is concerned, all directions are toward the middle. The Mississippi drains 33 states and two provinces of Canada—one-eighth of all of North America. Its watershed is the third largest in the world.

Two million years ago, following the massive uplift of the Rocky Mountains, the age of the glaciers began. Ice more than two miles deep covered the continent as far south as the Missouri and Ohio rivers. Four times the enormous ice sheets advanced and four times they retreated. Thousands of years intervened between each episode. So much water was frozen in the ice sheets that the level of the world's oceans dropped 300 feet.

Just when it seemed that the earth would forever exist as a planet with a third of its surface frozen solid, astonishingly the ice began to melt. The melting glaciers created a vast sea of fresh water—an expanse of water greater than all of the Great Lakes combined. Lake Agassiz, one of the largest fresh water lakes that ever existed in North America, was about 250 miles wide and 700 miles long and covered northwestern Minnesota, parts of North Dakota, much of western Ontario and Manitoba.

Water from Lake Agassiz, blocked from flowing north by three-mile-high glaciers, found its outlet to the south, pouring an unprecedented flood tide down the River Warren and carving the broad valley where the far smaller Minnesota River now flows. There the river collided with the modest stream of the Mississippi in a tumultuous embrace. The river that resulted from that union was monstrous. Engorged with water from the melting mountains of ice, the torrent of water cascaded 200 feet over a ledge of hard limestone into the valley below.

In geologic terms, the thundering waterfall had a brief existence. The upper layer of rock over which the water rushed was hard limestone but the underlying sandstone was soft. The pounding water in the cauldron at the base of the falls chiseled away at the softer sandstone, undercutting the limestone above. As time passed slabs of unsupported rock on the brink of the falls broke off and crashed into the valley. Century by century, as rock continued to break off from the top, the River Warren falls backed up. After retreating for two miles, the sheet of limestone ended, marking the demise of the falls.

The retreat of the River Warren left the Mississippi perched two hundred feet above its gorge. For a century a horseshoe-shaped cataract existed at about the distance a good outfielder can throw a baseball from the present City Hall of St. Paul. It may have been one of the greatest waterfalls of all time—a torrent of water twice as wide as Niagara and half again as tall. The roar of falling water reverberated through the forest for miles in every direction. Mist rising hundreds of feet in the air gave the region the appearance of a boiling cauldron in summer while hoarfrost coated the landscape in winter.

The same geologic condition that ended the River Warren falls doomed the falls on the Mississippi. The churning turbulence in the pools at the base of the falls eroded the softer sandstone, sending pieces of the hard caprock above crashing into the river below. The death march upstream of the falls went on for ten thousand years. In that time, the falls backed up about eight miles, from St. Paul to Minneapolis, and carved a deep gorge during its retreat. At Nicollet Island, as had occurred with the River Warren, the Mississippi approached the end of the limestone caprock. The cataract shrank to become a tumultuous stretch of rapids.

When Father Louis Hennepin first saw the falls on the Mississippi in July of 1680, he almost certainly exaggerated the height. He wrote, "This cataract is forty or fifty feet high, divided in the middle of its fall by a rocky island or pyramidal form." The falls were probably only about 30 feet high when Father Hennepin saw them but they may have seemed higher because of the great blocks of limestone that had fallen into the ravine below the falls. The cataracts were wide, extending about 500 yards from one side of the river to the other. The roaring of the torrents of water rushing over and around the jumbled rocks could be heard fifteen miles away.

Hennepin was not known for accuracy. His fellow explorers, examining accounts of his explorations, called them "rather romances than relations" and consigned Father Hennepin "to that amiable class who seem to tell truth by accident and fiction by inclination."

Hennepin was portaging his canoe around the falls when he got a good look at the foaming cataract. A place of wonder for the Europeans,

View of the Falls of St. Anthony (circa 1849) by Seth Eastman, at a time before bridges and mills were built. Courtesy of Pogo Press, Incorporated.

the falls were a sacred site to the Indians. A man was offering prayers at the cataract when Hennepin and Picard du Gay came upon him. The Ojibwe called the falls *Kakabikah,* meaning "severed rock" while the Dakota called them *Minirara* (curling water) and *Owahmenah* (falling water). Hennepin named them for his patron saint, St. Anthony of Padua.

From its joining with the glacial River Warren the Mississippi followed a course south that was millions of years old. Beginning below St. Anthony Falls the bedrock of the continent gradually rises until it reaches a crest near La Crosse, Wisconsin, where the bluffs tower six hundred feet above the river valley. Though they may appear to be old uplifted mountains, the bluffs are the product of erosion that took place over millions of years. The bottom layer is sandstone, laid down when the land was a vast inland sea. The weight of the water compressed the sand into sandstone. Lying atop the sandstone is a deep layer of limestone formed from the countless decaying skeletons of ancient sea life.

Over this plateau the waters rushed, carving the deep valleys and leaving standing the towering bluffs. The uplifted land near La Crosse was too much for the glaciers to overcome. Below the mouth of the Chippewa the rivers of ice split and flowed around this huge upland peak to leave a "driftless area"—ten thousand square miles of rugged highlands that were never covered by glaciation of any kind. Through this landscape roared the adolescent Mississippi, gouging out a valley twenty miles wide and 900 hundred feet deep in the 400,000,000 year old sedimentary bedrock. Here immense gumdrop-shaped hills rise 600 feet above the valley floor and extend for miles on either side of the Mississippi. The torrents of water that roared down the valley of the Mississippi from the melting glaciers during the Pleistocene Period carved out these hills. The Ordovian dolomite rock on the top of the bluffs was once the floor of an ancient sea and is pockmarked with fossils.

DE SOTO AND THE MISSISSIPPI

The first European mention of the Mississippi was in 1519 by Alonzo Alvarez de Pineda, a Spanish explorer who was searching for a transcontinental waterway between the peninsula of Yucatan and Florida. The first map on which the mouth of the river appeared was published in 1520. On November 2, 1528, Alvar Núñez Cabeza de Vaca, one of four survivors of the ill-fated Panfilo de Narvaez expedition, floated out into the Gulf of Mexico and reported "the mouth of a broad river, which poured so large a stream of water into the gulf that [we] took fresh water from the sea." It remained for Hernando de Soto to finally reach the banks of the Mississippi, probably in early May 1541. He called it the Rio del Espiritu Santo. De Soto's men spent two years in the vicinity of the river, exploring as far north as the Arkansas River, before building seven brigantines (the men hammered the nails to hold the boats together out of their armor), and sailing down river for eighteen days to reach the Gulf.

Though Spaniards discovered the river, they were not eager to explore it or find a way to put it to use. One hundred and thirty-two years were to pass after De Soto's men consigned his body to the river before Louis Jolliet explored the northern portion of the Mississippi in 1673. The French came in from the north where they were exposed to the frigid winters. To reach the vicinity of the river the French had to spend at least one summer traveling by canoe and then winter over at their outposts on the Great Lakes before they could continue on.

Despite the physical problems of weather and distance the French faced, the most significant obstacles to exploring the Mississippi were political. At various periods, the Spanish, French, British and Americans all competed for control of the river. French explorers traveled only part way down the river for fear of encountering the Spanish who controlled the mouth. Government officials were more concerned with issues of sovereignty than they were with exploration, with the result that more than 300 years went by before Schoolcraft identified the source of the river in Lake Itasca. As Mark Twain later noted in the first chapter of *Life on the Mississippi* (1883), "Apparently nobody happened to want such a river, nobody needed it, nobody was curious about it; so for a century and a half the Mississippi remained out of the market and undisturbed. When De Soto found it, he was not hunting for a river, and had no present occasion for one; consequently, he did not value it or even take any particular notice of it."

Rivers are not like other dramatic natural landmarks in that, to an extraordinary extent, they lend themselves to the needs of man. Great mountains, though they inspire awe, are often more of a barrier than a boon. A river such as the Mississippi draws life to it—from the wildlife that thrives on its banks, in its waters and in the flyway above it—to the people who build their lives on its shores. Like the Nile whose annual flooding made possible the ancient civilization of Egypt, the Mississippi is the engine that drove the social and economic history of the Upper

Midwest. Unlike the Nile, which is bordered by deserts, or the Amazon that is surrounded by a largely impassable tropical rainforest, the Mississippi runs down the center of the largest continuous area of fertile agricultural land on earth.

Life on the Upper Mississippi has been a series of accommodations to a river that can be maddening to live with. It deposits silt in colossal quantities, changes shape and direction repeatedly, creates islands only to wash them away, leaves former riverfront towns stranded inland, and is frustrating and exacting to navigate.

The peculiar characteristics of the Upper Mississippi River: its falls of St. Anthony, its meandering channel, its multiplicity of islands and sloughs, its devastating floods and frustrating shallows are the little-recognized forces that created the twenty-first century world of the Midwest. How people reacted to the river has determined what the region is today. Residents of the valley of the Upper Mississippi, to a great extent, are what they are because of their region's relationship to the river. The one constant through 200 years of conflict and struggle has been the river itself. A British historian asserts that "no single fact of nature played a bigger part in American progress than the Mississippi."

NOTES

Material in this chapter is based on Tom Weil, *The Mississippi River, Nature, Culture and Travel Sites Along the Mighty Mississippi* (1992); Norah Deakin Davis, *The Father of Waters—A Mississippi Chronicle* (1982); William J. Petersen, *Steamboating on the Upper Mississippi* (1968); and John Madson, *Up on the River* (1985). Charles Lanman's *A Summer in the Wilderness, embracing a canoe voyage up the Mississippi and around Lake Superior* was published in 1847. B. A. Botkin's *A Treasury of Mississippi River Folklore* (1955) was the source for the Schoolcraft story. For other explorers see John Gilmary Shea, *Early Voyages Up and Down the Mississippi* (1861) and Timothy Severin, *Explorers of the Mississippi* (1968). Charles Maguire wrote the story of Mary Gibbs for *The Minnesota Volunteer* (May-June 1992), while the Father Hennepin reference appears in an article by N. H. Winchell, "Hennepin at the Falls of St. Anthony," *Bulletin of the Minnesota Academy of Sciences* IV (1910).

CHAPTER 2

The First Inhabitants

The Europeans, seeing the country of the Upper Mississippi for the first time, believed themselves to be the discoverers of a virgin land. The land was indeed new to the Europeans but it was hardly "virgin"—the Indians had inhabited the area for millennia. While the explorers referred to the region as being largely empty, what they meant was it was empty of people like themselves. Nevertheless the native occupants piqued their curiosity. Many of the Europeans became keenly interested in the original inhabitants, learned their languages, painted scenes of their daily life and, in many instances, became valued members of their families.

Though anthropologists call the earliest residents Woodland, Mississippian and Oneota peoples, no one really knows who were the first occupants of the land along the Upper River. Curtis Campbell (*Wakan-hdi Sapa*—Black Lightning), retired chairman of the Prairie Island Dakota community, believes that the Oneota people he calls the "Khemnichan" were the ancestors of the Dakota and Winnebago.

Whoever they were it is clear that there were a great many of them and that the river played a significant role in their lives. The thousands of mounds they left behind provide dramatic evidence of their presence. Their meaning lost to living memory, the mounds presented the white settlers with unsettling earthen mysteries. What had happened here in the past that caused these mounds, some in the shape of birds and bears, to be built? And why were there so many of them?

The number and location of most of the mounds might never have been known if it had not been for two bachelors living in St. Paul in the 1880's. One was Alfred Hill, a civil engineer in the land office. Hill was fascinated by the mounds he saw scattered along the rivers and began to gather information about them. When he met Theodore Hayes Lewis, a young surveyor, Hill began his project to survey and map all of the mounds he could find in an eleven-state area north of St. Louis.

Hill paid Lewis $3 a day and his expenses to find and survey mounds. For the next fourteen years, until 1895, Lewis counted and surveyed mounds, traveling more than 54,000 miles, 10,000 of them on foot. Altogether Lewis found 2,000 village sites and 17,000 mounds; 7,700 in Minnesota. He identified 2,000 mounds at Red Wing, at least 66 mounds on the hills across the river from Prairie du Chien, another 900 a few miles north. Two groups of mounds lay within the town limits of Wabasha. One was a cluster of 80 mounds crowded together on a terrace about forty-four feet above the river. The other group contained five mounds ranging in size from 50 to 80 feet in diameter. Farmers hastened to plow under the mounds as if to exorcise unwelcome spirits. The Indians kept their own counsel where the mounds were concerned and honored their sacred places in secret. In later years at least some mounds have been preserved in parks, such as those on St. Paul's east side.

The size of the Indian population at the time of European contact has been hotly debated. Henry F. Dobyns initiated the controversy with the publication in *Current Anthropology* (Vol. VII, 1966) of his article, "Estimated Aboriginal American Population: An Appraisal of Techniques with a New Hemispheric Estimate." Dobyns estimated that at least 18 million people lived in North America at the time Columbus landed, four million of them in the valley of the Mississippi. Because Native Americans had no immunity to the diseases of Europe, Dobyns believed that 95% died of diseases brought by the Europeans and their domestic animals within the first 130 years of occupation.

When De Soto landed in Florida, with him were 600 soldiers, 200 horses and 300 pigs. For four years this entourage roamed over the south, crossing the Mississippi a few miles south of Memphis. De Soto's men reported seeing a thickly settled land, "very well peopled with large towns, two or three of which were to be seen from one town." The Spaniards encountered many clusters of small cities, protected by walls and moats. When, one hundred years later, Rene-Robert Cavelier, Sieur de La Salle, traveled over the same route he did not encounter a single Indian village for 200 miles. They had all disappeared. Dobyns suggests that De Soto's pigs, which can infect other species with a variety of diseases, may have wandered off and begun the contamination that afflicted an entire population.

When the first Frenchmen made their way to the Upper Mississippi they found a situation far different from what La Salle saw in the south. Here the area along the river was full of activity; vibrant with a culture and life of its own. Gary Anderson estimates the pre-contact Dakota population in the Upper Mississippi watershed at 38,000. Traffic on the highway of the river was heavy with Indians traveling to hunt, fish, gather nuts and berries from favored areas, attend feasts and ceremonies, trade with each other and defend tribal hunting grounds. Footpaths that ran for great distances tamed the forest and connected distant villages and trading partners. Hundreds of Indian lodges and teepees lined long stretches of the riverbank. The bounty of the land sustained a flourishing population.

Prairies of tall grass lay like a thick blanket over the upper two-thirds of Illinois, almost all of Iowa and much of southern Wisconsin and Minnesota. Bluestem grass grew as tall as a man. Although Charles Dickens found the prairie "oppressive in its barren monotony" to farmers it was the best soil in the world. The variety of grasses, flowers, animals and birds that lived on this fecund prairie overwhelmed the white settlers who first saw it. They compared the prairie to an ocean of meadowland dotted with islands of trees. Hardwoods of mammoth proportion grew along the banks of the Mississippi. Forests of oak, walnut, ash, maple, beech and hickory covered the cone-shaped hills. In the thickets gooseberries, blackberries, plums, crab apples, strawberries and wild cherries flourished.

The woods were alive with game—bear, deer, wolves, prairie chickens, turkeys and squirrels. Flocks of birds were so enormous that their passage darkened the skies and broke the branches of trees they alighted on. Birds flew in open windows and doors. One hunter brought down 30 birds with one shot. Fish in Lake Pepin grew so large that the Indians went on the lake in dugouts carved from cottonwood logs because a bite from a fish could tear apart a bark canoe. Buffalo grazed less than a day's journey to the west. Indians regularly cleared underbrush with fire to create open grassy fields that were favorable for game—sculpting entire ecosystems to support herds of elk and deer. Passengers on the *Virginia* saw a large fire on the prairie on the boat's maiden voyage up the Mississippi. Because the Upper Mississippi offered such a bounty of resources the Dakota lived well. Extended families of fifty or more individuals worked together hunting, fishing and caring for children. Prosperous villages held from five hundred to a thousand residents.

The Mdewakanton Dakota (the name means "Mystery Lake"—a reference to Mille Lacs Lake) had permanent summer villages along the Minnesota and Mississippi Rivers as far south as the present town of Winona. Chief Wapasha II, for whom the town of Wabasha is named, maintained a village of seventy bark lodges near present-day Winona and another village of two hundred at his hunting grounds at Wabasha. The bark houses were permanent residences made of six-foot long elm poles sunk into the ground. Walls and roofs were covered with strips of bark. Indians occupied the villages from early spring through the fall. Surrounding the villages were gardens where the women raised crops of corn, beans and squash.

Indian life followed a regular, predictable pattern. The Indians had intimate knowledge of their surroundings; they knew where the berry patches were located and when the fruit would be ripe, the location of groves of maples and the season the sap would be running, where to find medicinal herbs. In winter the entire village, including women and children, went on the winter hunt for deer. This was a major event requiring the labor of everyone in the band to hunt down, kill and dress as many as a thousand deer. While away on the hunt, the Indians lived in their ingenious teepees, portable homes made from 12 poles covered with eight dressed buffalo skins sewed together. The women owned the teepee, bark lodges and all possessions. Men owned only their clothing and weapons.

James L. Stokes, whose Dakota name is *Zitkadan Hota* or Gray Bird, remembers his grandmother explaining that, while the Indians lived in large villages, they often dispersed into smaller groups. The presence of a large village kept the animals away forcing hunters to travel longer distances to find game. The women's task of gathering firewood also became more difficult in a large village. "The other thing is the practice of burying their dead on scaffolds made it rather smelly. And there was the human excrement and excrement from dogs. To clean it up they just moved away for awhile," Stokes said.

Indian contacts were not limited to their own village or tribe. They traveled long distances and exchanged goods and ideas over two-thirds of the continent. Exchange with the Mississippian peoples to the south brought changing modes of religious rituals, pottery-making and jewelry. Indian traders journeyed long distances on the river to distribute items made from stone, bone, copper and exotic shells brought from areas as distant as the Gulf and Atlantic and Pacific coasts.

Group solidarity was a principle of Indian life. Consensus government was the key to the Indian political systems. Everyone had to work together if the tribe were to survive in the harsh climate of the Upper Mississippi. Indians resolved problems through long sessions of discussion that included all the male members of the tribe and could go on for days. They avoided coercion as they recognized the serious possibility of social disruption if one individual attempted to force his will on another. Because they governed by consensus and persuasion, oratorical skills were important. Indian leaders had to be not only skilled hunters but persuasive speakers. Samuel Pond noted that, "Speeches well made and well timed had a great influence over the minds of the Dakotas and a few words fitly spoken often changed the purposes of the inhabitants of a whole village."

An important value was to share what one had with others. Indians condemned hoarding or any sign of greed. An Indian gained prestige and status by giving his property away, not by accumulating it for his own use. Schoolcraft's companion, the Reverend Boutwell, observed that an Indian could not eat alone. If he killed a pheasant he brought his neighbors in to share it with him. In his history of the Prairie Island Dakota, Curtis Campbell refers repeatedly to the concept of "relatedness through sharing." The sharing of food demonstrated an individual's community-mindedness and generosity.

When the French made their way to the region around Lake Superior in the seventeenth century they encountered two groups of Indians, the Ojibwe and the Dakota. The French already knew the Ojibwe, from prior trading relationships, but the Dakota were new to them. The Dakota had originally lived in the Southwest but in the distant past they had migrated to the forested lands of northern Minnesota and Wisconsin. Here the Dakota encountered the Ojibwe. The Ojibwe, too, were newcomers, having lived in the East until pressure from the Iroquois forced them to move west in the late 1600's.

For a time the Dakota and Ojibwe coexisted peacefully, even joining together as allies to combat the Fox and the Sauk Indians. The Dakota say that they taught the Ojibwe about wild rice and that the two groups intermarried. Chief Wapasha I had an Ojibwe wife, whom he sent back to her own people when hostilities broke out between the two tribes. Two of their sons, Big Feet and White Fisher, grew up to become prominent leaders among the Ojibwe.

The period of good relationships ended when the Ojibwe obtained guns. For some time before the Dakota encountered Europeans the Ojibwe, living in the East, had begun trading furs with the French. The Ojibwe's long and close relationship with the French was cemented in 1671 when fourteen tribes met with the French at Sault St. Marie to establish trade relations. The recognition and attention the French showered on the Ojibwe gave them their first sense of themselves as a discrete people.

Far more than the British or the American traders, the French had expressed kindness and sympathy toward the Indians and respect for their sacred beliefs and rites. In return, the Ojibwe supported the French who were the most successful of all the Europeans in gaining the confidence of the Indians. The Ojibwe fought with the French against the British and American colonists in the French and Indian War. When a British officer told the Indians that the French had surrendered, an Ojibwe woman replied disdainfully, "Englishman! Although you have conquered the French, you have not yet conquered us."

The fur trade upset the balance among the tribes. Using their newly acquired guns, the Ojibwe clashed with the Dakota, forcing them back west across the Mississippi and, in some cases, into what became South Dakota. For more than a hundred years the two tribes engaged in sporadic fighting. Accounts written by the early French explorers indicate that the Sioux (Dakota) and Ojibwe nations were continually at war with each other. The Mississippi River valley above and below the Falls of St. Anthony was their principal battleground.

For a time the Mdewakanton band of the Eastern Dakota succeeded in forcing the Ojibwe back into Wisconsin. Later the Ojibwe reclaimed some of the land around the Mississippi. Eventually an informal understanding developed between the two tribes. The Ojibwe occupied the pine and birch forest of the north woods as well as some areas on the east side of the Mississippi. The Dakota retained control of the western shore of the river and the Big Woods of central Minnesota and the eastern Dakotas.

An area that both the Dakota and Ojibwe claimed and that separated the two groups was the "debatable zone," a strip of land many miles wide that ran from above the St. Croix River northwest into the Dakotas. The zone was a transitional area of mixed forest and prairie land, making it an ideal habitat for the game they depended on. With both groups hunting in and claiming ownership of the region, it inevitably became the site of many conflicts

In 1819 the Dakota chief, Little Crow, explained his rationale for the continual fighting with the Ojibwe. "A peace could easily be made but it is better for us to carry on the war in the way we do than to make peace, because we lose a man or two every year, but we kill as many of the enemy during the same time and if we were to make peace the Ojibwe would overrun all the country lying between the Mississippi and Lake Superior and have their villages on the banks of the Mississippi itself. In this case, we, the Dakota, would lose all our hunting ground on the northeast side of the river; why then should we give up such an extensive country to save the life of a man or two annually? I know that it is not good to go to war, or to make too much war, or against too many people; but this is war for land which must always exist if the Dakota Indians remain in the same opinion which now guides them."

The Dakota did not delay in establishing their own trading relationships with the French. To make it easier to trade with the French on Prairie Island the Mantanton, part of the Mdewakanton Dakota, moved from the Onamia Lake area to a site on the Mississippi near the end of the seventeenth century,

Following contact with Europeans the Indians began to refer to themselves in a new way. They called themselves "children" in need of the protection of a "Great Father." This did not reflect a belittling of themselves by the Indians but instead the establishment of kinship or relatedness relationships with the whites. A father-son relationship implied mutual obligations. To the Indians, trade was the exchanging of gifts to cement relationships. The value of the goods exchanged was secondary to the reciprocity that would result from the new bonds. Committed to this personalized interpretation of trade, the Indians eagerly sought relationships with the traders.

In 1695 the chief of the Mantanton Dakota, Teeoskahtay, persuaded Pierre Charles LeSueur to take him to Montreal to meet Count Louis Frontenac, the governor-general of New France. The chief went to pledge his allegiance to the French king and to establish the personal relationships the Indians believed necessary for trade. At the meeting the chief laid out twenty-two arrows on a beaver robe, explaining that the arrows stood for twenty-two Dakota villages that desired French protection. "Take courage, great captain," he said to Frontenac, "and reject me not; despise me not, though I appear poor in your eyes. All the nations here present know that I am rich and the little they offer here is taken from my lands." The French accepted the Dakota pledge of allegiance and welcomed them as trading partners. Sadly, however,

Teeoskahtay died in Montreal shortly after the council with Frontenac.

The arrival of the French traders radically changed the dynamics of Indian life. The Indians were enthusiastic trading partners, bringing in over 100,000 pelts in one season to exchange for metal cooking pots, knives, axes and guns. Eager as they were for trade, the Indians continued to view their activities with the traders as a social rather than an economic activity. Few grasped how profoundly their lives were changing. Once the Indians began dealing with the traders they were forever entangled in the economic system of the whites—a system that stretched from the interior of America across the Atlantic to Europe.

It was a Faustian bargain. For a brief time the Indians prospered as the new tools made them more efficient and productive. Soon, however, they became dependent on the traders' gifts and goods, which they called "iron," equating trade with life itself. As traders flocked to the Upper Mississippi to take advantage of the boom in furs, the Indians responded with such alacrity that game soon became scarce. No longer a self-sufficient people, as they had been for millennia, the Indians became dependent on the traders, the missionaries, the federal Indian agents, anyone who could help them survive.

It was inevitable that misunderstanding would develop between two such disparate groups as the Indians and the missionaries. The early missionaries to the Ojibwe and Dakota were affiliated with the American Board of Commissioners for Foreign Missions, a group dominated by Congregationalists and Presbyterians.

The missionaries spent their energies trying to change Indians into Euro-Americans. Indians were expected to adopt Christianity, change their mode of dress, cut their hair, learn English, have but one wife, stop the practice of holding goods in common and abandon hunting to become settled tillers of the soil. The missionaries were convinced that their program of "Christ and the plow" was the only form of economic organization that would support "civilized" human life. This was a difficult concept for Indians to accept, as gardening was believed to be women's work, linked conceptually to women's reproductive abilities. A shift from hunting to large-scale plow agriculture represented a cultural change of enormous magnitude for the Indians. Some Indian leaders— those who foresaw the depletion of the game and overrunning of the country by whites—agreed and believed it had to be done.

One of these leaders was John Johnson Enmegahbowh, an Ojibwe from Ontario who married *Biwabikogijigokwe* (Iron Sky Woman), the niece of two influential Ojibwe leaders, Hole-in-the-Day the Elder and Strong Ground. Enmegahbowh converted to Christianity and Bishop Henry B. Whipple ordained him an Episcopal priest, the first such ordination in the United States. In the summer of 1861 Enmegahbowh invited an Ojibwe chief and colleague, Nabunashkong, to talk with him about his people and their condition.

"Nabunashkong, tell me plainly and tell me as a friend, what is your hope for your people? You know as a nation we are fast sinking. Your country and your hiding places tell you, sooner or later, you will in one day be swept away from the face of the earth. And besides, a strong pressure is now upon our people. This great continent will be peopled by a higher class of nation—far stronger and more powerful than our chiefs and warriors were. And this great and mighty movement of the Pale-faces has already taken place and has gone forward like some great tidal wave, sweeping through to our beloved land and country. Now, Nabunashkong, tell me plainly, what is your future hope for our people?"

Nabunashkong's reply reflected the despair felt by Indian leaders who saw little hope for their people's survival. "I love and pity my poor people," he told Enmegahbowh. "I seek their interest. I have made no provision for them but this war-club and the scalping knife. I have defended them day and night, Why? Because I love them. I will follow the brave steps of my fathers and will seal my blood for my country and people." Enmegahbowh had come to the conclusion that it was hopeless for the Indians to resist accommodation to white demands. "To resist," he observed, "was like throwing a stone against a rock, it would bounce back."

The missionaries were among the first to document Indian life as they observed it and to assess the character of the Indians. Samuel Pond wrote of the Dakota, "It may be said of the Dakotas that they have good common sense. They were quick to distinguish between sound argument and sophistry and many of them could reason with clearness, precision and force. They were very close observers of men and things. Nothing visible escaped their notice and they were peculiarly quick to discern the true character of their casual acquaintances. They soon found out all the strong points and all the weak points of a white man with whom they had to deal and commonly knew a great deal more about him than he did about them."

In many ways the differences between the Indians and whites living on the frontier were small. Both groups were trying to survive in the same harsh country. Evidence of the two people's similarity is the fact that many hundreds of Indians passed imperceptibly into white society, losing in a generation or two most of their ethnic identification.

One of Dakota-descendant James Stokes' great-grandfathers, Henry Doughty, an Oneida-Delaware mixed-blood from the East, was apprenticed to a wagon maker and learned the trade. Other Indians became hired men on farms, learned farming and earned their keep by hunting for the farmers. A high percentage of the early settlers of Buffalo County, Wisconsin, across the Mississippi from Wabasha, were Indians posing as whites.

Stokes claims, "When the Dakota Uprising of 1862 occurred, a lot of these people were smart enough not to give their Indian identities. They had no choice; they had to take white names. It was survival. That's what they had to do. My great-grandfather who I am named after, Chief Grey Bird, was at the Battle of Birch Coulee and he just vanished, like many others. From Prairie Island they came over to Wisconsin. They were coached along by other survivors from eastern tribes who had been pushed over here, too."

The early explorers who first encountered the people living in the Upper Mississippi had little concept of the variety or complexity of Indian life. They would have been astounded to learn that at least 300 languages were spoken in North America at the time of European contact. Henry R. Schoolcraft, a pioneer ethnologist, marveled at discovering that Native American culture had produced its own rich body of oral literature. Like the often told *Iliad* and *Odyssey* of Europe, tribal storytellers had passed down tales through many generations. "Who would have imagined that these wandering foresters," Schoolcraft wrote, "would have possessed such a resource?" Schoolcraft chided his fellow explorers. "What have all the voyagers and remarkers (sic) from the days of Cabot and Raleigh been about, not to have discovered this curious trait, which lifts up indeed a curtain, as it were, upon the Indian mind, and exhibits it in an entirely new character?"

SETH EASTMAN—ARMY OFFICER AND ARTIST

In 1830 the army assigned a twenty-two-year-old graduate of West Point, Second Lieutenant Seth Eastman, to Fort Snelling. In addition to his career as an army officer, Eastman was an accomplished watercolor painter who was fascinated by the Dakota. Life for an officer at Fort Snelling was not demanding and Eastman took advantage of his free time to paint scenes of everyday Indian life. Among the 400 pictures of Indian life he painted are scenes of Indians guarding the cornfields, striking camp, making maple syrup, spearing fish and muskrats and conferring in council meetings. Eastman's paintings of Indian villages depict substantial houses of upright logs, walls of bark and roofs of bark strips held down by long poles.

Although the artists Karl Bodmer and George Catlin had preceded Eastman into Indian Territory, Eastman eventually spent more time among the Indians of the Upper Mississippi than any other artist of his day. Indians were a popular subject for artists as most people believed the Indians would vanish within a few generations. While living at Fort Snelling Eastman formed a relationship with the third daughter of the Dakota chief Cloud Man (*Wakaninajinwin*—Stands Sacred) and the couple had a daughter, Nancy. When Eastman was ordered to a post in Texas, he left his Indian family behind. Indian tradition says that when Eastman left Fort Snelling "on his last visit to his child he pressed it to his heart while tears ran down his noble young face."

The Indian agent at Fort Snelling, Major Lawrence Taliaferro, assumed guardianship of nine mixed-blood children including Nancy Eastman and a girl named Mary Taliaferro, his own child by another of Cloud Man's daughters. Eastman's daughter Nancy grew up to become a beautiful woman who married and died, while still in her twenties, after giving birth to her fifth child. That child was Charles Alexander

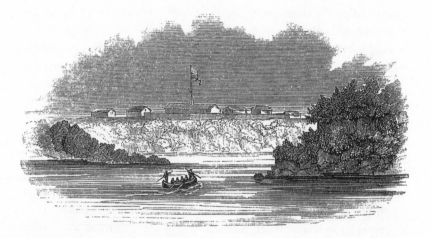

Laurence Oliphant sketched Fort Snelling as he viewed it from his canoe voyage on the Mississippi. From his *Minnesota and the Far West* (1855). Courtesy of Pogo Press, Inc.

Eastman, who became a prominent frontier physician and author of *Indian Boyhood* (1902). Nancy's death occurred just twenty-eight years after Eastman first came to Fort Snelling.

After leaving the territory Eastman married Mary Henderson. The two collaborated on books of Indian life that Mary wrote and Eastman illustrated. "A traveler in Indian country during the summer cannot fail to be struck with the taste of the Indians as regards the location of their villages," Mary Eastman wrote. "Even if it be a mere encampment on a hunting excursion, the point of resting is sure to be where all that is attractive in nature meets the eye." Eastman painted few portraits of individual Indians, preferring to depict them in groups going about the activities of daily life.

Eastman served a second tour of duty at Fort Snelling from 1841 to 1848. In 1850 the army transferred him to Washington, D.C., to create more than 300 illustration plates for Henry Rowe Schoolcraft's six volume *Historical and Statistical Information Respecting the History, Conditions and Prospects of the Indian Tribes of the United States* (1851-1857). Schoolcraft has been mentioned in connection with his expedition to find the true source of the Mississippi River. He served as an Indian agent in northern Michigan for nineteen years. There he met and married his wife Jane, a part Ojibwe woman who assisted in his researches concerning Indian culture. Schoolcraft's *Algic Researches* (1839) introduced the legend of Hiawatha to a wider public and especially to poet Henry Wadsworth Longfellow. "Song of Hiawatha" (1855) became one of Longfellow's most famous works. When a Mississippi tributary and its falls were given the name of Hiawatha's sweetheart, Minnehaha, the falls became a more popular tourist destination than Father Hennepin's Falls of St. Anthony. In 1912 a bronze statue of Hiawatha carrying Minnehaha, by the Norwegian sculptor Jacob Fjelde, was set beside the creek. Not far away is Ed Archie Noise-Cat's giant face of "Little Crow"(1994), thus uniting a mythical and actual Dakota near a spot their ancestors frequented.

NOTES

The reports of Alfred Hill and Theodore Hays Lewis were included in N. H. Winchell, *The Aborigines of Minnesota* (1911). David C. Anderson described mounds in Wabasha in his "City of Wabasha Historic Context Study, Final Report" (1995).

Sources on the Dakota include Curtis Campbell, Sr., *A Family Oral History of Prairie Island* (2000); Mark Dietrich, *Dakota Oratory* (1989); Samuel W. Pond, *The Dakota or Sioux as They Were in 1834* (1986 reprint); Rebecca Anne Kugel, "To Go About on the Earth," Ph.D dissertation, University of California, Los Angeles (1986); Gary Clayton Anderson, *Kinsmen of Another Kind: Dakota-White Relations in the Upper Mississippi Valley, 1650-1862* (1997); Rev. Edward Neill writes of the trip a Dakota leader made to Montreal in *The History of Minnesota* (1882). Comments on Indian dispersal come from an interview with James L. Stokes (July 2003). For information on John Johnson Enmegahbowh see *Enmegahbowh's Story: An Account of the Disturbances of the Chippewa Indians at Gull Lake in 1857 and 1862 and Their Removal in 1868* (1904). For Seth Eastman, see John Francis McDermott, *Seth Eastman's Mississippi, a Lost Panorama Recovered* (1973) and Sarah Boehme, Christian Feest and Patricia Condon Johnston, editors, *Seth Eastman: A Portfolio of North American Indians* (1995).

CHAPTER 3

Early River Craft

The French might have left the great river flowing down from the falls unexplored for far longer if it had not been for the Indian birch bark canoe—a craft the Spanish never learned to use—but which the French immediately adopted. Upon arrival in the New World the French explorers were amazed to see that the Indians, in their fragile craft, could paddle circles around European sailors in their heavy rowboats.

Laurence Oliphant visited the territory of Minnesota in 1854, traveling by canoe. When other lodging was not available a canoe, tipped on its side, had to suffice. The campfire of red cedar logs and pipesmoke provided warmth, comfort and protection against mosquitoes. From Oliphant's *Minnesota and the Far West* (1855). Courtesy of Pogo Press, Incorporated.

The Indian canoes were faster than anything the Europeans had brought with them and could be steered through dangerous rapids. The French left the ships that had brought them from Europe and immediately adopted the Indians' canoes for their activities. The bark boats drew but a few inches of water, could be hauled overland for long distances, did not require nails or other scarce items, could be repaired with materials from the forests, carried a ton of freight as well as a dozen men and could be turned upside down and used as shelters.

The canoes exhibited great skill in design and construction, evidence of a period of development that took place long before the coming of the white man. The Indians made their versatile craft from the outer bark of the paper birch tree that grows to a height of 100 feet. They peeled the bark in the fall or early spring when the sap was running, sewed the bark "skins" together with the thin roots of the black spruce, made ribs for the canoe of white cedar lashed together with rawhide thongs and carved the thwarts and paddles from hard maple.

They made the canoes watertight by coating the seams and sewing with spruce gum—the resin from the black or white spruce tree. Ojibwe and Dakota canoes used on the Mississippi had a high curve at the prow, a quarter again as high as the boat's midsection.

THE FLATBOATS

When the Revolutionary War ended, white settlers began to push west down the Ohio River to the Mississippi and the midsection of the country. Rivers provided the major route through the wilderness. Families loaded all their possessions—cows, horses, chickens, farm implements, furniture and tools—on rafts and floated downriver in search of new homes. The rafts drew about a foot of water and could only go downstream. Once at their destination, the family took the raft apart and used the lumber to build its home.

The ungainly flatboat that followed was a variation of the family raft. While a few flatboats measured a massive 100 feet in length, most were fifty feet long by fourteen feet wide, a dimension determined by the fact that a worker could tie two rows of horses across the beam of the boat. Flatboats carried forty to fifty tons of cargo stored in rows of barrels. Builders pegged the boats together with oak and steered them with oars forty feet long made by fastening a board to the end of a long pole. Forked sticks sunk in postholes in the rear held the two sweeps, called "broadhorns," that kept the flatboat in the river channel. Most flatboats carried a crew of five, two men to manage each sweep and one to steer. It was on such a craft that the young Abraham Lincoln floated down the Mississippi to New Orleans where the sight of a slave market shocked him into his lifetime abhorrence of slavery. Like the rafts from which they were descended, the flatboats could only go downstream. New Orleans sidewalks were paved with the planks from flatboats. George Caleb Bingham's famous painting of flatboat life, "The Jolly Flatboatmen" (1844), was reproduced in an engraving and widely distributed by the American Art Union.

THE KEELBOATS

The current on the Ohio forced the flatboats to turn south when they reached the Mississippi. Only canoes could navigate upriver. Traffic on the Ohio River and the lure of the Upper Mississippi, the need to bring far more trade goods upriver than could be stowed in a canoe, led to the development of the keelboat—a sturdy craft from 40 to 80 feet long and eight to ten feet wide. The keelboat had a keel-shape instead of a broad flat bottom, with a heavy four-inch square timber bolted to the bottom of the boat running from bow to stern to protect it against collisions with obstructions in the river. Keelboats were pointed at the bow. A crew of ten could propel a keelboat up river by either pulling it with ropes from the shore or poling it.

Poling the keelboat was unremitting labor. The men planted their long poles on the bottom of the river, tucked the ends in the hollows of their shoulders, and on a signal from the pilot, strained to walk from the prow to the stern, bending almost double from the effort. A contemporary sketch of a keelboat shows the helmsman leaning on the long handle of the tiller while the pilot reclines on a crate on top of the load as he calls the cadence for the toiling men. The men chanted as they toiled:

> *Working on a push boat*
> *For fifty cents a day*
> *Buy my girl a brand-new dress*
> *And throw the rest away.*
>
> *Working on a push boat*
> *Water's mighty slack;*

Taking sorghum 'lasses down
And bringing sugar back.

Pushing mighty hard, boys,
Sandbar's in the way
Working like a son-of-a-gun
For mighty scanty pay.

The weather's mighty hot, boys
Blisters on my feet;
Working on the push boat
To buy my bread and meat.

Another technique to move keelboats up the river was "bushwhacking." The pilot and crew leaned over the side of the boat and by grasping and pulling on the bushes at the river's edge painfully, by brute force, inched the craft up the river. On the upstream trip they carried a load of 3,000 pounds per man and the boats were fortunate to make eight to ten miles in a day. Freight charges on the keelboats for the trip from St. Louis to St. Paul in the early decades of the nineteenth century were around $7 per hundred pounds. The downstream rates were a bargain— one-third to one-fourth what it cost to move freight upstream.

Despite the difficulty of travel by keelboat, the craft provided access to the Upper Mississippi. No longer was the traffic on the river limited to Indians and fur traders who could paddle canoes. Adventurers, soldiers, tourists, settlers—the assorted denizens of the American frontier—rode the keelboats on their tortuous journey upriver into the Northwest Territory.

The keelboats quickly replaced the Indians' canoes and, for two decades, monopolized the hauling of trade goods. Blankets, tools, guns, trinkets, and whiskey moved up the river to supply the posts doing business with the Indians. Drifting back downstream the keelboats carried furs to Prairie du Chien at the mouth of the Wisconsin River and further south to Mound City (later named St. Louis) where the muddy Missouri deposited its load of silt into the crystal waters of the Mississippi.

When the breeze was strong, the keelboat crews hoisted sails and when night came the men tied their boats up to trees on the river bank where they sang songs of nostalgia while longing around camp fires and lightening the keelboat's load of strong drink. Richard Oglesby described

them as "half-men, half-horse, half-alligator keepers of the keelboat . . .
led by the biggest brashest member of the entire fraternity, Mike Fink."
For Oglesby the keelboatmen, and their stories, represented the first
American anti-heroes.

Keelboat men were a class apart, known on the river and in river
towns as wild, strong and joyous. Mostly French-Canadians, the men
wore scarlet shirts, bright blue jackets, wool trousers, leather caps and
moccasins. They claimed to drink a gallon of whiskey in 24 hours and
eat four pounds of bacon or salt pork in a day. The men assumed that
their way of life on the river would go on forever. Few dreamed that the
era of the keelboats would end so soon.

THE INNOVATIVE UPPER MISSISSIPPI RIVER STEAMBOATS

On September 24, 1811, a strange craft chugged out of Pittsburgh sailing
for Natchez, which it reached on Christmas day. Observers on shore
were amazed, for this boat had no sails nor was it propelled by human
effort. Many expected it to explode at any minute. The boat was the *New
Orleans,* built for $38,000 by partners Robert Livingston (a signer of the
Declaration of Independence) and Robert Fulton. It was the first boat
built by the Fulton-Livingston Company of Pittsburgh and it quickly
revolutionized water travel. Innovative as Fulton's early steamboat was,
it could not be used on the Upper Mississippi until it was modified.

Fulton's first steamboats were deep draft vehicles, modeled after
ocean-going ships. These vessels would not work on the Upper Mississippi because the upper river was shallow. In the fall, when the water was
low, cows could walk across the river in search of better grass on the opposite shore. Farmers drove their teams from shore to shore through the
water. One farmer, driving a load of hay across the river at night, scared
a riverboat captain half out of his wits. The load of hay looked to the
boat captain like a hill that had suddenly sprung up out of the water.
Sandbars had scarcely three feet of water flowing over them in the fall.

The man who adapted Fulton's steamboat for Upper Mississippi
River travel was Henry M. Shreve—for whom Shreveport, Louisiana, is
named. Shreve built a steamboat on the hull of a keelboat. Shreve's
steamboat sat on the surface of the water instead of sinking into it.
Rather than putting the machinery that drove the boat in the hull, as others had done, Shreve put it on the deck. He laid the twin boilers on their

sides (another innovation) and he switched to high-pressure engines which—though more hazardous—reduced the weight and increased the boat's capacity for freight.

To create more deck space, Shreve built a second deck above the first and placed the cabin between the two decks. It was a revolutionary design. Shreve's first boat was the four-hundred-ton *Washington*, and it skimmed over the surface of the river like a water bug. Some Upper Mississippi River steamboats drew as little as 18 inches of water. Their captains claimed they could sail them on dew, or run them for miles on the suds from a keg of beer.

The trip of the *Washington* upstream from New Orleans to Louisville in an astounding twenty-five days in the spring of 1817 was the turning point in the history of steamboating. "That was the trip that convinced the despairing public that steamboat navigation would succeed on the western waters," declared one writer. "After that memorable voyage of the *Washington* all doubts and prejudices in reference of steam navigation were removed. Shipyards began to be established in every convenient locality and the business of steamboat building was vigorously prosecuted." If anyone had thought to inquire how the Upper Mississippi River should be used he would have been thought daft for asking. It was for steamboating, of course.

The Mississippi River steamboat was essentially an engine on a raft with $10,000 worth of fancy jig-saw superstructure made of wood, tin, shingles, canvas and twine giving it the look of a wedding cake or, as one captain expressed it, of "a bride of Babylon." Steamboats ranged from a hundred to three hundred feet long and from thirty to fifty feet wide. They rose from 40 to 70 feet above the water but the largest models, when fully loaded, seldom descended more than four feet into the river. The boats had to be light because, as the river pilots explained, "if they were heavy they would stick to the bottom of the river and become an island instead of a means of transportation."

The unusual design of the riverboats, which allowed them to glide over the water instead of cutting through it, created a peculiar motion. With their top-heavy cabins and superstructure the steamers dipped and sheered—like a belle swaying on a dance floor. To the Mississippi steamboat men the movement of their boats on the water was the ultimate embodiment of grace and style—a unique and admired characteristic of their craft.

The early steamboats, called sidewheelers, had two paddle wheels mounted midship on the sides of the boat. This design resulted in a narrower hull and a greater draft—from four to six feet—limiting the boats to deeper water or travel on the Lower Mississippi. The sidewheelers had superior steering and handling qualities while the early sternwheelers were vulnerable to strong head winds. However, putting a single paddlewheel on the stern of the boat allowed for a wider hull and far less draft, making it possible for the boats to travel up the shallower Upper Mississippi. The ability to carry more cargo and to operate more weeks of the year tipped the balance in favor of the sternwheeler. In the end, the sternwheeler was cheaper to build and to run, had a shallower draft, could carry more cargo and so steadily displaced the more elegant and faster sidewheelers on the upper river.

The boats had a main deck where they put the engines, boiler and woodpile. The second deck was for the passengers. The third deck, called the *texas* deck, was for the crew and on top of this were the twin smokestacks and a twelve-foot-square room for the pilot. Sleeping arrangements on the early boats consisted of rows of open bunks with mattresses filled with hay or corn husks and separated by curtains. Staterooms, when they were later added, were tiny—barely six feet square.

The superiority of the steamboat over the keelboat was immediately apparent. Freight rates dropped. Where keelboats had once dominated, steamboats began to take over. In 1841 St. Louis recorded the arrival of 143 steamboats and 108 keelboats. By 1843, 244 steamboats arrived compared to 55 keelboats. By 1846 the keelboats had disappeared but not before one keelboat made a journey that was to determine the destiny of the Upper Mississippi for the next two centuries.

NOTES

George Caleb Bingham's famous painting of "The Jolly Flatboatmen" appears in an exhibition catalogue called *Westward the Way* (1954), edited by Perry T. Rathbone. Benjamin Botkin included the keelboat song in his anthology, *A Treasury of Mississippi Folklore* (1955). Richard Oglesby wrote about keelboatmen in "The Western Boatmen: Half-Horse, Half-Myth," in *Travelers on the Western Frontier* (1970), edited by John Francis McDermott. Important sources on steamboats and other river craft are George Merrick and William Tibbals, *Genesis of Steamboating on Western Rivers* (1949), Charles Edward Russell, *A-Rafting on the Mississipp'* (1928), and Mildred Hartsough, From *Canoe to Steel Barge on the Upper Mississippi* (1934).

CHAPTER 4

Lieutenant Zebulon Pike's Voyage to the North

O n the hot muggy morning of August 9, 1805, twenty-six-year-old Lieutenant Zebulon Montgomery Pike departed St. Louis for the North-west Territory with twenty soldier companions. They poled a 70-foot keelboat loaded with provisions. Just the year before Merriweather Lewis and William Clark had left from St. Louis on their journey to ex-plore the Upper Missouri. General James Wilkinson, Commander-in-Chief of American military forces in Upper Louisiana, dispatched Pike on his trip to inform the numerous British and French fur traders work-ing on the Upper Mississippi that this was now American territory. Pike carried instructions to win the loyalty of the Indians away from the British and to buy land for military posts on the Mississippi, most partic-ularly at the mouth of the Minnesota (then called the St. Peter's) River.

Progress up the river was slow. Pike and his men dragged their keel-boat across sandbars and, when the boat hung up on a log, cut the log off below the water to free the boat. When they reached the mouth of the Wisconsin River the men noted a high hill on the western shore. Beach-ing their boat, they climbed the hill (since named Pike's Peak) and planted the first American flag raised in the Northwest Territory. At the village of Prairie du Chien Pike abandoned his keelboat in favor of two flat-bottomed bateaux which the 21 men paddled resolutely on up the river. On September 11 he wrote in his log, "The river has never been clear of islands since I left Prairie du Chien. I absolutely believe it to be here two miles wide."

Pike reached the mouth of the Minnesota River in late September and found the Kaposia band of the Mdewakanton Dakota Indians living in a village on the west bank about four miles below the falls. The chief, Little Crow III (*Ce-Tan Wa-Ku-Wa Ma-Ni* or He Who Walks Pursuing a Hawk), welcomed Pike and his party to his village of twelve large bark and pole lodges.

On September 23, 1805, Pike held a council on an island (later named Pike Island) that lay squarely in the mouth of the Minnesota where it flows into the Mississippi. The young Pike, with his keelboat crew about him, sat in a circle with Indian chiefs whose ancestors had already fought in two of the white man's wars. They were an illustrious company including Chief Red Wing, known to the people as "*Tatanka-mani*" or Walking Buffalo.

Red Wing had fought with the British against the Americans in the Revolutionary War. Following the war Red Wing's son had gone to Washington where President James Monroe had treated him graciously. When the British would later urge Red Wing to again side with them in the War of 1812, Red Wing foresaw how the conflict would end and refused. As he explained to the British officer who had tried to recruit him, "I will not now fight the Big Knives [Americans]. You tell me that the lion on this [British] medal is the most powerful of all animals. I have never seen one but I believe what you say. This lion, like our tiger, sleeps all day but the eagle, who is the most powerful of birds, only sleeps at night; in the daytime he flies about everywhere and sees all on the ground. He will light on a tree over the lion and they will scold at each other for awhile. But they will finally make up and be friends and smoke the pipe of peace. The lion will then go home and leave us Indians with our foes. That is the reason for not taking up my war club." Red Wing was correct. The British lion made peace with the American eagle and the Dakota were left to work out their own future with the winners.

Red Wing impressed Pike who called him a "very celebrated war chief" and "a man of sense." Stephen Kearney, who met Red Wing later, had a similar opinion of him. "Red Wing," he wrote, "was an early example of the self-made American. Not born in a chief's family, he rose from warrior ranks by sheer force of character to be second only to Wapasha." To make it easier to trade with the Americans, Red Wing had moved his village of over a hundred people from the mouth of the Cannon River to a site on the Mississippi at the foot of a bluff. The bluff, more than a half-mile long and 334 feet high, reminded the French of a barn so they named it "La Grange."

Red Wing died on a hunting trip during the winter of 1828-29 and his body was first placed on a high platform by the Mississippi River. Later his bones, along with the 1801 medal Jefferson had sent him with Pike, were buried in a mound in his village. For the burial ceremonies, Taliaferro contributed a blanket, shroud, three gallons of whiskey, calico, ribbon and 25 pounds of tobacco.

Like most of the whites who sat in council with the Indians Pike had come to negotiate for land. When the speech-making and ritual smoking of pipes ended, Pike obtained from the Indians two pieces of land, one on each side of the Mississippi River. The first extended from Pike Island upriver to above St. Anthony Falls on the east side of the river. The second piece, intended for a military reservation, measured approximately nine miles and was located on the west side of the river.

The Mdewakanton Dakota of Kaposia gave up these two parcels of land for an initial payment of sixty gallons of whiskey and trade goods worth about $200. Since the treaty stipulated that the Indians could go on using the land as they had in the past many, quite rightly, got the idea they were agreeing to *share* the land with the white settlers—not give it up entirely. Pike's was the first U.S. treaty to be signed west of the Mississippi River.

Although a winter for which Pike and his men were ill prepared was coming on, the men continued north, following the Mississippi as far as the mouth of the Swan River. There, at a site just south of the present city of Little Falls, they built a log stockade and prepared to spend the winter, living on game, fish and wild rice. From their base at Fort Pike, the men pressed on north eventually reaching Cass Lake. The North West Company, made up mainly of British officials and factors, dominated the fur trade in this area.

Pike camped at Leech Lake on February 1, 1806, and, following his instructions, ordered Hugh McGillis, director of the British fur company's Fond du Lac department, to take down the English flag at his Leech Lake post. Pike also told McGillis to cease giving out medals with the image of the English sovereign to the Indians. McGillis took down the Union Jack as requested, but British traders continued to work around the Falls of St. Anthony, though some prudently obtained American trading licenses in St. Louis. As for the British medals, the Indians could not see why Pike attached so much importance to the shiny emblems. The Indians insisted that the British medals were merely a reward for good hunts and did not reflect their political allegiance.

Cass and Leech Lakes, Pike decided, were the principal sources of the Mississippi. On reaching Leech Lake in 1806 Pike wrote in his journal, "I will not attempt to describe my feeling on the accomplishment of my voyage, this being the main source of the Mississippi." Pike was wrong but not far wrong. The true headwaters was but a few miles away from his northernmost camp at Cass Lake. With the coming of spring, Pike and his men abandoned Fort Pike and pointed the prows of their crude bateaux downriver. His epic exploration of the Mississippi was over, but others would soon follow in his footsteps.

Jefferson waited for two years to send the treaty Pike had negotiated with the Indians to the Senate for ratification. Then he sent Major Stephen Long up the Mississippi in 1819 to confirm Pike's selection of a site for the military post. A few months later Lieutenant Colonel Henry Leavenworth followed to build the fort but before he could get started Colonel Josiah Snelling replaced him. In 1819 Snelling and his men from the Fifth Regiment of Infantry wrestled their keelboats up the river to build the army fort on the dramatic promontory Pike had purchased from the Indians thirteen years before.

The Mississippi, at this point, negotiates two sharp curves, like a giant S lying on its side. Soldiers built the fort at the bottom of the first curve, on the western side of the river seven miles below the falls. Named for its commander, Fort Snelling was a lonely outpost—built to assert U.S. authority over fur traders and Indians, many of whom were still loyal to the British crown. Control of the river was the key to control of the vast territory of the Upper Mississippi. Fort Snelling, perched on a bluff high above Pike Island and the meeting of the rivers, exposed to arctic gales in the winter, with its flag whipping in the wind, bravely proclaimed U.S. sovereignty over the Northwest Territory.

Life at the remote fort was not an easy one. The men laid the cornerstone for the first building on September 10, 1820. During the winter of 1820-21 they went into the woods along the Rum River to cut logs for their buildings and in the spring they floated 2,000 logs down the Mississippi. Dependent on the unwieldy keelboats for only the most essential of their supplies, the soldiers planted hundreds of acres of vegetables, wheat and corn, and cut hay for their horses.

Other soldiers worked at building a stonewalled sawmill on the west bank of the river, just below the falls and connected it to the rushing water by a wooden flume. Here they sawed logs of maple, oak, elm and basswood into lumber to build the fort. In 1823 the hard-working men installed a pair of millstones and ground the small amount of wheat they had raised into what they complained was poor quality flour. The first two buildings on the site of what would become the city of Minneapolis did not inspire awe. The sawmill measured 45 by 60 feet and the flour mill was about sixteen feet square.

The soldiers at Fort Snelling had company in their wilderness. Dakota villages, all on the western side of the Mississippi, lay to the east, west and south of the fort. Near the main gate to the fort was the St. Peter Agency where the Indian agent Major Lawrence Taliaferro mediated disputes and regulated the traders, Alexis Bailly (licensed by Taliaferro) conducted his fur trade business with the Indians, and visiting French voyageurs camped.

The social life at the Fort and in the tiny settlement, called for a time New Hope, was lively. Taliaferro, the most influential and important civil officer on the Upper Mississippi, was from an aristocratic Virginia family. Stubborn and patriotic, he fought with the trader Bailly. Taliaferro's task was to protect the Indians from intertribal warfare and from the unscrupulous dealings of the traders. This put him in continual conflict with Bailly and, at times, open warfare with the American Fur Company.

Alexis Bailly, who gave Taliaferro no quarter, was descended on his father's side from the French colonial aristocracy of Canada and on his mother's from the Ottawa Indian tribe that had once controlled much of the fur trade in eastern Canada. Bailly spoke and wrote faultless English and French and was fluent in several Indian languages as well as Latin. His wife was Lucy Faribault, herself the child of a French trader and a part-Indian mother.

Taliaferro had a nearly impossible task. With the help of only a subagent and a few interpreters he was charged with policing the fur trade throughout the vast territory between the Mississippi and Missouri Rivers. Traders illegally leased or purchased land from the Indians, hired foreigners even though only Americans were permitted to engage in the fur trade and sold alcohol to the Indians.

When the Europeans established trading posts in the interior they introduced a new and dangerous element—the practice of selling supplies to the Indians on credit. Indians needed kits of tools and supplies to carry them through a winter of trapping in the north woods. Traders sold supplies to the Indians on credit and charged interest—knowing that the federal government would pay off all Indian debts once the Indian lands were ceded to the government. The traders succeeded in getting exorbitant sums of purported Indian debt written into the terms of the treaties. When the federal government agreed to pay cash for Indian land the traders stepped between the tribes and the government and insisted that the traders be paid off before any of the money went to the Indians. As a result the traders grew rich on government money and the Indians became more and more impoverished.

Taliaferro regarded this practice as using the Indians to defraud the government. He was certain that the American Fur Company was scheming to get as much of the forthcoming treaty payments for itself as it could. At one point Taliaferro wrote in great frustration to his superiors in Washington, D.C., "The crisis is approaching. We have designing and unprincipled men at work. Gold is their brazen goal and they will act freely to destroy any honest man standing between them and the forlorn and helpless savages. Thousands and hundreds of thousands of dollars are now annually paid by the Treasury to a set of men who have defrauded the Indians and are now using them to defraud the government." Recognizing Taliaferro's threat to his business, Henry Sibley, an official of the American Fur Company, tried to get him dismissed from his post but was unsuccessful.

The missionary Samuel Pond saw a different Taliaferro. "He was a man of generous, friendly disposition and was more popular with both whites and Indians than agents usually are. He was very gentle in his treatment of the Indians, being averse to the use of harsh means in dealing with them. Some thought he was too lenient. Perhaps the prompt severity of the commanders of the garrison sometimes needed to be tempered a little by the mildness of the agent." Taliaferro's influence with the Indians was greatly enhanced when he had a child with a daughter of the Dakota war chief Cloud Man. This kinship relationship tied the agent into the traditional Dakota network system and gave him a base of political support for his policies.

Because of the good counsel he gave the Indians, his attempts to negotiate peace between the Ojibwe and Dakota and his battles with the American Fur Company, Indian agent Taliaferro never lost the confidence of the Indians, nor, in the end, the gratitude of the federal government. He was colorful, incorruptible and had a deep sense of justice. In the twenty-one years Taliaferro served as Indian Agent on the Upper Mississippi no whites were killed by the Indians.

Besides choosing the site for Fort Snelling, Pike selected the location for another fort several hundred miles south on an island in the Mississippi that he called "big island" but which was soon renamed Rock Island. On May 10, 1816, keelboats hauled 600 soldiers and their supplies to begin building Fort Armstrong, named for the Secretary of War, on the west end of the island. Major Stephen H. Long, who visited the fort a year later, said it was "situated immediately upon the lower extremity of Rock Island, at which place the shores are perpendicular cliffs of limestone overhang 30 feet high. In some instances the cliffs project over their base and even some parts of the Fort overhang the water." The actions of the youthful Pike—whose name graced a mountain in the west and a bluff and island in the Mississippi, who was captured by the Spanish at Santa Fe and died in Canada during the War of 1812—determined the sites of Minneapolis and St. Paul. His purchase of two pieces of land from the Indians guaranteed that not one, but two cities would develop around the falls and at the head of navigation on the Mississippi.

NOTES

For Zebulon Pike, see Elliott Coues, *The Expeditions of Zebulon Montgomery Pike*, Vol. 1 (1895). Quotations from Dakota leaders are found in Mark Diedrich, *Dakota Oratory* (1989) and his *Great Chiefs of the Eastern Sioux* (1987). On Taliaferro, consult a master's thesis written for Hamline University by Hubert W. Snodgrass, "The Major and the monopoly; a study of the relations of Major Lawrence Taliaferro, United States Indian Agent, with the American Fur Company, 1835-1837," (1948). Samuel Pond's memoir, *The Dakota or Sioux in Minnesota*, was first published in 1908 and reprinted in 1986. *The Northern Expeditions of Stephen H. Long, the Journals of 1817 and 1823* were edited by Lucile Kane, June D. Holmquist, and Carolyn Gilman and published in 1978.

CHAPTER 5

The Voyage of the *Virginia*

Though the keelboats were gone, replaced by the steamboats, the Upper Mississippi River had yet to be conquered. The Rock Island rapids in the river at Fort Armstrong were a formidable obstacle. While keelboats could be wrenched over the rocks, fifteen miles of foaming water blocked the more fragile steamboats. The last of the four great glaciers had formed the rapids. In the final ice age the Iowa and Tazell glaciers had collided and forced the Mississippi into its present channel, forcing it west for fifteen miles across a hard limestone outcropping before it met an older channel near Muscatine, Iowa. That outcropping, breaking up in massive chunks of rock that lay at right angles to the flow of water, formed the rapids. The fingers of rock, extending from both shores, created a twisting channel of cross currents, pools and shallows that were nearly impossible to navigate. The drop at the rapids was a little over twenty feet with about half of the total occurring in the last five miles. Boats had to zig-zag back and forth across the river to avoid the rocks and treacherous currents.

Illinois became a state in 1818 solely because the lower half of the state was settled. Above the Rock Island falls, the land was empty of white settlers. Immigrants, whose only mode of travel was by the river, were impatient to move onto the tall grass prairies. The rapids in the river at Rock Island blocked their way. Well aware that the rapids were an obstacle to settlement the federal government's Chief of Engineers, in 1837, sent a young West Point graduate, Lieutenant Robert E. Lee, to Rock Island to map the rapids and devise a solution to the problem. Lee lived on the second deck of a boat that had sunk in the river and while he was unable to solve the problem of navigation of the rapids, he reported that fishing was good from his window.

On April 21, 1823, the steamboat *Virginia*, weighing just over 100 tons and measuring 118 feet long with an 18 foot beam, set off on a journey that no steamboat had ever taken before. Her captain, John Crawford, was attempting to take her all the way up the Mississippi from St. Louis to the head of navigation at Fort Snelling. The principal obstacle to the trip was those fifteen miles of treacherous rapids at Rock Island.

No one knew if a steamboat could negotiate this turbulent section of the river and make its way up to Fort Snelling. The *Virginia* was a decidedly unimpressive boat for such an undertaking. She was little larger than a keelboat with no cabin (her passengers slept in a roofed cargo box on the stern) and no pilothouse. Her steam engine sat open on the deck. The *Virginia* reached Fort Armstrong at the tip of Rock Island on May 10, 1823, to the welcoming salute of cannon from the fort and musket fire from Sauk and Mesquakie Indians along the shore. To aid the *Virginia* in traversing the fifteen mile stretch of treacherous rapids, Crawford took on as pilot George Davenport, an Indian trader living on the island. The boat's departure was delayed when, despite Davenport's efforts, the *Virginia* hung up on the rocks for almost three days until rising water in the river floated her free.

Numerous Indian villages, some housing several hundred people, were on the banks of the upper river at the time of the voyage. The *Virginia* stopped at Wapasha II's and Red Wing's villages and the chiefs came aboard. Those weren't the only stops the steamboat made. Wood fueled the boilers, so every thirty miles the boat pulled in to shore while everyone, passengers and crew alike, got off to chop wood to keep the fires going. Since the captain was unacquainted with the river, the boat traveled only during the day—except for one night when the way was illuminated by a fire raging in the underbrush on the bank.

The passengers on the historic voyage of the *Virginia* reflected the times. One was a woman missionary bound for the lead mines at Dubuque to work among the Indians. Also on board was the young Indian agent Taliaferro, who was returning to his position at Fort Snelling following a visit to Washington, D.C. Accompanying them was a family from Kentucky headed for the lead mines at Galena who came aboard as a passenger described them, "with their arms and baggage, cats and dogs, hens and turkeys; the children too had their own stock."

Among other passengers on the *Virginia* was Great Eagle, a Sauk Indian chief who had gone to St. Louis to confer with General William

Clark. When Great Eagle boarded the boat he was wearing an officer's uniform that Clark had given him. After a day or two, Great Eagle shed the uniform and continued on, as a fellow traveler wrote, "in *status quo* of our first parents." Members of Great Eagle's tribe made their way along the riverbank as the boat bearing their chief beat its way upstream. At one point the chief differed with the captain as to the proper channel to follow. The captain ignored the chief's advice and promptly ran the boat onto a sandbar. Disgusted at the captain's intransigence, Great Eagle dove overboard, swam (or waded) to shore and joined his tribesmen, traveling the rest of the way to his destination on foot.

GIACOMO BELTRAMI'S EXPLORATIONS

Also aboard the *Virginia* was the eccentric Giacomo Beltrami, an Italian adventurer. Beltrami, who was on a tour of the United States, had encountered Taliaferro and General William Clark while waiting in a log house at the confluence of the Ohio and the Mississippi for a boat to

Giacomo Beltrami, Italian adventurer, came to Fort Snelling aboard *The Virginia* in 1823. Near the flagpole Beltrami hoisted his famous umbrella. From the painting by Ken Fox in the Collection of Captain William D. Bowell.

go downriver. The three men fell into conversation and Taliaferro and Clark convinced the Italian that there was much more to see and explore upriver than down. Beltrami, who had a deep interest in the Indians, changed his plans and boarded the *Virginia*. "To learn the habits of the Indian tribes was almost a mania with him," Taliaferro reported.

Beltrami had another obsession. He wanted to find the headwaters of the Mississippi. Though he had few woodsman's skills and could not paddle a canoe, Beltrami envisioned himself as an explorer and he could imagine no nobler task than to discover the headwaters of the mighty Mississippi. At the time, locating the precise source of the river was not a major interest among American explorers. They knew the river originated somewhere amid the bogs, lakes and swamps bordering Canada. Pike thought he had found it in 1806. In 1820 Lewis Cass, the governor of Michigan Territory and his companion Henry Schoolcraft, had taken the Savanna Portage Route from Lake Superior to the Mississippi, then followed the river north to a lake, later named Cass Lake, that they believed was the river's source. Doubts about the accuracy of Cass's claim lingered and the challenge of locating the exact source captured Beltrami's imagination. He was fascinated by everything he saw on the American frontier, including even the paddle wheel on the *Virginia*. Beltrami spent hours hanging over the side of the boat watching its progress up river.

Beltrami compared the bluffs and hills around Lake Pepin to the valley of the Rhine. (Lake Pepin, a wide "lake" in the bed of the Mississippi, is caused by the delta of the Chippewa River spreading across the gorge of the Mississippi at the lower end of the lake. The smaller Chippewa, because of its steeper grade, brought in more glacial debris than the slower moving Mississippi could carry away. The delta formed a dam and as water backed up, created Lake Pepin.)

When the boat stopped for wood Beltrami went ashore, armed with his rifle, pistols and sword, and fired at anything that moved in the woods. On one occasion he wandered off and when he found his way back to the river, discovered that the boat had departed without him. In a panic he fired off his gun and splashed along the shore after the boat— to find it only a short distance ahead, stuck on a sandbar.

The pioneering boat took twenty days to make the 700-mile journey upriver to Fort Snelling. Five of those days had been spent grounded on sandbars or stuck in the rocks of the Rock Island Rapids. The arrival of the *Virginia* at Fort Snelling on May 10, 1823, belching smoke from her chimneys and exhausting steam from her escape pipes, caused a sensation. The Indians were terrified at the sight and some fled into the countryside. The officers at the fort fired a cannon salute and rushed down to the landing to greet the boat. Besides supplies for the fort and goods for the Indian traders, the *Virginia* carried a cargo of lead, picked up during stops at Dubuque and Galena. Her cargo was a harbinger of the future. Lead was already challenging the supremacy of furs as the major commodity carried on the river.

Col. Josiah Snelling cordially entertained the passengers of the *Virginia*. But when Beltrami asked permission to go further into Indian tribal lands in his quest for the source of the Mississippi, Snelling refused. Beltrami's dream of exploration would have ended at that point if Major Stephen Long had not coincidentally arrived at the fort at the head of a company of soldiers sent to explore the Minnesota River. Beltrami convinced Long to let him tag along. They were scarcely underway when their association proved to be an unhappy one.

Long, a member of the army's elite corps of topographical engineers, was a brave, strict West Point-trained army officer who lacked both imagination and humor. Long's consistently pessimistic assessments helped popularize the idea that the west was a wild and barren waste. Beltrami, on the other hand, was a verbose Italian romantic. They took an instant dislike to each other. Long refused to tell Beltrami the route they were following but when the expedition reached Pembina on the Red River, Beltrami realized he was north and west of the Mississippi's probable source.

Refusing to be deterred from his quest, Beltrami left Long's company and, without equipment or experience, set off with two Ojibwe guides into the woods. A few days later his guides abandoned him when they were attacked by some wandering Dakota. Now, cast adrift and alone in the northern wilderness, Beltrami spent a short time meditating on the story of Robinson Crusoe and rather enjoying the drama of his situation. Then, tying a piece of rawhide to the bow of the canoe he was unable to paddle, he slung the leather strap over his shoulder and began wading upstream, towing his canoe behind him.

As he later explained, " I was totally unacquainted with the almost magical art by which a single person guides a canoe . . . the lightness of which is overpowered by the current . . . Instead of proceeding up the river, I descended. Renewed efforts made me lose my equilibrium, the canoe upset . . ." When it began to rain Beltrami unfurled a large red silk umbrella and wedged it upright in his canoe to protect his baggage. The sight of a canoe crowned with a red silk umbrella and towed by a white man rendered Beltrami an unforgettable sight to the startled Indians who came upon him.

If it had not been for his umbrella and the help of bemused Indians, Beltrami might not have survived. Instead he almost succeeded in his quest. He recognized Lake La Biche (Schoolcraft's Itasca) as one source of the Mississippi but believed another nearby lake to be the northernmost point of origin. He named it Lake Julia in memory of a close friend, the Countess Giulia Spada de Medini. His visit to Lake Julia took place nine years before Schoolcraft identified the true source of the river. Beltrami's red silk umbrella can be seen today in his native city of Bergamo in northern Italy.

The *Virginia* was to make but one more trip up the river to Fort Snelling that season before she had a mishap and sank. Though the *Virginia's* career on the Upper Mississippi was brief, the repercussions of her trip to the Falls of St. Anthony were enormous. The ramshackle craft demonstrated that steamboats could navigate the river and its rapids. With transportation assured, the magnet of the river began to draw commerce and settlers.

Tentatively, other boats followed the *Virginia's* lead. A door had been opened and what began as a trickle of people moving north on the river, soon turned into a flood. Tocqueville, on a trip on the Mississippi in 1831, wrote in his journal, "There isn't anyone who does not recognize that the discovery of steam has added unbelievably to the strength and prosperity of the Union and has done so by facilitating rapid communication between the diverse parts of this vast body."

In time, not just river craft, but towns were to emerge from the fertile womb of the river. The Mississippi was every village's "first cause," the reason for its being. The river had already brought the artifacts of Europe to the Indian in exchange for furs. Now it would lure explorers and adventurers, transport immigrant farmers to new lives in the north country and drain the forests and plains of their wealth. As a flyway for the migration of birds, waterway for commerce, bearer of human dreams, greed and sorrows, the highway of the Mississippi began its flow through the imagination of the nation.

NOTES

Giacomo Beltrami's tale of his travels was published in 1824. A later account of Beltrami's life is *The Man with the Red Umbrella* (1974) by Augusto P. Miceli. The voyage of the *Virginia* is recorded in William J. Petersen, *Steamboating on the Upper Mississippi, the Water Way to Iowa* (1968). The de Tocqueville journal is mentioned in Louis Hunter, *Steamboats on the Western Rivers* (1949).

CHAPTER 6

The Early Towns

The Mississippi is to [Westerners] everything. It is the
Hudson, the Delaware, the Potomac and all the navigable
rivers of the Atlantic States formed into one stream.

–James Madison, in a letter to Thomas Jefferson, 1803.

At the time of the *Virginia's* voyage one community dominated the
Mississippi above New Orleans. That city, founded in 1764, was St.
Louis. Pierre Laclede had received a six-year exclusive right from the
French to trade with the Indians of the Missouri as well as with all Indian nations residing west of the Mississippi River. With thirty men and
his fourteen-year-old stepson, Auguste Chouteau, Laclede traveled up
the river from New Orleans looking for a suitable location for his trading post. When he came to the mouth of the Missouri where it empties
into the Mississippi he chose a site on the west side of the river because
he knew France had recently ceded the land on the east side to England.
No self-respecting Frenchman would, at that time, knowingly live under
English rule.

Though Laclede was unaware of it, by choosing the west side of the
river he had established his trading post in Spanish territory, land which
remained under Spanish rule until 1804 when the area was ceded to
France. On March 9, before the formal transfer of the territory to France
could take place, the 900 citizens of St. Louis (including 268 slaves)
watched in bemusement as the Spanish flag was taken down and the flag
of France immediately raised on the pole. Then, the next morning, the
French flag came down and the flag of the United States was raised in its

place. In the space of twenty-four hours, the residents of St. Louis had the unique experience of living under the flags of three countries.

Located between the mouths of the Ohio and Missouri Rivers that flowed east and west, and on the Mississippi carrying traffic north and south, St. Louis grew exponentially. In one decade the population of the city leaped from 17,000 to 77,000. John Jacob Astor established a branch of his American Fur Company in St. Louis and when the fur trade began to decline, expanded into banking and wholesale goods—outfitting exploring parties, army detachments and wagon trains. St. Louis became the crossroads of river commerce and westward expansion. It was from this burgeoning city that Lewis and Clark left on their voyage of discovery up the Missouri and Pike began his exploration of the Upper Mississippi.

PRAIRIE DU CHIEN, WISCONSIN

When the *Virginia* began her historic voyage up the river there were only three non-Indian villages of any size above St. Louis where she could pay a call and take on cargo. These were Dubuque, Galena and Prairie du Chien. The oldest of the three was Prairie du Chien, located a mile from the mouth of the Wisconsin River. In 1673 Louis Jolliet and Jacques Marquette stood on a promontory and looked down at the meeting of the Wisconsin with the Mississippi. With the help of Indian guides, they had traveled from Green Bay, an arm of Lake Michigan, up the Fox River, across 128 miles of marshy prairie to the Wisconsin River and, after two days of paddling their birch bark canoes, reached the Mississippi.

The two Frenchmen immediately grasped the significance of this section of the Mississippi. They had discovered a major transit route for the great loads of furs that had enriched the French ports of eastern Canada for the past three decades. For ninety lucrative years the French had maintained sovereignty over the region. After the English won control, the Fox Indians, at a ceremony in Mackinac in 1781, sold the 15 mile long glacial terrace formed near the juncture of the Wisconsin and Mississippi rivers to the British for a fur trading post.

The site, called Prairie du Chien after the Fox Indian name for their leader, "Dog of the Prairie," was a logical choice. One reason was its celebrated history. Long before the whites arrived on the scene, Prairie du Chien had been a Fox Indian village and was considered by the Indians to be a neutral zone. In late May every year thousands of Dakota, Pottawatomie, Orielle, Winnebago, Mascoutin, and Fox Indians, many of whom were bitter enemies, came in fur-laden canoes to Prairie du Chien to barter and meet in council. For a few weeks in the spring they forgot their differences to trade, feast, smoke peace pipes, look for spouses, celebrate and play games. The Indians put aside all intertribal enmity during this time.

After the arrival of Europeans in the New World, customs from pre-contact times continued. Each spring about 6,000 Indians came from great distances up and down the Mississippi River to Prairie du Chien to trade their furs for the ammunition, tools and cloth provided by the French and Spanish. When Jonathan Carver, of Connecticut, visited Prairie du Chien in 1766, he found a village of 300 Indian families tilling the soil, and living in houses "well built after the Indian manner, and pleasantly situated on a very rich soil, from which they raise every necessity of life in great abundance. I saw here many houses of a good size and shape. This town is the great mart. . . ."

The original English community of Prairie du Chien was on an island of the Mississippi, called St. Feriole, separated from the eastern shore by a shallow lagoon. Clustered together on the island were log warehouses stocked with trade goods for the Indians, cabins and out-buildings, taverns, stables for animals and a landing area for boats. East of the island, across the lagoon, lay the broad, glacial terrace that rose gradually from the river to end at the base of distant hills. The river was over two miles wide at this point and strewn with a maze of channels and islands. Steep hills rose precipitously from the western shore.

During the early years of white settlement of Prairie du Chien a group of Winnebagoes threatened to attack the town. Concerned, the settlers appealed to the Dakota chief Wapasha II for protection. They made a wise choice. Wapasha II had the respect of both the whites and Indians. The son of the revered Wapasha I, Wapasha II was an imposing figure. He had lost an eye in his youth and wore an eye patch, had wide cheekbones, a strong nose, thin cheeks and a large head. In response to the settlers' pleas for help, he went before the council of Winnebago chiefs, plucked a hair from his head and held it out to them.

"Winnebagoes, do you see this hair?" he asked. "Look at it. You threaten to massacre the white people at the Prairie! They are your friends and mine. You wish to drink their blood? Is that your purpose? Dare to lay a finger upon one of them and I will blow you from the face of the earth as I now blow this hair with my breath where none can find it." Taking a deep breath, Wapasha II blew the hair from between his fingers. Then he turned and left. The Winnebagoes never attacked the village of Prairie du Chien.

The wars among the French, British and the colonists for control of North America brought about changes in ownership of Prairie du Chien with dizzying frequency. The Indians had good reason to be confused. Originally most Indians had allied with the French who were the first Europeans to claim sovereignty. When the Treaty of Paris ended the French and Indian War in 1763, many Indians transferred their allegiance to the British.

England's victory meant that France's lucrative fur trading franchise would now go to the great trading houses chartered by the British crown. Soon the English were taking over a million dollars worth of furs annually from the waters and forests of the Upper Mississippi region— furs obtained from the Indians and shipped north to the Great Lakes through the village of Prairie du Chien. For the traders, the river's usefulness was as the water conduit to move furs to markets in the East.

When the Revolutionary War was about to break out, the leading English trader, Robert Dickson, called the Indians together at Prairie du Chien and asked for their help against the "long knives" of the Americans. The spokesman for the Indians was Wapasha I who had been born in about 1718. Wapasha I was considered to be the most effective speaker and the most influential trader in the Indian councils of all the Dakota chiefs. His family had inter-married with the French fur traders and he was an uncle to one of Henry Sibley's fur trade associates, Augustine Roque.

The missionary Gideon Pond wrote of Wapasha I, "He was the courage, the heart, the grit of the Mdewakanton band . . . Dakota tradition has preserved the name of no greater or better man than Wapasha." Mary Eastman claimed, "There has never been a chief more honored and respected than Wapasha." Wapasha I, knowing how dependent the Dakota were on traders of any nationality, equivocated in his reply to Dickson's plea for help. "We live by our English traders," he said, "who have always assisted us and never more so than this last year at the risk of their lives and we are at all times ready to listen to them on account of the friendships they have always shown us." In other words, though he favored the British, Wapasha I kept Dakota trading options open.

Wapasha I was wise not to have committed himself. The Americans won the war and the Northwest Territory became the property of the United States. Despite having lost, it was years before the British relinquished their hold on the region. The French influence was also still strong. When Pike visited Prairie du Chien in 1805 he reported that 370 individuals, mainly French-Canadians, lived with their Indian wives in houses of logs plastered with mud and covered with strips of bark.

Through the signing of the Treaty of Paris all of New France was supposed to pass into the hands of the English. However, in a move to avoid having to turn all of America over to the British, France had taken the precaution of deeding its possessions *west* of the Mississippi, together with New Orleans, to Spain. In 1800 Spain had secretly handed the territory, called Louisiana, back to Napoleon and France.

When President Thomas Jefferson learned of the land transfer from Spain back to France, he was deeply concerned. The reason was the Mississippi River. Jefferson knew that the United States had to have access to the mouth of the Mississippi and the city of New Orleans or risk losing everything west of the Appalachians. He had not been worried when feeble Spain controlled New Orleans. But having Napoleon, the greatest military genius of the age, in control of the region was a decidedly different matter. Could Napoleon have designs on the Northwest Territory or on Canada? Jefferson sent his minister, Robert Livingston, to Paris to offer Napoleon ten million dollars for New Orleans and Florida.

Fortunately for the United States, travel across the Atlantic took time. By the time Livingston reached Paris, reverses in the French-held Santo Domingo (now Haiti) had changed Napoleon's plans to expand his holdings in the New World. He offered to sell—not just New Orleans and Florida—but *all* of Louisiana to the Americans. On receiving the offer Livingston was struck almost speechless. His instructions had said nothing about buying an area almost as large as the entire United States.

This was not something that Jefferson had foreseen or planned either. On the contrary, in his inaugural address Jefferson had expressed the opinion that the United States already had all the land it would need for a thousand generations. Since there was no way Livingston could consult with Jefferson he would have to make the decision himself. Fortunately James Monroe arrived in Paris the very next day to share the responsibility with Livingston. The two men dickered with the French and eventually signed a treaty agreeing to pay $15 million for all of Louisiana, as well as New Orleans and Florida. When Livingston asked the French minister Talleyrand where the boundaries of the purchase lay, Talleyrand replied, "I can give you no directions. You have made a noble bargain for yourselves and I suppose you will make the most of it."

Thus it was from France and not Spain that the United States purchased the Louisiana Territory. Jefferson's action guaranteed that the Mississippi River would forever be an American possession. No longer would the Mississippi River be the western border of the infant nation. Now it would become a seam through the heartland that, in time, would knit the two halves of the country together.

In 1814, when the second war with Great Britain was underway, William Clark, recognizing the strategic importance of Prairie du Chien, sailed upriver from St. Louis with 150 soldiers to establish a fort. Neither the resident British nor the French opposed him. Clark and his men built a fort they called Fort Shelby on the top of a large Indian mound that rose abruptly from the flat land of St. Feriole Island like a forgotten, buried castle. When the British in Canada learned of Clark's fort they sent an expeditionary force to Prairie du Chien. They quickly took back the fort and changed its name to Fort McKay.

In their struggle, both the British and the Americans sought the support of the Indians. Tamaha was a Mdewakanton Dakota who had been a friend to both Pike and Clark. Aware of Tamaha's influence as an orator with the Indians, Clark sent him on a mission to the Teton Dakotas living along the Missouri River to persuade them to remain faithful to the Americans. Tamaha was successful in his efforts but when he went to Prairie du Chien to do the same, he was imprisoned by the British fur trader Dickson, now a Colonel in the British army. Dickson ordered Tamaha, on pain of death, to report what he had told Clark.

Tamaha refused. "Tamaha is a good Indian," he said to Dickson. "He has no fear of death. He told his white chief, Governor Clark, that he would carry his talk to his people at Prairie du Chien. He had endeavored to do so. He was a prisoner of war. He could do no more. This and only this made the heart of Tamaha sad. Tomaha has no secrets to reveal to Colonel Dickson. The talk of his white chief to Tamaha should be buried with Tamaha in the silent earth. Why should Colonel Dickson kill Tamaha? What would he gain? The dead tell no tales. The living brave betrays no trust. Colonel Dickson, the heart of Tamaha is strong. If one word would save the life of Tamaha, Tamaha would not speak that word to save his life. As the forest leaf falls silently and calmly to the ground, so shall Tamaha go calmly and silently to the spirit land. The talk of Tamaha is ended." When Tamaha finished his speech and would say no more, Dickson knew he had met his match. Dickson was married to a Dakota woman and had spent years among the tribes. He did not take Tamaha's life and instead released him.

A few months later the War of 1812 ended with the signing of the Treaty of Ghent. It took a long time for news of the treaty to reach the American frontier. When word finally arrived, the British obediently withdrew from Prairie du Chien but not before burning the fort on the mound to the ground. Tamaha was in the town at the time and daringly rescued the American flag from the flames. The date was May 24, 1815. Governor Clark rewarded Tamaha for his patriotic act by giving him a captain's uniform with a stovepipe hat and a meaningless title. Tamaha treasured the uniform and hat for the rest of his life and wore them only on special occasions. The retreat of the British from Prairie du Chien was the last surrender of English forces on American soil. The heroic Tamaha lived for 100 years—long enough to see the complete removal of his people from their homelands.

After the British departed, General Thomas Smith of the U.S. Army lost no time in sailing back to Prairie du Chien with six companies of riflemen to again assert U.S. control over the Upper Mississippi. Smith carried with him orders to rebuild the burned down fort. Construction of a new fort, called Fort Crawford, began on July 3, 1816, on the same much-abused Indian mound.

The personnel stationed at this remote fort played major roles in American history. One of the first commanders was Colonel Henry Leavenworth. He had come to Prairie du Chien as Indian agent in 1817. Within two years he was a Lieutenant Colonel in the army. Leavenworth was followed at Fort Crawford by Major Philip Kearney, who later gained fame during the Mexican war for capturing Santa Fe without firing a shot. He was succeeded by Col. Zachary Taylor, who later became a U.S. president.

A member of Taylor's staff was a young lieutenant from the South named Jefferson Davis. Davis fell in love with Taylor's daughter, Knox. Colonel Taylor disliked Davis and ordered the lieutenant to abandon his suit. Instead, Davis resigned from the Army and continued his, now secret, courtship of Knox while she was visiting an aunt in Louisville. On the morning of her wedding day Knox wrote to her mother from Kentucky telling her she was marrying Davis. Less than three months after the wedding, Knox Taylor Davis died of cholera at the Davis plantation on the Mississippi. Davis, grief-stricken, became a recluse for eight years before he remarried.

Prairie du Chien, at the time the *Virginia* called on her way north, was the principal town on the Upper Mississippi and the second most important fur trading post in the Northwest Territory. Though business still centered on St. Feriole Island, the bustling town had grown far past the lagoon and extended up the terrace toward the hills. The leading citizen was Jean Joseph Rolette, a burly man who had moved to Prairie du Chien in 1804 as a junior partner to Indian trader Murdoch Cameron. Rolette had prospered and before long owned much of the town as well as several farms and a sawmill.

In 1819 the 40-year-old Rolette married 15-year-old Jane Fisher, a niece of prominent citizens Domitelle and Michael Brisbois. Jane had been educated in a Cincinnati convent and was beautiful, cultured and, despite her youth, the strong-willed equal of her husband. Jane's father, Henry Monroe Fisher, had been the first American to settle permanently in Prairie du Chien. Jane was also descended from the sister of an Ottawa chief, La Fourche. Though Jane's ancestor's Indian name has been lost, it is known that the woman converted to Christianity and was baptized "Domitelle," a name carried forward through several generations of her family. Domitelle's first marriage had been to a French trader named Daniel Villeneuve and, after his death she married Augustin Langlade, the younger son of an aristocratic French family.

Jane and Jean Rolette most certainly entertained the passengers on the *Virginia* at their home during its stop at Prairie du Chien. Though traffic on the river was busy (the town had begun levying a fee of $1 for every keelboat and fifty cents for every flatboat that tied up at its dock) the arrival of the *Virginia* would have been an extraordinary event and its passengers welcomed, fed and entertained.

The major business at Prairie du Chien and on the Upper Mississippi was the fur trade; everyone involved in it tried to monopolize it. In the beginning the Indians had succeeded in maintaining control, taking huge shipments of furs on a thousand mile journey to Montreal where they exchanged them for the French trade goods of firearms, tools, textiles, traps and cooking utensils. Indian middlemen journeyed on the rivers far into the interior to collect the furs. By the 1670's the French had pushed westward and shifted the location of the fur exchange from Quebec to the interior. For the Dakota and Ojibwe this was a great convenience. They no longer had to wait for caravans of canoes to return from the East to obtain goods from Europe. Each Indian could deal directly with the traders. Other tribes, particularly the Fox, realized that the coming of the French to the Mississippi valley and the establishment of trading posts meant the end of Indian control of the fur trade.

In addition to setting up trading posts the French, British (and later the Americans) married Indian women and became related by marriage and by blood to the leading Indian families. There was a strategy behind the unions. As competition among the traders increased, those who had strong kinship attachments to the Dakota fared better than those who did not. Traders were quick to purchase the most beautiful daughters of the leading Indian families and take them as wives.

Within a generation a large secondary population of mixed blood individuals grew up, many of whom were at home in both cultures. Some were fluent in Indian and European languages and became the intermediaries and interpreters of each culture to the other. While some continued to live in the manner of their Indian parent, others sought education and married into the leading white families. Having an Indian ancestor was no deterrent to social success. Throughout the first century or more of contact, racial feelings were not in evidence. There was no stigma attached to having Indian parents or grandparents. Indians were not seen as being "red" or looking physically different from whites until the eighteenth century. The fur trade, in particular, was ideally suited to the abilities of mixed-race individuals and many prospered.

For almost 150 years the fur trade was an economic bonanza for the country that controlled it. The French, British and Americans each, in turn, attempted to dominate the trade by establishing large trading companies, awarding licenses and offering traders cheap, duty-free trade goods to exchange with the Indians for furs. One such company was the North West Fur Company, formed in 1783, which for a time controlled much of the Upper Mississippi region. Relationships among the trading companies and the traders were constantly shifting, however, and many of the successful traders at Prairie du Chien managed to maintain their status as independent operators until 1820 when the American Fur Company dominated the trade on the Upper Mississippi.

The fur trade brought Henry Hastings Sibley, who would later become Minnesota's first governor, to Prairie du Chien. He was 26 when he became a junior partner of Jean Rolette and Hercules Dousman in the American Fur Company. Soon he went north to manage a portion of the company's territory from the village of New Hope, next to Fort Snelling, where he worked with Alexis Bailly.

Sibley's partner, the aging Rolette, a victim of imbibing too much of the alcohol he illegally sold to the Dakota, died in Prairie du Chien and his widow Jane married Dousman, who was only four years her senior. Dousman had made a fortune in fur trading, steamboats and land. Some of his fortune was invested in a mansion, later called the Villa Louis after his son. It was built on the same much-abused Indian mound that had earlier been the site of the two military forts. (Fort Crawford had since been moved up to higher ground.) The elegant house had stained glass windows in the upper story rooms that faced west toward the river and the sunset, a boat landing, library, drawing and morning rooms, and a conservatory. For the rest of her life, in her river mansion, Jane entertained the distinguished individuals who traveled up the river highway. Her two husbands had been leaders of the fur trade with the Indians and Jane lived to see the end of it. After the death of the last Dousman descendant the Villa Louis was given to the state of Wisconsin. This villa is now a museum operated by the State Historical Society of Wisconsin.

DUBUQUE, IOWA

Julien Dubuque, a French mineralogist, was floating down the Mississippi below the mouth of the Wisconsin River in 1774 when he recognized a familiar mineral on shore. If his eyes were not deceiving him, the Indian women on the west side of the river were melting pure lead from the rocks! Dubuque was not the first European to have observed the lead. A Fox Indian had earlier given a piece of lead-bearing ore, probably from Catfish Creek, to Nicholas Perrot. In 1700 Charles LeSueur had found Indians mining on the west bank of the Mississippi near what is now the city of Dubuque. He also took lead samples from the area. Father Hennepin's map shows a lead mine near Galena.

Though others had noticed the lead, Dubuque was the first European to mine the mineral. Since the west side of the river was Indian Territory and therefore not open to white settlement, Dubuque could, at first, do little about his discovery. The Indians were protective of their lead and would not allow whites on their land. Dubuque, however, had an Indian wife, Potosa, and through her in 1788 he received permission from the tribe to stake a claim and mine the lead, "tranquilly and without any prejudice to his labors." Dubuque moved onto the west bank of the river amid the towering black hills and bluffs where he mined lead and became a great favorite among the Indians.

When Pike visited Dubuque in 1805 the Frenchman told him he was manufacturing from 20,000 to 40,000 pounds of lead annually. Pike thought the wily Frenchman was vastly understating his production. Dubuque, who bequeathed his name to the mining settlement, became wealthy from mining and trading. He later lost his land when ownership of the region was transferred from France to the United States in the Louisiana Purchase.

After Dubuque's death in 1810—he was buried, at his request, in a solid lead coffin—the Indians continued mining, the work now being done by women and old men. After digging out the lead ore, they carried it in baskets to the banks of the Mississippi and ferried it to traders camped on the river islands. In 1830 English brothers named Langworthy made their way to Dubuque and negotiated permission from the Indians to mine lead on the west side of the river.

The Langworthys' activities at Dubuque presented a problem for U.S. government officials because whites were prohibited from staking claims or settling in Indian territory on the west side of the river. The problem had to be handled. Zachary Taylor, commander of the military post at Prairie du Chien, sailed down the river to Dubuque and ordered the settlers to leave. When they refused, Taylor threatened to force them out with his troops. Faced with the possibility of military action against them, the Langworthy group grudgingly abandoned their houses and mines and retreated to the east bank of the river where they watched with fury as the Indians helped themselves to the lead the miners had laboriously extracted from the rocks. Colonel Taylor well understood the frustration of the deposed settlers and he prudently established a garrison of troops at Dubuque to keep the frustrated miners from sneaking back across the river.

The standoff ended in 1832 with the outbreak of the Black Hawk War. The war, which lasted only a few weeks, was a futile attempt by the Indians, led by Chief Black Hawk, to regain their lands in Illinois. Showing remarkable generalship, Black Hawk held off two United States generals at Wisconsin Heights until the women and children of his tribe could escape across the Wisconsin River. The refugees made it as far as the mouth of the Bad Axe River where they were massacred by rampaging whites and enemy Sioux. The battle took place in August 1832.

At Bad Axe a century of Indian-white conflict, for the most part anyway, came to an end. The war was a dire object lesson to the Winnebago of Wisconsin and hastened their removal to so-called "neutral ground" across the Mississippi. With the defeat of Black Hawk, the new states of the Union gained what they had secretly wanted all along: the removal of all Indians from the state of Illinois and the opening of Iowa for settlement by whites. In the treaty that followed, the Indians gave up their lands on the west bank of the Mississippi and the miners went back across the river to their camps and lead mines in the hills of Dubuque.

No other Indian war had the participation of so many men who were later to achieve prominence. Abraham Lincoln and Colonel Zachary Taylor both became president. President Andrew Jackson sent General Winfield Scott, a later presidential candidate and the most famous soldier in America, from the East Coast to put an end to the uprising. And Jefferson Davis, the future president of the Confederacy, was called back from a furlough to take charge of Black Hawk after his surrender.

Following his capture and imprisonment at Jefferson Barracks in St. Louis, the Americans paraded Black Hawk through cities in the East to impress him with the white man's power. Artists and writers were equally impressed with Black Hawk. George Catlin visited him in St. Louis (and painted his portrait) while Washington Irving wrote a description of the Indian leader after meeting him. Before his death Black Hawk dictated his autobiography. In it, he is quoted as saying "Rock River was a beautiful country. I loved my towns, my cornfield and the home of my people. I fought for it. It is now yours. Keep it as we did." Black Hawk is remembered by an 1891 statue in Rock Island and another monumental work (dedicated in 1911) in Oregon, Illinois, beside the Rock River. This statue, forty-eight feet tall, was the work of Illinois sculptor Lorado Taft, and is of cast concrete. The U.S. Army has used the Indian leader's name for one of its larger helicopters.

GALENA, ILLINOIS

While Dubuque, with the cooperation of the Indians, mined lead on the west bank of the Mississippi, other Europeans and Indians on the east bank at the town of Galena, were also engaged in lead mining. At the time of Dubuque's death in 1810, the Fox Indians on the east side of the river were melting approximately 400,000 pounds annually. Galena is located on the Fever River—about five miles upriver from the

Mississippi—on a series of hills that rise abruptly from the flat terrain east and west of the town. The same quirk of geography that created the driftless area kept the glaciers away from this part of Illinois and as a result the town is hilly. Residents thought nothing of having to climb 100 steps to reach their houses. Five hundred steps led up to a school. One early settler sat on his roof to weed his vegetable garden and women claimed they could walk on the roofs of the houses built against the hills, look down the chimneys and see what their neighbors were cooking for dinner.

With the discovery of lead at Dubuque and Galena, the United States government moved quickly to take control of the mineral. In 1822 the General Land Office transferred responsibility for lead to the War Department which gave out leases for mining. Anyone wishing to dig for lead had to get a permit from a government agent and was required to sell his ore to a licensed smelter. Word of the lead deposits in Galena soon filtered east and a wave of immigration began. When the *Virginia* stopped at Galena in 1823 for a load of lead, fewer than 300 people lived in the town. Seven years later the population had swelled to over 1,000. Many miners came from the British Isles. Others came from the south, bringing slaves with them. Though the Northwest Ordinance of 1787 prohibited slavery in the Northwest Territory, the law was evaded by calling slaves "registered servants."

Life in the mines, though colorful, was brutal. The miners wore red flannel shirts, buckskin pants and red knit caps. In winter they wrapped themselves in blankets or, if they were fortunate, in overcoats. They lived on coffee, biscuits and fried meat as well as a prodigious amount of wild onions—perhaps due to a shortage of vegetables. They drank copiously and fought hard. Disputes were settled by force. The miners who had come from Cornwall and Wales engaged in a vicious practice called "stone fights," the poor man's version of a duel. To settle a dispute each man stood by a stockpile of rocks and threw stones at his opponent until one of the combatants was either unconscious or dead.

The lead deposits at Galena and Dubuque were shallow so they needed little costly machinery to extract the ore. Miners prospected by sinking a test hole in the ground. If lead were found, they would sink a four by six foot shaft into the vein. They dug tunnels following the veins for several hundred feet and raised the ore to the surface in buckets on a windlass. The blast furnaces used for smelting had chimneys that rose 30 to 40 feet into the air with flues eighteen inches in diameter. Galena, where smoke and flames belched day and night from the smelters, resembled a version of Dante's Inferno. Workmen maintained a constant current of air over the fires with bellows driven by water power. Ore sold for $17.50 per thousand pounds delivered to the furnaces. The smelters paid the government one tenth of the lead smelted. By 1845 the mines were producing 54,500,000 pounds of lead a year.

The lead would have stayed where it was mined in Dubuque and Galena if it had not been for the river. The Mississippi River linked the towns to the outside world. Because of the river the lead the region produced could reach world markets. The state of Illinois north of Peoria and Springfield was sparsely inhabited by a scattering of people living in primitive conditions. By contrast, because of its lifeline to the river, Galena was a luxurious city—an oasis of culture.

Boats on the river brought in the best of French wines and liquors, elegant furniture and accessories. Department stores advertised the latest in Parisian fashions permitting wealthy women in Galena to be as well dressed as women in New York, Philadelphia or Boston. Eighteen riverboats at a time, loaded with the exotic goods of the world, tied up at Galena's wharves. In the 1850's Galena was the busiest port and most important wholesale point above St. Louis. Of the boats arriving in St. Paul in 1853, 65 were from St. Louis and 99 were from Galena.

In April of 1859 a middle-aged man got off the crowded steamboat *Itasca* at Galena carrying a battered chair under each arm. His wife and children followed him down the ramp. The man attracted little notice for he had lived in Galena before, left home to go to school, and had since failed at every occupation he had attempted in his life. He had failed as a farmer, failed in real estate and, as a last resort, had come back to Galena to work in his father's store. As it turned out the man would be a near-failure there as well as he could never remember the prices of the merchandise.

Barely six years later, on April 19, 1865, the attitude of people in Galena toward the man had changed. The individual who had been considered a failure, Ulysses S. Grant, returned to Galena to the cheers of 10,000 people. Among the many signs held up by the welcoming crowd was one that read, "General, the sidewalk is built." The sign referred to the fact that when Grant had lived in Galena he had often wished for a sidewalk in front of his house so he would not have to walk in the mud when he went downtown. Now there was a sidewalk as well as an appropriate residence presented by the city to the general. As well as producing lead, the small town of Galena, Illinois gave the United States eight Union army generals and one president.

Galena reached the pinnacle of her prosperity in 1856. Besides lead mines, the residents of the town owned and controlled a large share of the steamboat activity on the Upper Mississippi, including a line of daily packet boats that ran downriver to Rock Island and upriver to St. Paul. Beginning with a single boat running to St. Paul in 1848, the Galena and Minnesota Packet Boat Company expanded operations until, in 1852, boats left Galena three times weekly for St. Paul. By 1857, the town had thirteen boats running on the Upper Mississippi, mainly above Galena.

Galena's dominance of the steamboat traffic was difficult for Dubuque, its rival community across the Mississippi, to accept. While Galena residents owned two steamboat lines, Dubuque citizens did not possess a single boat. The boats plying between Galena and St. Paul often went up the river without stopping at the rival town which was galling to the citizens of Dubuque who decided they must have steamboats of their own. They held public meetings, organized a stock company and canvassed the town for subscriptions. Eventually they purchased one boat, the *Lamartine*, captained by James Hartlow. Galena's businessmen, whose large wholesale warehouses covered all areas of trade, were unperturbed by the competition. Galena merchants supplied the entire northwest including northern Iowa, Minnesota Territory and western Wisconsin. Even the emerging lumber companies got their supplies from Galena.

The development of steamboating and of the lead-mining towns of Galena and Dubuque went hand-in-hand. Beginning around 1830, builders of steamboats recognized that the transportation of lead presented them with an economic opportunity and they moved with alacrity to take advantage of it. For their part, the lead producers recognized their total dependency on the steamboats and the steamboat industry. In no other way could a product as heavy as lead move to market except on the great river highway that flowed five miles from Galena. By 1834, 65 steamboats had made about 850 trips to Galena. The steamboat owners profited handsomely from their partnership with the lead producers, earning as much as two-fifths of the value of the upstream trade just for transporting it.

Within a period of twenty-five years miners at Dubuque and Galena shipped 472,000,000 pounds of lead down the Mississippi River. Its total value was $114,178,000, an enormous sum when compared to the value of the fur trade which, in 1848 at St. Louis, amounted to only $300,000. The annual trade on the famous Santa Fe Trail came to barely $500,000 compared to $1,654,077 for lead mined the same year. Lead, used principally to make shot for guns, was king, kept on the throne by the busy steamboats plying the river. Lead mined at Dubuque and Galena was the single most important factor, between 1823 and 1848, in the development of steamboating on the Upper Mississippi.

The boom in lead brought not only steamboats to the Mississippi; it brought people. Thousands of hardy, adventurous settlers made their way in ever-increasing numbers up the Mississippi from St. Louis, drawn by tales of adventure and riches. Their rambunctious arrival moved the shifting line of the frontier further and further north and west. Captains of the steamboats that had been built to transport lead from and luxury goods to Galena discovered another profitable cargo with which to fill their boats—immigrants and all the goods the immigrants brought with them.

Thanks to the influence of the lead mines in spurring the development of steamboats, when the immigrants arrived and needed transportation up the river, fleets of steamboats were available to carry them. When the pioneers needed an ever-increasing supply of goods—tools, farm animals, lumber—for their farms and towns, the boats on the river were there to bring it to them. When the immigrant farmers began producing wheat, barley and vegetables, the boats were on hand to carry the produce down the river to market.

Fur had been the first commodity to rule the economy of the river. Lead was second. Soon other products of the Northwest Territory would eclipse lead. The one constant that remained was the Mississippi. Without the river and the boats that sailed on it there could have been little economic activity of any kind in the region. The river was the key to the success of every enterprise. Money could be made in furs and lead only if the rivers and boats were there to bring the products to market. The river was the indispensable connecting link that tied Fort Snelling to St. Louis, Prairie du Chien to Galena and Dubuque—and all of them to the outside world.

NOTES

In the first chapter of *Three Years Travels Throughout the Interior Parts of North-America* (1797) Jonathan Carver recorded his visit to Prairie du Chien. On Prairie du Chien see Constance M. Evans and Ona B. Earl, *Prairie du Chien and the Winneshiek* (1928); Bruce Mahan, *Old Fort Crawford and the Frontier* (1926); Alice Plehal, "History of Prairie du Chien, 1760-1800," (an unpublished manuscript dated 1924 in the collections of the Minnesota Historical Society) and Rhoda Gilman, "How Henry Sibley Took the Road to New Hope," *Minnesota History* 52:6 (Summer 1991). Tamaha's speech is given in Mark Dietrich, *Dakota Oratory* (1989). The quotations from Gideon Pond and Mary Eastman are presented in Dietrich's *Famous Chiefs of the Eastern Sioux* (1987). For Galena see Carl Johnson, *The Building of Galena, an Architectural Legacy* (1977). On Dubuque, see "Reminiscences of Mississippi" in *The Dubuque Telegraph Herald* (July 15, 1906). Also see *Ma-Ka-Tai-She Kia Kiak. Black Hawk. An Autobiography,* edited by Donald Jackson (1955). The first edition appeared in 1833, five years before Black Hawk's death.

CHAPTER 7

New Towns on the
Upper River

*The valley of the Mississippi is, on the whole, the most
magnificent dwelling-place prepared by God for man's abode.*

—Alexis de Tocqueville, *Democracy in America* (1835).

News of the successful voyage of the *Virginia* was like the distant
firing of a starting gun for a race. At first little occurred. Then immigrants, pressing down the Ohio River, began to appear in what, at that
time, was called the West. At the junction with the Mississippi they no
longer floated south but turned north, drawn by tales of unlimited land,
fertile prairies and forests alive with game that lay to the north along the
route of the great upper river. Every month more newcomers appeared,
taking passage on the steamboats, riding a distance before off-loading
their mules, trunks, tools, hopes and dreams on some lonely levee and
continuing their journey into the hinterland. Most were farmers; a few
were traders, lawyers or businessmen.

The common element in all of their dreams was land. The idea that
land could be obtained for almost nothing was an unbelievable concept to
immigrants recently arrived from Europe. In Europe land was scarce
whereas in America, if he were willing to work, every white settler
could expect to own some land. The country was immense. The physical
surroundings, the awful isolation that enveloped the immigrants, the
sense of having cut all ties with home and past lives, transformed them.

They had to face westward and construct a new life or perish—if not of hunger then of loneliness.

Cheap and fertile land in the West was a major inducement to New England farmers exhausted from trying to wrench crops from fields of rocks. The hopes of the farmers seldom extended beyond owning their own land and making a living. Others, the lawyers and businessmen, dreamed of making fortunes, earning their money in the towns that would inevitably grow up along the banks of the Upper Mississippi. Farmers, even those on the most remote farms, would need towns in which to buy supplies and sell their produce.

The extraordinary rapidity with which immigrants settled the vast tracts of the Louisiana Purchase fed into Americans' belief that they were destined to take over the continent. It was a religious impulse as well as a nationalistic one—a belief that God, the republic and democracy all called on citizens to settle and civilize the west. The 1840's were known as the "Roaring Forties," in part because Americans "roared" west, looking for more lands to conquer. A congressman expressed the national mood in 1845: "This continent was intended by Providence as a vast theater on which to work out the grand experiment of Republican Government, under the auspices of the Anglo-Saxon race."

The national mood demanded that towns be founded. And so they were. From the settlers' perspective, the prime purpose of the river was as a site for towns. Every promoter had a town plan in his vest pocket. Accessibility to the river was the single consideration governing a town's establishment. A promising location for a town was at the mouth of a smaller stream that emptied into the Mississippi, or along a level stretch of glacial drift that made a likely landing spot for a steamboat. Towns were the essential points of access to the river for settlers in the hinterlands. They were the openings in the trees that led to the river and the outside, wider world.

Fifty-four communities now flank the river from Rock Island to the Twin Cities. Some of their histories follow.

LA CROSSE, WISCONSIN

Despite the plans of the promoters, the founding of most towns on the Upper Mississippi was a haphazard, accidental process. The spontaneous actions of ordinary citizens gave birth to many of the communities.

Some towns were founded simply because their location was a convenient place for a steamboat to take on wood.

Nathan Myrick was nineteen when he paddled up the river from Prairie du Chien on November 9, 1841, to become the first white settler on the site of La Crosse where, living on Barron's island, he cut wood for the paddle wheelers and traded with the Indians. Though he later moved to the mainland to avoid flooding on the island, he maintained his location by the river.

In October of 1844 the isolated Myrick had visitors from downriver. About twenty families of Mormons, led by Lyman Wight, suddenly appeared to settle at Mormon Coulee, a valley five miles south of Myrick's trading post. The group had abandoned the Mormon Church's river town headquarters of Nauvoo, Illinois, following the assassination of Joseph and Hyrum Smith and fled the mob violence that had scattered the residents of the town.

The winter was a hard one and the traumatized Mormons kept strictly to themselves, seldom visiting their neighbor. Myrick was surprised one day the following spring to discover that the colony had mysteriously abandoned the coulee during the night after first setting fire to all of its log cabins. The departure of the Mormons was a loss. By 1846 Myrick's entire settlement still consisted of just nine men and four women, all whites. Though many Indians lived in the area and traded with Myrick, they were not counted in the census. Myrick continued as an Indian trader after he moved to St. Paul in 1848, according to J. Fletcher Williams.

In 1851 Samuel Freeman published *Emigrants Handbook and Guide to Wisconsin* which was designed to lure immigrants from the British Isles to La Crosse and other Wisconsin towns. Freeman contrasted the "miserable wage" paid to farm laborers in England with that paid in Wisconsin where "the laborer gets the fullest amount of wages, can live cheap and meets with few temptations to spend his money." Freeman added that children would not be an economic burden to their parents because "it is the custom here to send children out to employment as early as 9 or 10 years of age . . . There does exist a prejudice in favor of 'old country' children, especially females. Girls from the age of 11 or 12 are sought after as day-helps."

Competition for immigrants was apparently keen, for the author actively discouraged newcomers from going south: "The climate is bad and a laborer, exposed as he is to much of its vicissitudes, cannot long continue in active employment." As for the climate in Wisconsin, the writer rhapsodized, "The brightness of the American winters in the West with a brilliant and glowing sun beaming from a cloudless sky, while the surface of the earth is covered with snow and the gay and lively equipage of the sleigh, with the warm buffalo skin of the closely wrapped party and the jingling bells of the delighted horses as they glide along the streets makes the season far more cheerful than a winter ever is in England." The sunsets of Wisconsin, he claimed, "surpass even those of Italy and Greece." Freeman's book must have been widely read, for the British were the leading national group to immigrate to La Crosse, followed by Germans and Norwegians.

ALMA, WISCONSIN

Two Swiss bachelors, Victor Probst and John Waecker, came upriver from Galena and filed a claim in 1848 at a spot on the river pilots called "Twelve Mile Bluff" because it was twelve miles below Lake Pepin. The two Swiss chopped wood on the heavily forested islands for the steamers. The work was strenuous. The trees had to be chopped down, sawed into four-foot lengths, hauled to the riverbank and stacked into cords for sale to the steamboats. Other Swiss soon joined the woodcutters and a riverfront village they called "Alma" took shape.

In the early days of Alma a stranger came to town and entered a business on Main Street, a store run by W. H. Gates. After buying his supplies, the stranger asked for directions to the Post Office. Gates replied that his store was the Post Office. The stranger then asked for the Register of Deeds. That, too, was in the store. Finally, the stranger asked where he could find a room for the night and Gates informed him that he was keeping a hotel. This was too much. "Good God," the stranger exclaimed. "Are you the only man in town?"

Gates, who was also the justice of the peace, gave the village the name of Alma. As he explained it, "I took an atlas and commenced to look for a short name that could be spelled and pronounced. I ran across the name 'Alma' on the map of Russia and adopted it at once." Though only two blocks wide and wedged between the river and the 500 foot-high bluffs, Alma, from the 1860's to 1880's, housed as many as 1,500 loggers at a time. The men brought logs down from Boeuf Slough at the mouth of the Chippewa River, assembled them into rafts and sent them on down the river.

In the late 1980's the entire town of Alma was placed on the National Register of Historic Places. Not too far away another unusual site was also preserved. The Kohler Foundation restored the folk art environment created by Herman Rusch, known as the Prairie Moon Museum, and gave it to the river town of Milton in 1995.

WINONA, MINNESOTA

The boilers on the boats required vast quantities of wood that had to be replenished at frequent intervals. Captain Orren Smith, of the *Nominee*, noted that a level sandbar at an area known as Wapasha's Prairie was a likely spot for a steamboat to take on wood. He dropped off an immigrant named Erwin H. Johnson with the suggestion that he cut wood for the boats. Boat captains paid $2.50 to $3.00 a cord for oak cut into the proper length to feed the boat's boilers and the hills were heavily forested. Having no other plans, Johnson agreed, built himself a shack and cut wood for the steamboats. In time he was joined by others and the town of Wapasha Prairie—later Winona—grew up on the riverbank.

Among the first to join Johnson was George Washington Clark, who, in November 1851, along with five other bachelors claimed land where Clark planted what may have been the first apple orchard west of the Mississippi. The first woman to locate permanently in Winona County, Augusta Pentler, came the following year. That spring the government brought a herd of cattle from Missouri up the Mississippi for the Indians and Clark and two of his brothers arranged to buy two of the cows. From the milk they hoped to make cheese, a process familiar to these New York farmers. Their problem was that they had no way to coagulate the milk. Finally one brother shot a meadowlark and used the contents of the bird's stomach to make the rennet. The brothers became the first cheese makers in the area. They also made butter "which was much in demand at gatherings where ladies were expected to be present."

Within a few years of Johnson's arrival, woodsmen around Wapasha Prairie were cutting hundreds of thousands of cords of wood every year. Every hour of every day when the river was free from ice, men unloaded a dozen wagons of cordwood onto the Wapasha Prairie riverbank. No one wondered what the denuding of the hills might do to the river or the impact that rainwater rushing unimpeded down steep slopes would have on hillsides. Was it not the river's purpose, its destiny to serve the boats? And was not the supply of hardwood inexhaustible? A large sternwheeler used 25 cords (a cord measured four feet by four feet by eight feet) of hardwood a day. The piling of wood in cords was an art and a good cord-piler could make seven cords of wood look like ten.

One of the woodcutters on the Wapasha Prairie used his rowboat to move the wood from where he cut it to the landing where the steamboats could pick it up. Woodcutting had its hazards. Rowboats were popular with thieves and boat owners went to unusual lengths to protect their boats. The Wapasha Prairie woodutter fastened a chain to his boat and ran it up the bank of the river to his shack. Boring a hole in the wall of his bedroom he threaded the chain through the hole and fastened the end of it to his bedstead. A little Swiss bell hung on the bedstead was set to ring if the chain moved. Loading his shotgun, he propped it up by the window facing the river and, thus prepared, slept soundly. No one ever stole his boat.

RED WING, MINNESOTA

Missionaries established their schools at trading posts that quickly grew into towns. Assisted by John Johnson Enmegahbowh, the Swiss Presbyterian Samuel Francis Delton established the first mission to the Indians at Red Wing in 1837. The Swiss departed after a few years to be followed by the Reverend J.W. Hancock and his wife Martha who arrived in Red Wing on June 3, 1849. There were only two other white men in Red Wing at the time but an Indian community of 300 occupied the island opposite the lower end of Barn Bluff. To stimulate the Indian children's attendance at school Hancock went to Prairie du Chien and brought back a dozen big boxes of raisins to use as rewards for the students. As a result of Hancock's efforts, many young Dakota learned to read and write. The Dakota called Martha Hancock *"Washe-ween"*— good woman. Martha died at age thirty-one and was buried, at her request, on Indian ground.

Seemingly overnight, the town of Red Wing became a boomtown. By 1856 it supported twenty-four saloons and twenty hotels bearing names such as "Hack House, Chillson House, Kelly House, Goodhue House, Tepeetonka Hotel" and the "Metropolitan Hotel." The Metropolitan was so close to the river that passengers from the steamboats could walk across a plank directly from the deck of the boat onto the porch of the hotel. Travelers often had to wait more than a day for boats, as schedules were irregular.

The manufacture of lime was a major Red Wing industry. Lime burners covered the east side of Barn Bluff from the top to the bottom of the hill. Workers hammered rocks off the side of the cliff and then placed the stone in ovens. Drafts drew the fire to the topmost oven from the fires at the base of the cliff. The stone heated up until the impurities burned away leaving white lime that workers hauled away in wheelbarrows.

The early population of the river towns was a diverse mix of French and French Canadians, Indians, and "old stock" Americans, principally from the New England states, Pennsylvania and New Jersey. Immigrants from Europe came from German-speaking countries, Ireland and from Scandinavia. Irish, fleeing famine and British landlords, also flocked to the Upper Mississippi.

By 1850 Illinois had 27,786 Irish immigrants. Within a decade their numbers had swelled to 87,573. The Irish in Iowa settled mainly around the lead district of Dubuque and numbered 28,072 by 1860. Wisconsin had 49,961 Irish. A song composed by immigrant Thomas D'Arcy McGee expressed the feelings of the Irish who had moved to the Upper Mississippi:

> *Tis ten long years since Eileen bawn*
> *Adventured with her Irish boy*
> *Across the seas and settled on*
> *A prairie farm in Illinois.*
>
> *Sweet waves the sea of summer flowers*
> *Around our wayside cot so coy*
> *Where Eileen sings away the hours*
> *That light my task in Illinois.*
>
> *The Irish homes of Illinois,*
> *The happy homes of Illinois,*
> *No landlord there*
> *Can cause despair*
> *Nor blight our fields in Illinois.*

In Germany scores of travel books and immigrant guides promoted a romantic picture of life in the hills of the Upper Mississippi. A German immigrant wrote in 1851 from Davenport: "One third of the people [of Davenport] are German, and in the country perhaps one-half of the people are Germans. One hardly realizes that one is in America because one hears German spoken everywhere. . . . I would advise all my countrymen, who like to work. . . . to come to our beautiful and free America. . . . Here people are not divided into classes as in Germany. One person is as good as another."

Notwithstanding the rosy pictures painted in immigrants' letters home, the first few years of pioneer life were bleak and hard. While the river teemed with fish and the land on both sides of the Mississippi River abounded in wildlife—deer, wolves, raccoons, foxes, prairie chickens, quail and partridges—the pioneer's diet was meager. The first crop most of the settlers planted was rutabagas. They harvested these tough root vegetables before the first hard frost in the fall and stored them away in dugouts to use as food for both cattle and people.

Houses were tiny, typically measuring 10 by 12 feet, and were made of logs or of sod cut from the prairie. The unbroken soil was so dense farmers had to use axes rather than hoes to chop holes for seeds. Women cooked on big, black, iron cook stoves shoved against a wall so the stovepipe could go up the chimney. The women hated the stovepipes, as they had to be held up with wires and always seemed to be dirty. Soot collected in the pipes and caught fire, at times burning down the entire house. Children carried ashes out every day and put them on an ash pile. Sugar was a precious commodity, as settlers had to bring it upriver from Rock Island. Indians came to the door begging for it and women buried their sugar in a hole in the ground so they could be telling the truth when they said they did not have any.

Tragedy was a constant companion. According to the records of the Holden Lutheran Church, of the 56 deaths in the congregation between December 1861 and December 1862, 40 were children under five and four were mothers 35 or younger. One pioneer wrote of the long, dark winter, "[In winter] the silence of death rests on the vast landscape, save when it is swept by cruel winds that search out every chink and cranny of the buildings, and drive through each unguarded aperture the dry, powdery snow."

The founding stories told in the towns along the river have certain aspects in common. There is an obvious "Manifest Destiny" theme.

Women are seldom mentioned and Native Americans are presented first as obstacles to civilization and, once conquered, as sentimental subjects for nostalgia. Humor is significant and stories of mishaps and misadventures are told as jokes. Because the river was the focus of community life, many incidents involved boats.

As the Indians drifted away there was little to hold back the tide of white settlement. In a remarkably brief time the native peoples had vanished and even the memory of their presence grew dim. Before many years had passed the only reminder of thousands of years of Indian occupation of the land was in the names the whites chose for their towns.

WABASHA, MINNESOTA

When it came time to select a name for the white settlement on Chief Wapasha III's hunting grounds, the name of Wabasha seemed to the settlers to be a logical choice. Many of the prominent residents of the town were related by blood or marriage to the old chief who had assumed leadership of his band following the death by smallpox of his father in 1836. Though he had participated in the Dakota War of 1862, Wapasha III was opposed to it and was among the first to make proposals of peace. Toward the end of the conflict he had withdrawn from Little Crow's camp and, setting up a new camp of over 100 lodges, had protected many whites and mixed-bloods.

On the appointed day in 1843 to mark the official naming of the community of Wabasha, citizens dug a hole in the ground on the levee and sealed a bottle with a paper containing the name of the town and the particulars of its founding. They placed the bottle in the bottom of the hole and set up a pole and a board with the name "Wabasha" on it nailed to the top. Then, to properly celebrate the occasion, they opened a bottle of whiskey and shared it with all. The sealed bottle with the note has never been retrieved and may still be sunk in the levee somewhere between Allegheny and Pembroke streets in the town of Wabasha.

The town was still small, consisting of one street along the river, when the settlers saw what appeared to be a war party of Ojibwe men in three war canoes landing on the gravel bottom of the slough used for a boat landing. The settlers locked themselves in their houses as the Indians made their way to the local wagon-maker, who also painted wagons and buggies. To the townspeople's great relief, they soon learned that the Ojibwe were out to avenge some insults by the Dakota and wanted the wagon-maker's help in painting their bodies in preparation for an attack. The wagon-maker was glad to be of assistance.

Though Wabasha was now a town of whites, one Indian, a man named *Ne-Ka-Ka-Eda* still lived in a shanty on the site of the old Indian camp at the edge of town. On his occasional trips to town the man traded with the owner of the general store and over time a relationship developed between the two men. The storekeeper recognized and admired the dignity and self-respect with which the Indian conducted himself. The man never came to the store except to trade.

The white leaders of the community were regular visitors. For a few hours every day they occupied a row of chairs in the back of the store, near the side door and in front of a mammoth wood-burning box stove. The residents of Wabasha understood that this row of chairs was reserved for the inner circle of the community. Men who were members of the group attended regularly.

One Christmas morning the store was closed but a fire was burning in the stove and by mid-morning the regulars had slipped in the side door of the store and filled the chairs. Then the side door opened again and *Ne-Ka-Ka-Eda* came in. Instead of his customary blanket he was wearing a regulation British army red coat. He faced the storekeeper and, with a slight bow, greeted him. The storekeeper got to his feet and returned the greeting. Solemnly the two men shook hands. Then the chief, with the erect posture of a soldier, turned to the row of startled men who were now standing before their chairs out of respect to the storekeeper and his friend and, striking his chest with his right hand, introduced himself. The men returned the introduction and each one, in turn, stepped forward to shake the man's hand. The storekeeper took a tin pail of smoking tobacco from the shelf saying, "A Christmas present for you, *Ne-Ka-Ka-Eda*. Have a seat and smoke." The Indian seated himself and lighted his pipe in silence. When it was finished he rose and, with a nod to all, departed.

The Wabasha city fathers recognized that the Indian had paid a formal visit to the white man's council and they were grateful for it. As long as he lived, *Ne-Ka-Ka-Eda* repeated the visit in precise detail each Christmas. At no other time did he wear the red coat or sit in the row of chairs in the general store at Wabasha.

Besides providing a landing for the steamboats that ran up and down the river, each community maintained a ferry that went back and forth across the river to its sister community on the opposite shore. The ferry at Wabasha was called the *Bull-of-the-Woods*. The owner of the boat had set his heart on his son becoming a riverboat pilot and had arranged to apprentice him to the ferry boat captain.

The day arrived when the boy took the boat across the river for the first time. His father was at the dock in Wabasha to watch him make the landing, the critical test of a pilot's judgment of distance, the speed of the boat, the river current and the timing of signals to the engine room. At first all went well. The young man quartered up stream in proper fashion, correctly timed the signal for shut-off to allow the final reversing roll of the wheel to offset the boat's headway before reaching shore. At the last moment the boy rang "full-speed ahead" by mistake. The engineer gave him what he asked for and the *Bull-of-the-Woods* hit the shore with such a rush that her bow rode up high over the gravel bank and the smokestack toppled over.

The *Bull-of-the-Woods* was to have other mishaps. A farmer loaded a number of cattle on the boat and herded them onto the deck where they were kept in place by the raised apron at the bow and a high guardrail that completely encircled the boat. Once the cows were aboard, the ferry backed away from the landing and swung around to head for the Wisconsin shore. As it started steaming across the river the waves, raised by a downstream wind, began to throw spray through the guardrail on the upstream side of the boat onto the nervous cattle. At first the cattle simply moved away from the spray. Then they stampeded, crowding around the circular deck from both directions onto the lee side of the boat until their pressure broke the lee guard rail fence. Over the side went the crazed cattle into the river. The man in charge of the cattle was mounted on a horse. When he saw the last of his animals go through the rail he spurred his reluctant horse to jump overboard as well and, after a long struggle, managed to herd the entire group of animals safely to shore.

MCGREGOR, IOWA

Several towns grew up because of the need to cross the river. When an increasing number of immigrants wanted to cross the Mississippi from Prairie du Chien to the Iowa shore Alexander McGregor built a ferry in 1836 consisting of a flatboat propelled by poles. This proved to be so popular that, in 1844, he upgraded to a rope-ferry called the *Rob Roy McGregor* propelled by four horses walking on a circular wheel in the middle of the boat. Though he had lived in Prairie du Chien for twelve years (and had been a representative to the Wisconsin territorial legislature) in 1847 McGregor and his family moved over to the Iowa side where he founded the town that bears his name. When gold was discovered in California, hundreds of "forty-niners" crossed the Mississippi on McGregor's ferry. The business became so profitable that, in 1857, McGregor replaced the horse ferry with one operated by steam, called the *Wanamingo.*

For a time the village of McGregor thrived in its narrow corridor, squeezed between the river and the towering bluffs. In 1860 a harnessmaker named August Ringling moved to McGregor where four of his seven sons were born. They held their first Ringling Brothers Circus in McGregor and for several years located the circus's winter quarters in Prairie du Chien. Dr. Lucy Hubbs, the first woman in the world to receive a Doctor of Dental Surgery degree, operated her dental office in McGregor from 1862 to 1865 and Samuel Merrill, a McGregor businessman, was governor of Iowa for two terms from 1868 to 1872. The golden era of McGregor ended around 1866 and the town looks today about as it did in 1879.

Cassville, Wisconsin, had a horse-powered river ferry. In this postcard view the ferry captain poses, perhaps waiting for passengers, as horses and wagons disembark. A Cassville car ferry still carries passengers and vehicles from the Wisconsin side of the Mississippi to Iowa. Courtesy of Gregory Page.

READ'S LANDING, MINNESOTA

Augustine Rocque and his Indian wife were the first residents of Read's Landing, a village at the foot of Lake Pepin. Augustine and his son (also named Augustine) maintained trading posts up the Chippewa River and when they abandoned their post on the west bank of the Mississippi an Englishman named Hudson moved in and named it "Hudson's Landing." When Hudson died his widow, part Indian, married Louis Rocque, the son of Augustine, Jr. and the trading post came back into the Rocque family after an absence of twenty-five years. In 1847 an Englishman named Charles Read came up the river and bought Hudson's old warehouse from Louis Rocque and began trading with the Indians. The place then became known as Read's Landing.

John Knapp, of the lumber company Knapp, Stout and Co., recognized the strategic location of Read's Landing across the Mississippi from the mouth of the Chippewa and built a warehouse in the community. The town, wedged between the steep rock formations and the river, became the center of the log-rafting industry and, though there was scarcely room for them, soon had seventeen hotels and twenty-one saloons. All the river towns had reputations for boisterousness but at Read's lawlessness was a way of life. The town also boasted a general

Once Lake Pepin froze steamboats stopped travelling north and tied up at river docks until spring. This real photo postcard shows Read's Landing with steamboats "in Winter quarters," circa 1907. Courtesy of Gregory Page.

store with wholesale and retail stocks of wines, cigars, ice, and fruits. A nursery stocked with 2,000 apple trees grew on the hillside. One late spring as many as thirty-two boats waited impatiently at Read's Landing for the ice to go out of Lake Pepin.

HASTINGS, MINNESOTA

In 1850 the trader Alexis Bailly obtained government approval to establish another of his trading posts on the west side of the Mississippi at the mouth of the Vermillion River. This was in Indian Territory and any settlement other than a trading post was illegal. Contrary to what they told government officials, Bailly and his partners Henry Sibley and Alexander Faribault, had no plans to trade furs from that location. Instead they viewed it as an excellent site for a town. There was a broad landing area with deep water for steamboats and a good crossing point for a ferry. The land rose gradually from the riverbank with a supply of timber and limestone for buildings. The Vermillion River dropped 100 feet in a series of falls that could provide power for mills. Owners of excellent town sites, they knew, made fortunes in a few years. Bailly, Sibley and Faribault were reasonably certain that Minnesota Territory would soon be legally opened to white settlement and they wanted to record their claim before the rush began.

As the speculators had anticipated, Indians signed the treaty opening the land to white settlement in 1851 and the men laid out their new town. Bailly's cabin became the village's first hotel and tavern, called the Buckhorn. The name of "Buckhorn" might have become permanently attached to the village if the men had not put other suggestions in a hat and drawn them out. After some negotiating, they settled on Henry Sibley's middle name of Hastings and began selling lots in the new town in 1853.

Bailly and Sibley were not the only ones who found Hastings a valuable location. The Indians had long used the site as a spring sugar camp where, every year, they had made maple sugar from a big stand of old maple trees. After the town was established the Indians continued to visit the trees in their seasonal round of food gathering. One spring the Indians arrived at the grove of maples to discover that the white settlers had already tapped the maples dry. Angered, the Dakota plotted to attack the settlers to teach them a lesson. An Indian who was friendly to the whites revealed the plot and the attack never came off. His own people now ostracized the friendly Indian so the whites of Hastings took him in. They built a house for him and his family and saw to it that he had work in the town. The Indian family became members of St. Luke's Episcopal Church and the beautiful grove of maple trees, the cause of the dispute, was cut down and sold for fuel for lime kilns.

By the 1880's Congress required all stationary bridges over the Mississippi (those without a swingspan to allow boats to pass) to be built with a minimum clearance of 52 feet at high water. (To accommodate lower bridges some steamboats had hinged their smokestacks so they could be tilted to go under the bridges.) The mandated height of the bridge above the level of the water presented a problem for bridge builders in Hastings, Minnesota, who devised a memorable solution.

Hastings badly wanted a bridge of its own across the Mississippi River. A bridge towering 52 feet above the water would be so high that the end of the bridge would pass over the business district of Hastings and deposit customers far from the center of commerce. That would not do. The citizens of Hastings solved the problem by designing a spiral bridge, the only one of its kind in the country. The bridge was designed so that, once across the river, the bridge deck spiraled down, like a chambered nautilus, to deposit traffic at the foot of Sibley Street, a mere half block from the city's commercial center. Two special bills in the U.S. Congress as well as a bonding bill from the State of Minnesota were

From 1895 until 1950 visitors to Hastings, Minnesota, crossed the Mississippi and then entered the town via this unique spiral bridge, shown in a real photo postcard, circa 1895. Courtesy of Gregory Page.

required for permission and the $39,050 to build the bridge. The unique spiral bridge of Hastings was dedicated on April 27, 1895.

Some citizens of Hastings opposed the idea of a new bridge. "It would be the worst thing that could happen to our town," complained one. "We have a good rope ferry already," said another. Despite the opposition, once it was built, the bridge became the pride of Hastings. To celebrate its completion the town served a free meal to 5,000 people and a local musician composed a waltz celebrating the spiral bridge. A city ordinance prohibited any speed over the bridge faster than a man could walk. Women of the community, disgusted at the unsightly refuse that soon collected under the spiral bridge approach, formed the Clio Club which, in just 29 days, turned the area into a park. Rose McLoy contributed two 27-year-old century plants originally grown in the Shaw Gardens in St. Louis and St. Paul florist L. L. May gave 800 packets of flower seeds for the project.

The spiral bridge across the Mississippi was in continual use at Hastings until 1950. In 1930 highway officials placed load restrictions on the structure and a decade later announced plans for a new highway bridge a short distance upriver. When new floorboards for the pedestrian section of the spiral bridge needed to be replaced at a cost of $5,000, the city fathers decided it was a waste of money to repair the historic bridge. Rather than finding a way to save the bridge they heeded a petition from 71 individuals that called for the removal of the bridge because "it would be an expense to the city and the value of the approach would be less than the expense incurred." Last minute efforts to save the only bridge of its kind in America failed and the extraordinary spiral bridge of Hastings was razed the same year.

Hastings, in 1872, aiming to become a more decorous community, passed an ordinance that horses, cattle, sheep and hogs could no longer run wild foraging for food in the town. Most animal owners ignored the ordinance until the police rounded up forty of the violators and put them in an impound lot. Their owners were incensed but they gradually began confining their livestock behind fences.

A larger animal problem in Hastings was the rats attracted to Hastings and the other river towns because of the large piles of wheat waiting to be shipped to market. Wheat, the immigrant farmers' principal cash crop, required relatively little labor to produce and could be stored for later shipment. Moreover, there was a market for wheat in the East. As early as the 1850's Wisconsin and Minnesota had become among the top wheat-producing states in the nation. Wheat, like the lead of Galena and Dubuque, could be sold only if it could be moved. The only route to the market was through the towns that dotted both sides of the river and provided outlets for farmers eager to get their grain to their customers. If wheat farmers lived within three days by team from a river town, they considered themselves fortunate.

Beginning around 1857, the river of water carried another river on its surface—a burgeoning river of grain. By 1872, wheat grew on more than 61% of the land under cultivation in Minnesota—the largest proportion in any northern state. From 1857 to 1880 farmers shipped their wheat to market in bags on the riverboats. Hastings became a major grain terminal, the third largest in the state. Wagons lined up two-abreast for miles on their way to the Hastings market. Workers stored wheat everywhere. The grain warehouses were lunchboxes for rodents and their population grew exponentially. People bought arsenic over-the-counter from local stores to control the rats that grew to a startling size. When, in 1878, Hastings organized a rat slaughter, hunters killed 680 of the rodents. They shot one that measured three feet from its nose to the tip of its tail. The rat's incisors were three quarters of an inch long.

Winona was an even larger wheat-shipping port than Hastings. Officials had named the town for Chief Wapasha's daughter but they got the spelling wrong. The chief had called his daughter *"We-no-nah,"* a name that the Indians gave to a first-born daughter. During the steamboat era Winona was the largest wheat market in Minnesota and, in 1868, the fourth largest in the United States. Shippers stacked wheat in two-bushel sacks on board walks, on sidewalks, on the streets and in warehouses, waiting for boats to take it down the river.

By 1862 Winona had thirty warehouses for storing wheat ranging from 5,000 to 100,000 bushel capacity. In the cash-short economy farmers traded wheat for lumber and the lumbermen began dealing in wheat. The Laird, Norton and Company sawmill became a major Winona business. A long line of wagons laden with wheat wended their way around Sugar Loaf bluff from as far as 150 miles away over roads that were little more than rutted, muddy trails.

Wheat and lumber replaced fur and lead to become the warp and woof of the Upper Midwest economy. The river towns of Winona, Hastings and Red Wing competed to be the state's primary grain market. At first Winona led when it shipped a million bushels of wheat to beat Hastings, which had recorded 600,000 bushels. Then, in 1873, Red

Wing passed them both by shipping 1,800,385 bushels valued at more than two million dollars—allowing Red Wing to claim the title of the world's largest primary wheat market. The indispensable partner in all this activity was the river. During the season of 1873 one boat pushed barges containing 75,000 bushels of wheat down the river each week. Two of the barges came from Red Wing and five from Winona. In 1855, 583 steamboats landed at Winona. The next season 1,300 steamboats landed there and in 1857 the number grew to 1,700. More boats landed those years in Winona than went to St. Paul.

STOCKHOLM, WISCONSIN

The shipping of quantities of wheat on the riverboats was not limited to the larger towns of Hastings, Red Wing and Winona. Roads were in an abysmal condition so farmers hauled their wagon-loads of wheat to the nearest villages on the river which, on the Wisconsin side, were Stockholm, Alma and Pepin. Even though Alma's labor force was principally engaged in rafting, by 1873 five warehouses were doing business in wheat. Some days Alma's Main Street was choked with 100 wagons waiting to unload grain.

Twenty-nine-year-old Erik Pettersson, an immigrant from Carlskoga, Sweden, spent the winter of 1850-51 cutting trees in the pineries on the St. Croix. He was part of a raft crew on its way down the river when the crew tied up for the night in a small bay on the eastern shore of Lake Pepin. Pettersson climbed to the top of Maiden Rock and fell in love with the river and forested hills he saw below him. Writing to his married brother, Jacob, in Carlskoga, he urged him to emigrate and, together with Eric, found a Swedish colony on the Mississippi.

When several months had passed and Jacob had not replied, Eric became impatient and, in 1853, set off on the long return journey to Sweden. When he arrived back at Carlskoga he learned that his brother and family, along with friends, were on their way to America in response to Eric's invitation and the two brothers had passed each other going in opposite directions. Undaunted, Eric organized a second immigrant group and in 1854 headed back after Jacob. Eric's five thousand mile journey ended when the *War Eagle* brought him back to the bay by Maiden Rock where he and his brother Jacob founded the town they named "Stockholm."

For twenty-five years the industrious Swedish farmers near Stockholm, Wisconsin, delivered their grain to the long "government pier" that jutted into Lake Pepin. Owned by the Larson and Swanson Company, the enterprise was the longest-running business in the history of the town. A line of ragged black roustabouts carried the grain aboard in sacks, dogtrotting up and down the gangplank, urged on by a flow of profanity from villainous-looking bosses. To the Swedes of Stockholm, it was the Deep South scene brought to the North by the steamboats.

When the Pettersson brothers founded Stockholm there were already six tiny communities clinging to the shores of Lake Pepin, three on the Wisconsin side and three in Minnesota. They were North Pepin, Lakeport (then known as McCain's Landing) and Saratoga (a lumbermen's colony later named Bay City), Wisconsin. In Minnesota were Wacouta, Florence, and a community later to be called Frontenac. The principal residents of the settlement that would become Frontenac were the trader James "Bully" Wells and his Dakota wife.

In 1854 Wells sold his land on the river to Everett Westervelt who laid out a town, calling it after himself. There might have been a Westervelt, Minnesota, if—the same year—Israel and Lewis Garrard with their mother, Mrs. Sara Belle McLean, the widow of a Supreme Court Justice, had not come to Minnesota and become partners with Westervelt. They changed the name of the community to Frontenac and gave the village its exclusive resort-community character. They kept the first post office in the home of Henry Lorentzen who would go out in his rowboat to get the mail from passing steamers. He could tell which boats had the mail because they had white stripes on their chimneys. Lorentzen's dog knew the mail boats as well and, when Lorentzen was sleeping on the shore at night waiting for a boat to come, his dog would wake him up.

In 1857 a sudden change in the flow of the Mississippi threatened Winona's connection to the river. The problem that riveted the townspeople's attention was the fact that flooding water had begun to dredge a new main channel on the river through a slough north of Latsch Island. This created, in effect, two boat channels, the old one that ran by Winona's levee and a new channel past the more distant island. When this occurred some boat captains, none too friendly to the river settlement founded by their rival Captain Orren Smith, began to follow the new course of the river, bypassing and ignoring Winona.

Winona officials knew that this bypassing could mean the death of their town. To bring the boats back to the Winona landing the town officials concocted an elaborate scheme. First they voted to build a large stone courthouse in Winona. Next they awarded the contract to build the courthouse to one of their associates who immediately set out to bring the required stone from quarries across the river in Wisconsin. A huge load of stone was piled on a barge and moved carefully down the river. Just as the barge reached the opening of the new channel it met with a sudden and unfortunate accident. The barge sank, dumping its load of stone into the river and permanently blocking the new channel. Once again, to the relief of the residents of Winona, steamboat captains had little choice but to swing their boats into Winona's landing.

Many towns were founded, only to soon disappear. One was Central Point in Goodhue County, Minnesota. Settled in 1853, the town soon had three stores, a hotel, three grain-warehouses and sawmills. Farmers brought wheat to Central Point for shipment on the riverboats. However, the town died when steamboat captains determined that the harbor and loading facilities at Lake City were better and refused to stop at Central Point.

Just as towns came and went, so did their names. The town of Alma was once "Twelve-Mile Bluff," LaCrosse was "Prairie LaCrosse," Hastings was "Oliver's Grove," Fountain City was "Holmes' Landing," Prescott was "Prescott's Claim," Winona was first "Montezuma," then "Wa-Pa-Shaw's Prairie,"and then "Johnson's Landing," Stillwater on the St. Croix was "Mrs. Carli's," St. Anthony was "Cheevertown" and Bettendorf, Iowa, was at first "Lillinthal" and then "Gilbert Town" before it became Bettendorf. And, most unforgettably, St. Paul was once known as the spot where Pig's Eye Parrant lived.

NOTES

References include Robert George Wingate, "Settlement Patterns of La Crosse County, Wisconsin, 1850-1875," Ph.D dissertation, University of Minnesota (1975); for Nathan Myrick in St. Paul, see J. Fletcher Williams, *A History of the City of St. Paul and the County of Ramsey, Minnesota* (1876); Samuel Freeman, *Emigrants Handbook and Guide to Wisconsin* (1841); Barbara Anderson-Sannes, *Alma on the Mississippi, 1848-1932* (1980); for Red Wing, the *Daily Republican Eagle* (December 10, 1960); and Frederick L. Johnson, *Goodhue County, Minnesota* (2000); for the Irish, Mark Wyman, *Immigrants in the Valley* (1984). Several manuscripts in the Wabasha, McGregor and Hastings public libraries brought local history to life, while aspects of financial business are found in Richard Hoops, *A River of Grain—Evolution of Commercial Navigation on the Upper Mississippi River* (1987). A series of articles on Stockholm's history by Mrs. Eric

Forslund and E.J.D. Larson appeared in the Pepin *Herald* (September 7, 1939—January 23, 1941) and were republished as *Stockholm's Saga: History of Stockholm,* Wisconsin in 2001. For the Hastings Spiral Bridge see Jack El-Hai, *Lost Minnesota—Stories of Vanished Places* (2000), and Hazel Jacobsen, *The Spiral Bridge of Hastings. Its Beginning and End* (1976).

CHAPTER 8

The Ill-Fated Nininger
and Rolling Stone

Ignatius Donnelly, air castle builder,
'Apostle of protest,' writer of note,
Political leader, Lieutenant Governor,
Labored and toiled for a Populist vote.

– From "Ignatius Donnelly" (1954)
by Anthony Philip Londroche

The Upper Mississippi River, the Father of the Waters, was the birth-mother of communities. Promoters saw the river as a silver umbilical to which towns could be attached that would grow like husky babies and make their fortunes. Surrounded by fertile prairies, the river was made-to-order for development. Land bought from Indians for seven and a half cents an acre or from the government for $1.25 could be worth hundreds of dollars when platted as a town and thousands if it were located near the center of a growing city. Lots in river towns doubled in value every year.

The real estate boom on the Upper Mississippi was contagious. Unscrupulous individuals, motivated by greed, used the magic of the Mississippi River to lure innocents to fraudulent town-building schemes. By the early 1850's word of the boomtown atmosphere created by speculators hoping to make fortunes in real estate on the Upper Mississippi had spread throughout the country.

Speculators began platting towns that existed only on paper and selling lots to gullible people in the East. Everyone, it seemed, was willing to gamble on town properties so long as they lay along the Upper Mississippi River. Boosters launched great enterprises with little or no capital to support them, developers grossly exaggerated opportunities, shysters and well-meaning enthusiasts competed for the attention of an eastern populace newly aware of the promising great Northwest with the high road of the river running through it.

One company purchased 500 acres of land north of the mouth of the Wisconsin River and sold shares for $200 and a percentage of the profits. They platted a town on a big sheet of paper showing a courthouse, parks and streets named for presidents of the United States. Unfortunately, the land was low and swampy. A passenger on a steamboat passed over the town site and reported that the land was below twelve feet of water. When the swindle was exposed, the promoters quickly disappeared.

In the summer of 1856 a brother-in-law of Alexander Ramsey, John Nininger of Philadelphia, extolled the beauties of a town he had platted on the Mississippi River that he called, with a certain lack of modesty, "Nininger." Nininger's description of the town captivated a twenty-five-year-old Philadelphia lawyer named Ignatius Donnelly who became his partner. Together the two men filed claims on several hundred acres of land on the Mississippi River five miles above the town of Hastings and laid out 3,800 town lots which they advertised for sale at $100 to $250 each. Riverfront lots were priced at $500.

To promote their enterprise the partners flooded the country with advertisements. Every journal seemed to contain a notice about Nininger. The partners held mass meetings in eastern cities to interest prospective settlers and distributed thousands of small cards describing the advantages of Nininger through the mail. Donnelly published *Emigrant Aid Journal* that was filled with testimonials for Nininger.

In one of Donnelly's promotions called "Pamphlet in Reference to Nininger City," published September 10, 1856, a J.R. Case wrote, "I came to Minnesota knowing nothing of the enterprise or its projectors and I joined it only in view of its intrinsic merits after a very thorough examination. I have taken one hundred and twenty lots in the town at the original price, six dollars each. They are now all worth $100 and many of them I would not sell for $500 each. I can only say that before one year I expect every one of my lots to be worth $1,000 each. I consider the success of the town certain." Real estate speculation ran rampant.

Donnelly's community of Nininger had, on paper, a courthouse, four or five churches, warehouses, stores and a levee crowded with steamboats bringing eager residents. The partners even published a newspaper, the *Daily Bugle,* full of local advertising and stories. A printer who helped produce the *Daily Bugle* recalled, that the sheet was filled with a wealth of local advertising—dry-goods, groceries, hardware, millinery, shoe stores, blacksmith shops—every class of business found in a large and prosperous city was represented in those columns. But every name and every business was fictitious. . . . It was enough to deceive the very elect—and it did. . . . The paper was filled with local reading matter describing the crush at the opening of the latest emporium, that Brown had gone East to purchase his spring stock, that Mrs. Newbody entertained at her beautiful new residence on Park Avenue with the names of fifty of her guests.

Nininger was promoted as a get-rich scheme that could not fail. Unfortunately for the investors it did.

Nininger could not compete with the nearby, better situated town of Hastings. Any town founded on the Upper Mississippi in the middle of the nineteenth century could not survive without regular service by steamboats. Regrettably for Nininger, the steamboat captains refused to stop there, preferring instead the better landing at Hastings. More blows followed. The panic of 1857 dried up capital. The editor of Nininger's *Daily Bugle* lived in St. Paul and mailed the paper from the rival town of Hastings as there was no post office at Nininger. Although about 400 people eventually moved to Nininger, by the summer of 1858 the town was doomed. The owners of the Blakeley and Lewis steam sawmill, built in 1856 in Nininger, tore it down in 1862. The Eaton flour mill built in 1858 burned within three years and the owners did not rebuild. The Eagle Sawmill built in 1857 closed three years later and the machinery was sold.

Donnelly discontinued his *Emigrant Aid Journal* and forfeited the $500 check he had sent as a deposit on a steamboat. When the manufacturer wrote in the fall of 1857 that the boat was ready, Donnelly failed to claim it as he was out of money. Hopeful pioneers who had built houses at Nininger took them apart and moved them to Hastings. John Nininger never did live in the town named for him. Donnelly, however, did and remained faithful to the dream, building his own home in Nininger. He later served three terms in the U.S. Congress, became Lieutenant Governor of Minnesota and wrote several books including a speculative treatise arguing for the existence of Atlantis. By 1860 the town he founded had become a ghost town, and Ignatius Donnelly, because of the wide range of his interests and activities, became known as "the sage of Nininger."

ROLLING STONE, MINNESOTA

The town-site disaster that most outraged the river captains was that of Rolling Stone. Rolling Stone began with an advertisement placed by the printer William Haddock in the July 21, 1851, issue of the *New York Tribune*. Haddock was looking for 200 families to found a utopian community in the west. He promised a bountiful life on cheap land, fresh air, safety from urban crime, a healthy existence and, most tantalizing, the opportunity to make money. Each participant was to have a four-acre village plot and 160 acres of farmland nearby. Haddock's followers formed an organization called the "Farm and Village Association" and corresponded with Henry Sibley who enthusiastically extolled the limitless virtues of the Upper Mississippi Valley.

In the winter of 1852 Haddock and Arthur Murphy made their way to Wapasha's Prairie in search of land on which their community could settle. At the time, Wapasha's Prairie had only a few settlers, mainly woodcutters, living in shacks. After spending a few days with the woodcutter Johnson, Haddock and Murphy set off on ice skates upriver. Immediately above Wapasha's Prairie the main channel of the Mississippi swings far over to the Wisconsin side of the valley.

It was at this point that Murphy and Haddock made a serious and eventually fatal mistake. They mistook Straight Slough, a backwater that enters the main flow of the river at the head of Wapasha's Prairie on the Minnesota side of the river, for the navigation channel. They skated up Straight Slough for several miles to a beautiful little valley. The valley was actually a network of smaller valleys that converge to join the Mississippi about six miles above Wapasha's Prairie. Haddock loved the location and named it Rolling Stone, not realizing that his town site was separated from the nearest possible steamboat landing by several miles of backwaters and swamps.

Haddock remained behind at Wapasha's Prairie while Murphy returned to New York to prepare the settlers to emigrate. A large group left for the Upper Mississippi in late April and early May of 1852. Captain Russell Blakely of the *Dr. Franklin* was startled when 400 of his passengers with their farm implements and pets, asked to be let off at Rolling Stone. When he told them he had never heard of it, they responded with disbelief, showing him their beautiful maps illustrated with pictures of houses, a village square and a dock along the river's edge.

Refusing to follow the captain's recommendation that they get off the boat at Wapasha's Prairie, where the woodcutter John Johnson had now erected his cabin and filed a claim, they disembarked upriver where they waded through cold floodwaters to reach the site of their new home. Later arrivals, who left the boat at Wapasha's Prairie, faced the problem of traveling the last six miles to Rolling Stone. There was no road of any kind and the water at Straight Slough was at a high level, flooding the surrounding lowlands. Soon after arriving, the settlers faced yet another problem. The land where they hoped to settle was still owned by Chief Wapasha III who demanded an annual rent in the form of barrels of flour. When the snow melted the settlers discovered swamps and marshlands where solid ground was supposed to be.

Few of the members of the colony had farming experience. They built sod houses for themselves and dug burrows for shelter in the river-banks. In its first meeting on May 6, 1852, the group, still clinging to its dream, changed the name of the community from Rolling Stone to Minnesota City. Unfortunately, little was holding members of the group together other than the prospect of gain. Most found that they were unable to cooperate and work together. Many became ill and died, including William Haddock's wife. When fall came the survivors abandoned Minnesota City and most returned to New York.

Nininger and Rolling Stone represented the reality of pioneer life. No matter how fertile the soil, abundant the game, available other natural resources, if settlers were poorly prepared for pioneer life on the frontier they failed. For towns to survive on the Upper Mississippi, a special combination of circumstances were required. Though the specifics varied from community to community, there was one ingredient that—if it were lacking—doomed a town to failure. That was its connection to the river.

NOTES

Anthony Philip Londroche's poem about Ignatius Donnelly appears in his *I AM Mississippi* (1954). On Rolling Stone see Christopher Johnson, "The Rolling Stone Colony. Labor Rhetoric in Action," in *Minnesota History* 49:4 (Winter 1984). A number of writers have studied the career of Ignatius Donnelly and the sad tale of Nininger. See the biography by Martin Ridge, *Ignatius Donnelly: The Portrait of a Politician* (1962). Under "Town-Site Frauds" both Rolling Stone and the story of the Nininger printer are mentioned in B. A. Botkin's *A Treasury of Mississippi River Folklore* (1955).

CHAPTER 9

Davenport and the
Quad Cities

George Davenport, the first white settler on the rocky island below the rapids in Illinois, was better prepared for life on the frontier than had been the hapless New Yorkers. Though he was born in England, Davenport became an Indian trader on the American frontier. Having a British accent greatly facilitated Davenport's relationships with the Indians as many had supported Great Britain in the war and they instinctively trusted him. Davenport established himself on Rock Island where he built a log trading post using buffalo robes for a roof.

The Mississippi, at this location, is at one of its narrowest points. A stretch of water called Sylvan Slough flows between the island and the Illinois shore while the main channel of the Mississippi runs down the western side of the island. Davenport was soon operating a ferry across the river, and when Fort Armstrong was built on the tip of the island he became the suttler—the man engaged to supply provisions for the fort. Though no longer a trader, Davenport maintained his good relations with the Indians. When Andrew Jackson ordered the Indians removed from their lands and moved west Davenport went to Washington to ask that the Indians at least be paid for the land they were being forced to leave. Jackson refused.

On Rock Island, Davenport became a friend and business partner of Antoine LeClaire, the son of a French-Canadian father and a Potawatomi Indian mother. LeClaire spoke French and Spanish in addition to numerous Indian dialects and General George Rogers Clark, impressed with his ability, sent him to school to learn English. In 1820 LeClaire married Marguerite LePage, the daughter of a Frenchman and grand-daughter of the Sauk chief Acoqua. Because of their mixed French and Indian ancestry and through the provisions of the Treaty of 1832, both LeClaire and his wife received sections of land. LeClaire's land lay at the head of the Rock Island rapids.

LeClaire promptly formed an investment company with George Davenport and laid out two towns. One he named after his friend Davenport and the other he named for himself. By 1840 the population of Davenport was 300. The village of LeClaire grew more slowly until 1855 when the Iowa legislature merged two other tiny settlements along the river into LeClaire. Because of its location at the head of the rapids the town became a boat repair and boat building center.

Both LeClaire and Davenport were extraordinary men, involved in all aspects of their communities, from their founding to the coming of the railroads. Between them they operated the first ferry, the first foundry and first hotel. LeClaire was the first justice of the peace and first postmaster. His house served as Davenport's first railroad depot and his donation of land and money helped bring the county seat to Davenport rather than to Rockingham. LeClaire planted trees in the business district and donated land for Catholic and Protestant churches alike. He was only five feet eight inches tall, weighed 385 pounds and drove around Davenport in a buggy pulled by a white horse. Like Davenport, the Indians trusted LeClaire. After Black Hawk's return from the East the chief lived in a small house in Davenport where LeClaire worked with him, translating his memoirs and biography into English.

The town that grew up on the Illinois side of the river across from Davenport was called Stevenson. In 1840 Stevenson was twice the size of Davenport with 600 inhabitants. Immigrants coming to the area seldom called the village "Stevenson," referring instead to the rocky island in the Mississippi. Capitulating to the inevitable, in 1841 the Illinois legislature changed the name of the town from Stevenson to Rock Island. Industry began in 1837 when David Sears built a 600 foot-long dam over Sylvan Slough and began to produce power, sawing wood and grinding wheat for the local farmers. Sears also platted the village of Moline on vacant land next to the town of Rock Island. Manufacturing came first because of the waterpower and settlers slowly followed. It was the dam on the river that created the community. John Buford also had a waterwheel on Sylvan Slough and he offered power to a farmer-turned-inventor from Vermont named John Deere.

John Deere invented a device that would cut through the soil without becoming jammed with clods of dirt. By properly shaping and polishing the mould board of a plow Deere discovered that it would be self-scouring, making the breaking of the prairie sod a less daunting task than it had previously been. The invention had enormous significance for pioneers and once farmers saw the Deere plow in operation they wanted to buy one. Deere and his partner Robert Tate moved their fledgling manufacturing operation from Grand Detour, Illinois, to the Sears Dam on Sylvan Slough in the summer of 1848, a move that eventually gave Moline, Illinois, worldwide fame as the "Plow Town." Moline developed as a separate community from Rock Island in large part because one or two individuals controlled the land in Rock Island, forcing new business to settle in Moline.

John Deere was 43 years old when he established his plow factory at Moline. There were no banks in the region so conventional financing of his enterprise was not possible. To pay his employees, since there was little money in circulation, Deere traded plows to merchants in surrounding towns and gave the resulting store-credits to his workers so they could buy supplies. Despite the shortage of cash, his business flourished. In April 1852 Deere informed readers of a local newspaper that he "was prepared to furnish plows to all that favored him with an order on reasonable notice and at rates to suit the times. . . . I can increase from 4,000 (the number now manufactured) to 20,000 annually if necessary."

Though the towns of Rock Island and Moline developed side by side on the Illinois side of the river, they were very different communities. Influential southerners who were pro-slavery had settled Rock Island. Anti-slavery New Englanders had settled in Moline. Rock Island residents hurled insults at the people of Moline by calling them by the then pejorative term "abolitionists." In the 1860 presidential election the town of Rock Island cast 412 votes for Douglas while Moline cast 392 for Lincoln. Davenport, across the river in Iowa, was also pro-Lincoln and the North.

The community directly east of Davenport on the river (the Mississippi runs east to west between Davenport and Rock Island) was the little town of Gilbert, Iowa. Dred Scott had homesteaded the land for his owner, Dr. John Emerson. When a fire destroyed the metal wheel factory founded by the brothers William and Joseph Bettendorf, Gilbert town officials offered to name their community "Bettendorf" if the factory would rebuild there. Almost overnight, the quiet community of Gilbert, where the residents raised onions and flowers and retired at sundown, became a whirlwind of industry. Chimneys smoked and noisy, mammoth hydraulic presses stamped out iron wheels from boilerplate. The wheel plant opened in 1902 with 300 employees and the next year the residents of Gilbert voted to incorporate as "Bettendorf."

On July 4, 1845, while residents of Davenport, Moline and Rock Island, including George Davenport's family, were celebrating the national holiday robbers burst into Davenport's island mansion and, after a struggle, fatally wounded him. Boaters, out for an excursion on the river, heard Davenport's cries for help and came to his assistance. He had been shot in the thigh, choked and beaten by three men who demanded to know where he kept his money. Davenport died a few days later. A jury convicted three men, brothers John and Aaron Long and Granville Young, of the murder and sentenced them to hang on October 19, 1845.

Among the convicted men's last requests was that their bodies not be given to doctors. Their request was not honored. Officials gave the bodies of the three to Dr. Patrick Gregg who shipped two of them to friends in St. Louis and Alton. Gregg articulated the body of the third, that of John Long, and gave the skeleton to the Davenport high school where it hung for many years until the building accidentally burned.

The river towns on the Upper Mississippi evolved a settlement plan so similar to each other as to create a special genre of town building— an urban geography unique to the region. The Mississippi River was the dominating presence. Every day residents noted the color and texture of the water and the flow of the current. The departure of the ice in the spring was the signal event of the year. The steamboat landing area on the river bank, the place where boats could tie up to unload cargo and passengers, was the first location settlers marked off in their village and the single most important piece of real estate in the town. The first street back from the river was the commercial street. It ran parallel to the river and, if the town prospered, was soon lined with two-story brick buildings, the year they were built proudly emblazoned on the false fronts of the upper stories. There were warehouses for goods, hotels and numerous saloons to serve the steamboat passengers and crews.

All principal streets ran parallel to the river; all commerce, all travel, all news came by way of the river. In Wabasha, Hastings, Prairie du Chien, McGregor, Alma, St. Anthony and Red Wing, the commercial street is called "Main Street." In Davenport, La Crosse and LeClaire the street fronting the river is appropriately called "Front Street." In Davenport and La Crosse, Main Street runs perpendicular to the river, from the levee up to the bluffs above the town.

Daily life in the river towns was fulfilling. Because they existed as market centers to serve the isolated farmers in the surrounding countryside, every town offered essential services. The smallest of villages had harness-makers, blacksmiths, boat-makers, shoemakers, hardware and dry-goods stores, hotels, bakeries, gunsmiths, milliners, tailors, banks, newspaper publishers and photographers. Social life was complex and rich. Every community had one or more churches, singing societies, marksmen's clubs for men and women, debating and literary societies, bands and baseball teams.

A few towns could claim famous (or infamous) citizens. Pepin claimed the writer Laura Ingalls Wilder who was born in a log cabin near the village on February 7, 1867. William "Buffalo Bill" Cody was born in LeClaire, Iowa. In 1922, 18-year-old Ralph Samuelson invented water skis and rode them on Lake Pepin, towed by an airplane because boats did not yet have enough power. In Lake City, a sculptural image of a wave by artist Jack Becker commemorates Samuelson's achievement.

The son of the town photographer in Alma went on to become Dr. Arnold Gesell, director of the famed Yale Clinic of Child Development. Alma's pride turned to ire when Gesell published an article entitled "The Village of a Thousand Souls" in the October, 1913, issue of *American Magazine*. The village described in the article was thinly disguised Alma with every incidence of alcoholism, feeblemindedness, insanity, suicide and criminal activity identified with markers on a street map of the town. It turned out that Gesell's mother had supplied him with much of the personal information and his father's photographs illustrated the article. According to Alma historian Barbara Anderson-Sannes, "Even today the mere mention of "The Village of a Thousand Souls" in Alma elicits a negative response; and Arnold Gesell, distinguished child psychologist and author of some 27 books, is known, if at all, as the infamous writer of this one article."

All economic and social activity of the towns centered on the river. Farmers a hundred miles away patronized a particular village because that town provided an outlet to the Mississippi. Dependence on the river was a given, akin to a farmer's reliance on rain. Every settler and each business felt in its bones the ebb and flow of the Mississippi.

Without the recurring visits of the riverboats, no town, as Nininger's promoters learned to their sorrow, could long survive. The rhythm of the arriving and departing steamboats was the pulse that kept each community alive. If a town could not be reached at low water by a steamboat—that ridiculous machine with an explosive exhaust that could be heard for miles around and a boiler so full of power that it hourly threatened to blow its fragile hull out of the water—the town was fated to fade away while still in its infancy.

A visitor from France commented on the importance of the boats to the region. "Today steamboats are the salvation of the valley of the Mississippi. They are among the most essential agents of social life and if it were possible to imagine them wiped out for a time the rising civilization of those extensive regions would disappear with them. Everywhere in these thinly settled districts people await the steamboat with an impatience of which the arrival of newspapers in a period of revolution alone can give us an idea."

NOTES

References include Roald Tweet, *The Quad Cities: An American Mosaic* (1996). For Moline see Bess Pierce, *Moline—a Pictorial History* (1993); for Rock Island see the John Hauberg Papers in the Rock Island County Historical Society. Concerning Alma see Barbara Anderson-Sannes, *Alma on the Mississippi, 1848-1932* (1980). Steamboat comments come from Louis C. Hunter, *Steamboats on the Western Rivers* (1949).

CHAPTER 10

The Removal of the Indians

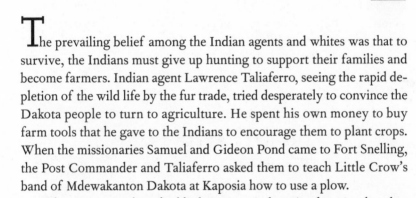

The prevailing belief among the Indian agents and whites was that to survive, the Indians must give up hunting to support their families and become farmers. Indian agent Lawrence Taliaferro, seeing the rapid depletion of the wild life by the fur trade, tried desperately to convince the Dakota people to turn to agriculture. He spent his own money to buy farm tools that he gave to the Indians to encourage them to plant crops. When the missionaries Samuel and Gideon Pond came to Fort Snelling, the Post Commander and Taliaferro asked them to teach Little Crow's band of Mdewakanton Dakota at Kaposia how to use a plow.

The Kaposia Indians had little interest in learning how to plow, but Taliaferro was able to convince Cloud Man that his people should become farmers instead of hunters. Actions of the American Fur Company influenced Cloud Man's decision. When Henry Sibley achieved a near monopoly of the fur trade in the region in 1827 he immediately raised prices on goods to the Indians by 200 to 300 percent. A tin kettle that had cost nine muskrat pelts now sold for 30 pelts. A $5 musket overnight cost $18. When the time came for the spring hunt, Cloud Man and his fellow Dakota hunters discovered that they owed three times as much as they had expected to the traders. They could see for themselves that game was becoming scarce. Yet animal pelts were the only currency the Indians had to spend with the traders.

Together, in 1829, Cloud Man and Major Taliaferro selected a site on the banks of Lake Calhoun (within the present city limits of Minneapolis) for a new village. The band began farming, raising corn, potatoes, squash, pumpkins and cabbage. Within ten years Cloud Man's village had become the largest in the area, housing almost 400 residents.

The Pond brothers moved their mission to the village. There they built a 12 by 16-foot log house with walls of tamarack poles and bark for a roof. The floor was made of split logs, laid the flat sides up, and the single window in the house was a gift from Taliaferro. The tiny building served as home, school for Indian children and church. The total cost of the structure was twelve and a half cents—money spent for the wrought iron nails used around the door. In 1839 Cloud Man's people had a major conflict with the Ojibwe and moved the farming community to the summer village of Chief Good Road near the present city of Bloomington.

Cloud Man's agricultural village was not a typical Indian community and it did not convince other Dakota to take up agriculture. Three of Cloud Man's daughters had had children by whites. Numerous other women who had children by soldiers from the Fort lived in the village, making it more an appendage of white society than Indian. The village survived economically because soldiers brought rations to their family members and Taliaferro gave the community a portion of the $2,000 annuity granted the Indians by the treaty of 1830.

THE HALF-BREED TRACT

Despite the limited nature of the success at Cloud Man's village, Taliaferro continued to believe that assigning land to the growing population of mixed-blood individuals would encourage them to become European-style farmers. This well-meaning attempt to provide for the Indians resulted in major unintended consequences. At a congress of tribes held at Prairie du Chien, at which the Indians surrendered claims to land in Iowa and Missouri, Taliaferro persuaded the chiefs Red Wing, Black Dog, Little Crow, Wacouta and Wapasha II to insert a special article in the treaty for the benefit of their half-blood relatives.

The article conveyed to mixed-blood Indians a tract of land from Barn Bluff, near the village of Red Wing, fifteen miles wide and thirty-two miles long, running south along the west shore of Lake Pepin to the mouth of the Boeuf River. The land became known as the "half-breed tract." Taliaferro strongly supported the measure as did the fur traders Alexis Bailly, Augustin Rocque and Oliver Cratte who were protecting the interests of the children they had fathered with Dakota Indian women.

The Prairie du Chien Treaty of 1830 was the Dakotas' first cession of their ancestral lands. In exchange for their land the Indians were to receive $25,000 worth of food and farm tools for twenty years. They were also promised a yearly annuity of $15,000 that would come from a permanent trust fund of $300,000. A sum of $90,000 was set aside for debts to the traders and another $110,000 would go to the mixed bloods.

The treaty reserved the tract of land near Chief Red Wing's village for exclusive settlement by children descended from early white traders and their Indian partners. When the U.S. Land Office opened in Red Wing in August 1855, officials sent a list to Washington of those who were qualified to share in the reserved land. Washington responded in the spring of 1857 with government scrip for those on the list along with a statement of the amount of land to which they were entitled. The scrip could be exchanged for titles to the land. Most Indians had been assigned 480 acres.

Among the whites there was a strong suspicion that land speculators had inspired the provisions of the treaty, as few mixed-bloods appeared eager to take up land and become farmers. As the whites had feared, speculators immediately bought up much of the scrip. This brought them into conflict with about 200 whites who had already settled on the tract without holding the required scrip. Titles to their land were legally worthless and speculators forced a few settlers off property they had improved. Since there was no court of law in Red Wing to enforce the land assignments, vigilante committees of whites took control of the land dispute until May 1858, when the federal government stepped back in and granted the whites who had illegally settled within the tract, rights to the land.

James "Bully" Wells was one of the speculators who went into the controversial business of buying up scrip for tracts of the half-breed lands at Red Wing. Wells served three terms in the territorial legislature. He and his Dakota wife, Jane, had seven children who were legally qualified for scrip and Wells had already made one land purchase in the area. Then Wells made the mistake of appearing in Red Wing with additional scrip for registration at the land office run by the vigilante committee. It was winter and a thick layer of ice lay on the river. A member of the committee cut a hole in the ice, took Wells out to it and gave him a choice of handing over his scrip to the half-breed lands or going into the water. Wells handed over the papers and departed. Other speculators were also given this icy option. Taliaferro's well-meaning efforts to transform the Indians into farmers had failed.

While settlers competed for land in the half-breed tract, the rush of events in other parts of the country swept the region along in its wake.

Minnesota had originally been a part of Wisconsin Territory. When Wisconsin was admitted to the Union in 1848 the western boundary of the state was set at the St. Croix River. That left the land west of the St. Croix without a recognized government. To remedy that situation a group met in Stillwater and elected Henry Sibley a delegate to Congress with instructions to see that Minnesota was recognized as a territory of its own. Stephen A. Douglas wrote and successfully sponsored the bill naming the village of Mendota as the territorial capitol. Sibley, aware of the importance of St. Paul's strategic location at the head of navigation of the Mississippi, convinced Douglas to make St. Paul the capitol.

MINNESOTA TERRITORY

The population requirement needed to become a territory was 5,000 and by the summer of 1849 Minnesota could count 4,535 Euro-Americans living within its borders. As many as one third were mixed-blood but if they lived and dressed as whites they were included in the census. The Indians, who probably numbered at least 25,000, were not counted.

The year Minnesota became a territory (March 3, 1849) was also the year of the California Gold Rush and everything happened very fast. The news that the bill had passed Congress reached St. Paul on April 9, when the steamboat *Dr. Franklin No.2* forced its way through the ice to the town. Within three weeks, the population of St. Paul doubled in size. Seventy new buildings were quickly built, bringing the total to 149.

President Zachary Taylor appointed Alexander Ramsey as the Territorial Governor and Ramsey arrived to take office in May, accompanied by judges and other territorial officials—a full complement of government officials. James M. Goodhue launched his newspaper, the *Minnesota Pioneer*. Officials quickly incorporated the village of St. Paul as a town. In 1840 there had been a total of nine cabins on the site of St. Paul. Ten years later 257 families consisting of 1,294 residents lived in the growing community. In 1854, the year of the Grand Excursion, St. Paul was incorporated as a city.

Steamboat captains kept the growing community supplied with goods and settlers. One hundred newcomers at a time, eager to make their way in the new territory, disembarked at the Lower Landing from a single boat. St. Paul's location on the north-south fur trade route where Red River ox carts connected to the head of navigation on the Mississippi was a major advantage for the growing community. The carts made the

448-mile trip to St. Paul laden with furs and returned to the settlements of the Hudson's Bay Company overflowing with supplies purchased from St. Paul merchants.

Ellen Rice Hollinshead described the carts in St. Paul. "The Red River carts from Pembina made their annual pilgrimage here until the year of 1860, about the last of June or the first of July, bringing furs, pemmican and dried buffalo tongues, the latter being considered a great delicacy. The carts were made entirely of wood and were drawn by oxen and Indian ponies whose harnesses were made of strips of buffalo skin. The drivers were French half-breeds. Sometimes they [the carts] numbered between 2,000 and 3,000—five hundred were owned by Culver and Farrington. They passed in procession through Third Street to deliver their goods to the fur companies and encamped on the prairie near St. Paul."

The decade of the 1840's was a feverish one for white Americans. The United States defeated Mexico in 1848 and added 529,017 square miles to its territory—an area larger than Spain, France and Italy combined. And that was without counting Texas. Iowa joined the Union in 1846 and Wisconsin in 1848. Oregon became a territory in 1844.

The flood of immigrants coming up river to the new Territory of Minnesota or heading west to the gold fields in California turned Rock Island and Davenport into major steamboat ports. In 1854 Rock Island averaged 175 arrivals a month during the season while arrivals and departures from Davenport totaled 1,587 in 1857. Davenport, Rock Island and Moline quickly grew from river towns into mercantile and industrial centers. By 1856 Davenport had grown to 10,000, Rock Island to 5,000. By 1856 both towns had new gas streetlights. "Now 400 train passengers won't have to grope their way to hotels," the *Rock Island Argus* bragged.

THE SIGNING AWAY OF INDIAN LANDS

Minnesota's achievement of territorial status put enormous pressure on the Ojibwe, Dakota and Winnebagoes. Whites, arriving by the hundreds daily, wanted land that was still legally defined as Indian Territory. The pressure to change that definition was overwhelming.

Beginning in the 1830's whites had, step by step, forced the Indians off their ancestral lands. The 1837 treaty dispossessed the Indians of all of their land east of the Mississippi. In that treaty the Ojibwe were awarded $870,000 payable over 20 years, less the deductions that had aroused Taliaferro's ire ($170,000 for the traders and half-breeds.) The Dakota were awarded $475,000 over a 20-year period plus an annuity of $15,000. The allowance for the traders and half breeds was $215,000. The annuity payments promised to the Dakota were cancelled after the Sioux Uprising of 1862.

Governor Alexander Ramsey negotiated the 1851 treaties of Mendota and Traverse des Sioux that ended the Dakota claims to land in Minnesota west of the river except for a small reservation along the Minnesota River. In two treaties, initialed in the summer of 1851, the Dakota signed away rights to twenty-four million acres of prairie that had been their tribal hunting grounds in Minnesota and parts of Iowa and South Dakota. The federal government agreed to keep $1,360,000 in the Treasury for the Dakota and pay them 5 percent interest annually ($68,000) for fifty years.

The money was never put in the treasury and Congress had to appropriate the interest annually. A special sum of $305,000 was carved out, supposedly to help establish the Indians on farms. Instead the traders planned among themselves and government officials to get most of this money—ostensibly to satisfy their claims against the Dakota.

The chiefs who signed the treaty knew what they were doing and felt that they had no choice. The game was gone and the Indians could no longer live by hunting. Very few had become farmers. Many were starving on land that no longer supported them. The only way the chiefs could assure the survival of their people was to exchange their land for promised government annuities. Fear of starvation forced them to sign. Hindering the Dakota's ability to negotiate were their ties of kinship to the traders and the decades of close relationships they had experienced with government officials. When their white relatives spoke, the Indians felt they had to listen and heed their advice. In the end the Indians had no realistic alternative to the selling of their Upper Mississippi land.

Red Iron, whose village was on the Yellow Medicine River, was one of the chiefs who signed the Treaty of 1851. In November 1852 Governor Ramsey called Red Iron to a meeting to urge him to sign receipts authorizing the handing over of large sums of Indian money to the traders. Also scheduled to be in attendance were 45 soldiers from Fort Snelling. When Red Iron heard that soldiers would be present, he asked to bring some of his own warriors to stand with him.

When Ramsey refused, Red Iron ignored the summons. Ramsey then threatened to have Red Iron removed from his position as chief.

When that failed, Ramsey had Red Iron picked up and brought to a meeting where Ramsey insisted that Red Iron sign the receipt for the traders. If the Dakota did not agree to pay their debts to the traders, Ramsey said, he would refuse to pay the Dakota the annuities promised in the treaty.

Red Iron refused to be cowed. "Take the money back," he said. "If you don't give us the money I will be glad and all our people will be glad for we will have our land back. That paper [the treaty] was not interpreted or explained to us. We are told it gives about $300,000 of our money to some traders. We don't think we owe them so much. We want to pay our honest debts but not the fraudulent ones. Let our Great Father send three good men here to examine the accounts and tell us how much we owe and whatever they say we will pay."

Ramsey rejected Red Iron's suggestion but he agreed to pay out some of the annuities owed to the Indians. Red Iron replied, "We will receive the annuities but will sign no papers for anything else. The snow is on the ground and we have waited a long time for the money you promised us. We are poor and have nothing to eat; you have plenty. Your fires are warm, your teepees keep out the cold. We have sold our hunting grounds and the graves of our fathers. We have no place to bury our dead and yet you will not pay us our money for our lands."

Ramsey's response was to take Red Iron into custody to compel him to sign the receipts. Ramsey held back annuity payments until he had secured all of the chiefs' signatures on the traders' papers. Red Iron and the other chiefs wrote out a declaration on December 2 that they wanted only $130,000 to go for traders' debts. Ramsey ignored their statement and turned over $250,000 of the Dakota money to his secretary Hugh Tyler for distribution to the traders.

Between them, Ramsey and Tyler took a fee for themselves of from 10% to 15% of the Indians' money for distributing it. Tyler received $50,000 and Ramsey probably took a similar sum. The American Fur Company received over $105,000 of the Dakota Indians' money. Ramsey would not allow the Indians to apportion the money to their own people themselves and eventually gave a total of $510,000 to the traders for purported Indian debts and for costs associated with the removal of the Indians to the reservation.

Though the 1851 land treaties at Traverse des Sioux were not legal until ratified by the U.S. Senate, white settlers did not wait before moving onto the Indians' land. Basing their claims on the Preemption Act of

1841 that allowed whites to claim government-owned land *before* it was put on sale, they built cabins and claimed land up and down the western side of the river. Settlers believed in their "natural right" to occupy land before it was surveyed or purchased from the Indians because the settlers had braved the rigors of the wilderness. They justified their illegal actions by claiming they were rendering a national service.

The preemption law favored male claimants, either single men or heads of families. *The Immigrants Guide to Minnesota* (1856) stated that "There is nothing in the law to prevent a single unmarried woman from pre-empting providing she be the 'head of a family'. We have known instances of women who, without having been married, could make it appear that they were the 'head of a family' and who have accordingly been permitted to pre-empt. But such instances are not common. A widow may pre-empt who is not the head of a family." The writer added a coy observation. "This premium offered by Uncle Sam for getting married, ladies would do well to 'make a note of.'"

Government agent Nathaniel McLean estimated that by late summer of 1852, 5,000 whites were living illegally on government land in Minnesota Territory. The white population continued to increase. In 1854 it was more than 30,000 and by 1857 it was over 150,000. The Red Wing band, returning from a winter hunt in the spring of 1853, found its homes burned to the ground. Overwhelmed by the tide of settlers moving onto their village sites and hunting grounds, members of the Red Wing and Wapasha bands abandoned their homes on the Mississippi to the invading whites and by September 10, 1853, were camped at Little Crow's village near St. Paul. That same year Superintendent of Indian Affairs Robert G. Murphy chose the site for the Sioux Indian Agency on the Minnesota River, about 15 miles above Fort Ridgely.

Despite the encroachment of whites on Indian lands, individual relationships between whites and Indians often reflected mutual understanding and helpfulness. Indian and white children played together. The whites gave the Indians food and supplies, attempted to doctor their sick and made coffins for the dead. One pioneer woman remembered an Indian who visited her cabin, gently held her daughter on his lap and measured her foot. A few days later he appeared with a pair of beautifully made moccasins for the child.

A family had homesteaded near the Red River in northern Minnesota. The woman was in the last days of a pregnancy, her husband was away on a trip, a storm had washed away part of the sod roof of their home and she began to give birth. As her grandson recounted the event, "She was in pain and obviously suffering. All of a sudden two Indians appeared in the house. They looked at my grandmother, saw the condition she was in and without a saying a word turned and walked out. Within ten minutes two squaws were in the house and they delivered my Aunt Sarah. They never knew where those Indians came from."

THE SIOUX UPRISING

The treaties of 1851 left the Dakota in a desperate situation. Some tried to hunt but game was scarce and they had lost over 90% of their land. The government money that could have sustained them went to the traders who sold goods at exorbitant prices. Supplies promised by the government often did not come. Many of the barrels of flour and pork that the government shipped arrived spoiled and inedible. Other goods sent to the Indians, such as castanets and handkerchiefs, were wildly inappropriate.

Even as the Indians plotted to attack the whites in the Sioux Uprising of 1862, many believed that it was an act of desperation doomed to fail. Resentment of their betrayal by the whites had become so powerful that it overrode centuries of tribal conflict between the Ojibwe and Dakota. The Ojibwe chief, Hole-In-The-Day the Younger, joined his traditional enemy, the Dakota chief Little Crow, in an alliance to fight the settlers. "Come, my fellow warriors, let us go forth to war," Hole-In-The-Day entreated his braves. "For we are a dying people anyhow. We might as well hasten the day of our sufferings and death."

Enmegahbowh, who heard Hole-In-The-Day the Younger's entreaty, advised against it. "If you knew as much as I know of the greatness and power of the whites against whom you are expected to fight, you would not entertain the idea to thus strike against heavy rocks. You may kill a few in the beginning, but in the end you will all be swept away from the face of the earth and annihilated forever. I love you all. I see and know just exactly how the war will terminate. As a friend who loves you, I would ask you all as wise men to think and well consider whether your present plan is to your salvation or death." Hole-In-The-Day the Younger agreed with Enmegahbowh's assessment but believed that events had run beyond his ability to change them. "The plan has already come into its maturity. I am not able to control it, " he said.

The leaders of the Upper Dakotas were bitter that they had not been consulted about the proposed conflict prior to its outbreak. Many considered themselves to be white men. Paul Mazakutemani, a brother of Cloud Man, urged the Dakota to end the war and give up their captives. In a speech to the Dakota chiefs after the fighting had begun he said, "You Mdewakanton and Wahpekute Indians have been with the white men a great deal longer than the Upper Indians. Yet I, who am an Upper Indian, have put on white men's clothes and consider myself now a white man. I was very much surprised to hear that you have been killing the settlers. . . . Why did you not tell us you were going to kill them? The reason was, if you had done so, and we had counseled together, you would not have been able to have involved our young men with you. When we older men heard of it we were so surprised that we knew not what to do. By your involving our young men without consulting us you have done us a great injustice."

"I have heard a great many of you say that you were brave men and could whip the whites. This is a lie. Persons who will cut women and children's throats are squaws and cowards. . . . I am ashamed of the way you have acted toward the captives. Give me the captives and I will carry them to Fort Ridgely. I hear one of you say that if I take them, there are soldiers [who] will shoot me. I will take the risk. I am not afraid of death, but I am opposed to the way you act toward the prisoners. If any of you have feelings of men you will give them up. You may look as fierce at me as you please, but I shall ask you once, twice and ten times to deliver these women and children to their friends."

The Sioux Uprising of 1862 lasted about six weeks. Sibley led the army that marched against the Indians. Approximately 500 settlers died. No one knows how many Indians were killed. Following the Battle of Wood Lake the Dakota sent a message to Sibley that the captive whites and people of mixed blood were in the hands of friendly Indians and that the braves who had made war on the whites were gone.

Sibley marched his army to the Indian village opposite the mouth of the Chippewa River and established Camp Release. That afternoon, at precisely two o'clock, Colonel Henry Sibley marched into the Indian camp, attended by his staff, senior officers, and two companies of infantry. The troops marched up with bayonets glistening in the bright sun, colors flying, drums beating and fifes playing.

Paul Mazakutemani, the spokesman for the friendly Indians, met Sibley at the village. Taking Sibley's hand in his, he said, "I have grown up like a child of yours. With what is yours, you have caused me to grow, and now I take your hand as a child takes the hand of his father. My hand is not bad. With a clean hand I take your hand. I know whence this blessing cometh. I have regarded all white people as my friends, and from this I understand this blessing has come. This is good work we do today, whereof I am glad. Yes, before the great God, I am glad." Sibley took over the prisoners and hired Paul Mazakutemani to serve as an Indian scout under mixed-blood Gabriel Renville who, in the confusion of blood-lines that existed, was a relative of Mazakutemani.

Many were unaware that hostilities had broken out between the Indians and white settlers. Henry Doughty and his brother Asa, mixed-blood Indians who had learned the trade of wagon building, left Lake City, Minnesota, with a caravan of wagons and farm implements they had assembled to sell to the German farmers along the Minnesota River. They reached St. Peter where they encountered a group of Sibley's militiamen who commandeered their wagons and supplies and hired the two men as wagoneers. The Doughtys continued with the army during the campaign and were present when about 2,000 Dakota, including many women and children, surrendered to Sibley.

Among the prisoners were two people Henry and Asa recognized as they had played together as children. They were Sophia Wapasha (*Mahpiyahotawin*—Grey Cloud Woman) and her brother Tatatespin. Sophia was the "winona" or first-born daughter of Chief Wapasha II and the wife of Paul Mazakutemani. Amazingly, though taken prisoner by the soldiers, Sophia and her brother had been able to preserve tribal heirlooms that had once belonged to the legendary Wapasha I, including a 12-foot long red chief's blanket with the three feathers insignia, a British officer's coat and hat, and a unique pipe axe.

The British had awarded these to Wapasha I at a ceremony on Mackinac Island for his participation in the Revolutionary War. The relics had been preserved in his village ever since. When the soldiers began organizing the prisoners for transport back to Fort Snelling, Sophia appealed to Henry to hide the artifacts in his wagon and to let her ride with him. During the journey to the fort, although white settlers attacked the wagons as they drove through villages, hurling stones and bottles at the prisoners, Henry protected Sophia.

After defeating the Dakota, Sibley put 400 men on trial with five military officers serving as judges. No one defended the Indians. At the end of the trial, officials sent the names of 303 Dakota braves to President Lincoln whose approval was needed for the death penalty. Lincoln recognized the injustice of the trial and refused to sign warrants for all but thirty-eight. These Indians were hanged on December 26, 1862. Among those executed were several Indians who had tried to stop the killings and save settlers' lives. One of the condemned was Chief Wapasha III's son-in-law who wrote the following letter before his death:

> Wapasha—you have deceived me. You told me that if we followed the advice of General Sibley and gave ourselves up to the whites all would be well. No innocent man would be injured. I have not killed, wounded or injured a white man or any other person. I have not participated in the plunder of their property and yet today I am set apart for execution and must die in a few days while men who are guilty remain in prison. My wife is your daughter, my children are your grandchildren. I leave them all in your care and under your protection. Do not let them suffer and when my children are grown up let them know that their father died because he followed the advice of his chief and without having the blood of a white man to answer for to the Great Spirit. . . . Let them remember that the brave should be prepared to meet death and I will do so as becomes a Dakota.

Following the executions, the government imprisoned about 1,200 Dakota in a stockade built along the Mississippi River below Fort Snelling. Among the Dakota who were imprisoned was Sophia Wapasha and many who had little understanding of what had taken place. Curt Campbell's great-grandmother was a girl of fourteen when she and her mother were arrested by soldiers and imprisoned at Fort Snelling. That winter hunger and sickness killed about 130 including Cloud Man who had been opposed to the fighting.

SOPHIA WAPASHA'S JOURNEY

Stories recounted in Campbell's family credit the women prisoners with saving many lives. "Most of the women were in the Medicine Lodge. They got sticks and found the roots under the snow that sustained them through the winter months." James Stokes, whose great-great-grandmother was Sophia Wapasha, says that to survive the Indians picked the corn from the dung of the cavalry horses and with it made a stew of cottonwood bark and grasshoppers. "The Army fed the horses better than the Indians. The meat the army gave them was usually spoiled and inedible. They had to survive on whatever they found. The hillsides were covered with graves," he said.

Sophia had amazing endurance. She survived the winter at Fort Snelling and even worse conditions at Crow Creek in Dakota Territory where the army sent 1,700 prisoners by boat. Crow Creek was a place of "drought-stricken desolation, a land with almost no lakes, almost no timber." There was no game, no berries and no edible roots. Even the Commissioner of Indian Affairs called it "one wilderness of dry prairie for hundreds of miles around."

No one went to Crow Creek willingly. The elderly Shakopee, whose name is perpetuated in a Minnesota town, expressed the Indian attitude: "Tell the Great Father that Shakopee will never leave his country voluntarily, that when he sends his soldiers to take him away, they will find old

Sophia Wapasha Paul (Grey Cloud Woman), the Dakota woman who survived years at Crow Creek and on the Santee Reservation in South Dakota, returned to her ancestral lands in Wisconsin long after the Sioux Uprising. Courtesy of James L. Stokes.

Shakopee lying on his belly holding on to his country with his teeth, toes, fingernails and eyelids and they will have to tear him away."

Sophia and two sons survived three years at Crow Creek before they were sent to the Santee Reservation near Yankton, South Dakota. Here Paul Mazakutemani, who had received $1,700 for his services to the U.S. government, found Sophia and sons Fred and Paul II. The family put on "white man's garb" they purchased from a trading post at Yankton, secured passage on a Missouri riverboat and, together with Henry Doughty who aided them, sailed downstream to St. Louis. There they outfitted themselves to settle on land in Buffalo County, Wisconsin, across the river from Wabasha. They identified themselves as "German Immigrants" and called themselves the "Henry Paul" family. The land they settled was familiar as it had been the hunting ground of Chief Wapasha's band for many generations.

A son of the Pauls later married a daughter of one of the Doughtys. Three generations later their descendant, James L. Stokes, was given the Dakota name *Zitkadan Hota* or Gray Bird on his twelfth birthday. Thus the daughter of Wapasha II and the brother of Cloud Man, whose descendants now number in the thousands, sank into the American melting pot. Yet the ongoing generations have not forgotten their roots. The culture of the Dakota and memories of their fateful encounter with white civilization run like an underground river below the surface of contemporary life.

Modern day Dakota have a fairly good idea where the great Wapashas are buried. James Stokes believes that the Tiffany Bottoms at the mouth of the Chippewa River, an area rich in medicinal plants and wildlife, may be the final resting place of some of the famous chiefs. The Dakota still hold private ceremonies at sacred river sites they prefer not to identify. As Curtis Campbell says, "I hear the clear voices and the medicine songs of my ancestral people. I feel their emotions and concerns and I carry all the memories of their importance in all phases of my work in this modern day. From time to time, when the wind is blowing softly, I often wonder if one of my ancestors, *Ta-ton-ka Maẓẓa*, Iron Buffalo, is guiding me so far." The artifacts of Wapasha I, the red chief's blanket and the rare pipe ax saved by Sophia Wapasha and Henry Doughty, are still in the possession of their direct descendants.

The moving of the Mdewakanton and Wahpekute Dakota to the new reservation began, halted for a few months, and then continued intermittently over several years. According to the 1880 census only two

Indian families were left in Red Wing following the removal. Beginning in the early 1880's a few Mdewakanton Dakota began to move back to their ancestral homes on Prairie Island, a piece of sandy land formed where the Vermillion River runs into the Mississippi fourteen miles from Red Wing.

The Secretary of the Interior purchased about 500 acres on the island for the Mdewakanton Dakota. The agent assigned to purchase the Prairie Island land wrote in 1889, "These Indians are of the Red Wing or Wacoute band and this is their old home, therefore though the soil is poor they are loath to leave it and we have no means of compelling their removal." Campbell says the Indians came back to Prairie Island for two reasons, to honor the graves of their ancestors and to hunt the medicinal herbs that had great significance for the tribe. "The philosophies of medicine gathering and the medicine lodge of the Holy Being were a way of life and a practice among the Dakota," he wrote.

The construction of Lock and Dam Number 3 reduced the area of the reservation and flooded community land including burial sites. Prairie Island is also the site of the Xcel Energy nuclear power generating plant where spent fuel rods are stored above ground in huge barrels, called dry casks. The nuclear storage containers are only three blocks from the Indian community. Of all the uses envisioned for the Mississippi River, few could have foreseen its use as a storage site for spent nuclear fuel.

NOTES

See Rhoda Gilman, "How Minnesota became the 32nd State," *Minnesota History* 56: 4 (Winter 1998-1999). There are many sources on the Sioux Uprising of 1862, beginning with William Watts Folwell, *A History of Minnesota*, Vol.II (1924). Ellen Rice Hollinshead's papers are in the collection of a descendant, Dr. William Hollinshead. Information on the Quad Cities can be found in Roald Tweet, *The Quad Cities: An American Mosaic* (1996), and on Red Wing in Frederick L. Johnson, *Goodhue County* (2000). Sources for Sioux history include Gary Clayton Anderson, *Kinsmen of Another Kind: Dakota—White Relations in the Upper Mississippi, 1650-1862* (2000); Mark Diedrich, *Dakota Oratory* (1989); Curtis Campbell, Sr., *A Family Oral History of Prairie Island* (2000); James L. Stokes, *A Buffalo County Saga* (2000); and an interview with James L. Stokes (July 2003). John Johnson Enmegahbowh's statements come from the book *En-me-gah-bowh's Story: An Acount of the Disturbances of the Chippewa Indians at Gull Lake in 1857 and 1862 and their Removal in 1868* (1904). Linda Mack Schloff recounted the story of Indian kindness to Red River homesteaders in *And Prairie Dogs Weren't Kosher* (1996).

CHAPTER 11

The Emergence of the Twin Cities

The cities on this river must be three
Two that are built and one that is to be.
......

When one great city covers all
The ground from Pig's Eye to the Falls,
I then will claim Saint Paul for mine,
The child of 1849.

— James M. Goodhue

Three factors determined the location of the Twin Cities of Minneapolis and St. Paul. One was the river itself and its Falls of St. Anthony. Without the river and the falls, there would be no Minneapolis or St. Paul. Second was Pike's purchase of two pieces of land, one on each side of the Mississippi River. Third is the fourteen years which separated the opening of the two parcels of land to white settlement.

The building of Fort Snelling, which occupied the military reservation land on the west bank of the river, was the beginning of significant white residence at the head of navigation of the Mississippi. From its first lonely years Fort Snelling maintained a lively presence with visits from military officers, traders, Indians, and explorers. The American Fur Company established its headquarters at nearby Mendota in 1825. Henry Sibley, sent up from Prairie du Chien to manage the business,

118

built a stone house for himself at Mendota in 1838 and added to it in 1845. Jean Baptiste Faribault constructed his stone home in 1840. (The Sibley house, maintained for many years as a museum by the Daughters of the American Revolution, was added to the list of historic sites managed by the Minnesota Historical Society in 2003.)

The first individuals, besides the soldiers and fur traders, to move onto the military reservation land were a group of Swiss farmers who had been part of the ill-fated Hudson Bay Company's Selkirk colony on the Red River. Discouraged by floods and plagues of grasshoppers and fearful of the Indians, they straggled south in 1827 to the government mill at the Falls of St. Anthony looking for protection. Colonel Josiah Snelling, sympathetic to their plight, allowed them to establish their small farms on a portion of military reservation land just north of the fort.

The other whites allowed to take up temporary residence on the military reservation were the Pond brothers who were missionaries. Neither the east nor the west bank of the Mississippi was open for white settlement. Whites could legally live only on the military reservation land or at the trading post community of Mendota. In 1837, in what would become an inevitable process, a group of Dakota chiefs had gone to Washington and signed treaties ceding some of their Indian lands to the whites. These treaties gave all of what would become Washington and Ramsey counties—the east bank of the river—to the United States. The treaty set in motion a series of fateful events.

The moving of whites onto Indian lands before they were surveyed and clear lines of ownership could be established occurred continually up and down the river. Greed for land was especially keen around the Falls of St. Anthony because everyone recognized the value of the falls for producing power. One man who clearly understood that whoever staked the first claim on the east shore of the Mississippi would control half of the power of the falls was Henry Sibley's brother-in-law Franklin Steele, a twenty-five-year-old from Pennsylvania. Though the agreements with the Dakota opening up the east side of the river were negotiated in 1837 the treaty would not become law until it was ratified by the Senate. Many individuals in the Fort Snelling and Mendota community, besides Steele, were scheming for ways to claim the land adjoining the falls as soon as it became legal to do so. Among the plotters was the commander of Fort Snelling himself, Major Joseph Plympton.

Plympton was clearly in the most powerful position. Realizing that the boundaries of the Fort had never been surveyed or clearly defined on a map, he decided to turn that omission to his advantage. If the land around the falls could be "detached" from the military reservation and the Indians' title to the land extinguished, he reasoned, settlers could move in and stake claims to the land before it was surveyed by exercising their privilege of preemption. The building of a shanty on the land was all that was needed to file a preemption claim. Later, when the government offered the land for sale, the holder of the preemption could purchase the land at the minimum price.

Plympton began by conducting a survey of the people living on the military reservation and found 157 squatters, including the Swiss farmers from Selkirk and a sorry group of whiskey sellers and loafers who hung around the fort. When he sent this information to Washington he was ordered to define the borders of the reservation and assert his military control over the property.

Plympton responded with alacrity, forwarding in 1838 a map outlining a reserve of approximately 34,000 acres. When the wily Plympton drew the boundary line at the Falls of St. Anthony he excluded the eastern shore, land that had always been considered a part of the Pike purchase, but kept in the reservation the western bank where the army's mills had been built. Land that was not included in the reservation would, by law, revert to the Indians. Moreover, Plympton was well aware of the treaty negotiations in progress. By drawing that little jog in the reservation boundary he was carving out a piece of land he fully intended to claim for himself.

All summer Plympton waited for news of the treaty's ratification by the Senate. In the meantime, to carry out his second directive from Washington to assume military control of the area, Plympton ordered the Selkirkers, whiskey sellers and squatters off the reservation land. He told everyone, except the residents of Mendota, to leave. There is a suggestion that Plympton personally disliked the Swiss who seemed to him like foreign invaders (they spoke French) and sometimes allowed their cattle to graze on the fort's parade grounds.

The Swiss and assorted undesirables crossed over to the east side of the Mississippi and, moving down river, settled near a landmark called Fountain Cave located at the second great bend in the S curve of the river. The cave, called by the Dakota "*In-yan ti-pi*," was over a thousand feet long with a 150 foot long winding hall that led to a beautiful circular room about fifty feet in diameter. Pierre (Pig's Eye) Parrant, one of the whiskey sellers expelled from the military reservation, had earlier built himself a cabin at the mouth of the cave.

Other structures were later targets of Major Plympton's house-cleaning zeal. Deeming the log church constructed by the squatters to be an illegal structure on military reservation land, he ordered it removed or torn down. Augustin Ravoux, the Catholic missionary at Mendota, had other ideas. He had the church taken apart and loaded on a raft where it was floated downstream to Wabasha. Set up on a point of land by the shore, it served for fourteen years as a Catholic chapel, then as the first newspaper office in Wabasha and, finally, as a school.

A month following the June 15, 1838, Senate vote to ratify the treaty, the steamboat *Palmyra* brought word of the ratification to Fort Snelling. Plympton was not the only man eagerly awaiting the news. Within hours of hearing that the treaty had been ratified, Steele, with a crew of men, raced across the river to the east side of the falls and, working all night, built a simple cabin and chopped blazes on the trees to mark the boundaries of his claim. Steele and his men were eating their breakfast around a campfire the next morning when Captain Martin Scott, with a party of soldiers, arrived from the fort to stake Plympton's claim for him. After a tense standoff, Scott ended up filing a claim for his commander on less desirable land near Steele's.

ST. ANTHONY

Plympton and Steele were two of many who plotted to take over Indian land for themselves. Others from the fort and Mendota—army officers, frontiersmen, traders, French-Canadians, businessmen—also filed claims and built shacks along the east bank. When the settlement claims were finally sorted out and resolved, Steele and Pierre Bottineau, a noted scout and trapper whose father was French and mother Ojibwe, ended up with most of the river frontage on the east side of the river from above Boom Island to below the falls. It was valuable property. Within their claim the Mississippi River dropped fifty feet, creating falls greater than those which supported the industries of Lowell and other major manufacturing cities in Massachusetts. There was no question in any-one's mind on how the river should be used. They were going to use it to generate power.

Steele planned to harness the waterpower to operate a second mill, this one for civilians, on the east side of the river. In July 1847 the first effort toward a permanent modification of the falls began. Steele and his business partners hired a millwright from Maine to superintend the building of the dam and mills. The business had a rocky beginning.

Steele's first attempt to get logs from the Rum River failed and he ended up chopping down the beautiful stands of maple and elm trees that covered Nicollet and Boom islands. Then the boat carrying the tools and hardware he had ordered from east coast suppliers for his new mill sank in the Erie Canal and he lost the entire shipment.

Undaunted, Steele and his partners ordered more mill irons from Maine and by September 1848, he had two saws running. Newcomers found the new settlement of St. Anthony to be a welcoming community. A settler who arrived with her family from Maine in 1850 remembered, "When we reached St. Anthony the people were lovely to us. We did begin to feel at home at once. We had to find a place to live. One of them went with us to the 'Stranger's House,' a slab house standing near the falls. Anyone who came and had no place to live was welcome to live in this house until they had a home of their own. A French Red River family was living in one-half of it. We scrubbed it out and moved in." Soon three hundred people lived in the village. Roswell P. Russell opened the first store in a log house opposite the falls in the fall of 1847. Anson Northrup built a hotel in 1849. A freight and passenger line of wagons went into business on the rutted territorial road connecting St. Paul to St. Anthony.

By 1850 the population of St. Anthony had doubled. Three thousand people called the place home when it was incorporated as a city in 1855. Though St. Anthony was now officially a city, it was a messy one. Pigs roamed muddy streets that were dotted with stumps; piles of lumber lay in scattered heaps; houses built of green lumber warped and oozed pitch; blowing sawdust filled the air and the whine of saws at the mills could be heard above the roar of the falling water. Steele's four lumber mills were sawing 100,000 board feet a day and over twelve million feet per year. Carts and stagecoaches rumbled on the road from St. Paul where the steamboats dropped off people bound for St. Anthony.

In 1856 the writer of a guidebook could advise visitors with a day or so to spend in the area to rent a conveyance at a livery stable and proceed through St. Anthony to Cheever's observatory. The tower stook one hundred feet high and afforded a splendid view of the Falls and of the wire suspension bridge connecting Minneapolis and St. Anthony. The view was charming and all the tourist had to do was "pay your dime and climb." Then, wrote Nathan Parker in the *Minnesota Handbook for 1856-57*, the tourist could continue on to Minnehaha Falls, Fort Snelling, Fountain Cave, and arrive in time for tea in St. Paul.

ST. PAUL

The first to live on the bank of the river that would become St. Paul were the hapless Selkirk farmers who Plympton had thrown off the military reservation. Before they could file legal claims to the land where they had established new homes and farms, they ran afoul of Plympton yet again. In their down-river location the Selkirkers had believed they were well beyond the boundaries of Fort Snelling, which they were until 1840 when Major Plympton arbitrarily extended the military boundaries of the fort to include the land where the Swiss farmers had settled. He ordered them to move yet again. Some complied and others ignored his order.

On May 6, 1840, when the farmers who had ignored Plympton's directive were peacefully planting their gardens, the troops arrived, carried the farmers' belongings out of their houses and destroyed them. Henry Sibley was dismayed. The soldiers, he wrote, "fell upon [the settlers] without warning, treated them with unjustifiable rudeness, broke and destroyed furniture wantonly, insulted the women . . . and killed cattle." The discouraged Selkirkers gave up and moved out of the Territory.

While the first residents of the area that would become the capital city of Minnesota were the Selkirk farmers, the first to formally claim land was the illiterate Canadian voyageur in his sixties, Pierre Parrant, who had hung around Mendota and Fort Snelling. Indian agent Taliaferro loathed Parrant, probably with reason. Taliaferro was so sure Parrant was up to no good that he prohibited him from entering Indian Territory for any reason whatsoever.

Parrant was an evil-looking ruffian. Taliaferro described him as "a coarse, ill-looking, low-browed fellow with only one eye. He spoke execrable English. His habits were intemperate and licentious." One of Parrant's eyes was "blind, marble-hued, crooked, with a sinister white ring glaring around the pupil, giving a kind of piggish expression to his sodden low features." Not everyone shared Taliaferro's low opinion of Parrant. The man provided a much-needed service to the area—at least so far as the soldiers at the Fort were concerned. He sold whiskey. Parrant's business location at Fountain Cave made it easy for suppliers of illicit alcohol to make deliveries and for soldiers from the fort to paddle their boats down to his establishment. The Dakota called the cave "the place where they sell Minne-wakan [alcohol]."

Major Plympton could easily have run Parrant off if he had wanted. Instead he allowed Parrant's business to continue. When Parrant left

Fountain Cave in 1848, it was not because of any pressure from Plympton but because Parrant could not pay off a loan of $90. Land claims were a common medium of exchange and were traded to buy whiskey or to settle debts. Giving up his claim to the land at the cave to pay his debt, Parrant moved downriver three miles where he took up a new claim on a patch of riverbank flats that extended from the water's edge to the bluff.

Parrant reopened his business and became known to river travelers up and down the Mississippi. In 1839 Joseph R. Brown stopped at Parrant's tavern and desired to send a letter to a friend on Grey Cloud Island. Lacking a return address and half as a joke, he wrote in "Pig's Eye," the name by which Parrant's establishment was known to the riverboat captains. In a short time Brown received a reply, directed to him at Pig's Eye.

Parrant could not stay out of trouble. He became embroiled in a dispute with Michel LeClaire over the boundaries of their neighboring claims. LeClaire brought Parrant up before Brown—who by now had become the justice of the peace. Brown, in a bizarre decision, ruled that since neither man had a valid claim to his land, each should race back to his claim and post a notice, a distance of eight miles, presumably in a contest to settle the matter. The aged Parrant was not able to compete in a footrace and so lost. Shortly afterward he left the area and was not heard from again.

FATHER GALTIER'S CHAPEL

The name of Pig's Eye, begun as a joke, might have clung to the frontier settlement for years if the Catholics at Dubuque, taking note of the Protestant missionary activity and growing churches at Kaposia and Mendota, had not decided to assign a priest to the area. They sent the 29-year-old Frenchman Lucian Galtier to minister to the 185 Catholics— mostly French from Canada—living at Mendota and at Pig's Eye. Galtier wanted to build a chapel for his services and considered three sites. One was at Pig's Eye but that location lay on the flood plain and was likely to be flooded out. "The idea of building a church which might at any day be swept down the river to Saint Louis did not please me," he wrote. A parishioner offered him a piece of land on Dayton's Bluff but that site did not please him either.

Galtier's final decision was an astute one. He resolved to build his chapel as near as possible to Fountain Cave because it was a convenient point from which to cross the river to Mendota and "because also it would be the nearest point to the head of navigation outside of the [Fort Snelling] Reservation line." Two "good quiet farmers," Benjamin Gervais and Vetal Guerin, agreed to give Galtier pieces of their land (the extreme eastern part of Guerin's and the extreme western part of Gervais') for a church site, a garden and a small graveyard. In October 1841 Galtier built a log chapel facing the river, a rustic building 25 feet long, 18 feet high and 10 feet wide. "On the first of November," Galtier wrote, "I blessed the new basilica and dedicated it to Saint Paul, the apostle of nations. I expressed a wish, at the same time, that the settlement would be known by the same name and my desire was obtained."

Soon after the church was built Henry Jackson opened a tiny store at the foot of the Gervais claim. Captain Louis Robert, of the steamboats *Greek Slave* and *Time and Tide*, built the first house. The presence of the store gave the steamboats a reason to land and the settlement became known as "St. Paul's Landing." Boat captains left letters with Jackson for the settlers. Jackson put a wooden case, about two feet square, on his counter which settlers could riffle through looking for their mail. Thus, almost by default, Jackson became St. Paul's first postmaster.

A young girl remembered Jackson's hospitality. "The family arrived at St. Paul in 1843 on the *Otter*. When mother saw Pig's Eye, as St. Paul

The chapel of St. Paul from J. Fletcher Williams, *A History of St. Paul and the County of Ramsey, Minnesota* (1875). Courtesy of Pogo Press, Inc.

was then called, she did not like it at all but father loved a new country. On landing we climbed up a steep path. We found only six houses there. One was Jackson's. He kept a store in part of it. In the kitchen he had three barrels of liquor with spigots on them. The Jacksons were very kind and allowed us to live in their warehouse which was about halfway down the bluff. We only slept there nights for we were afraid to cook in a place with power stored in it the way they had, so we cooked outside."

St. Anthony and St. Paul were not the only towns on this section of the river. Little Crow V's substantial village of Kaposia was on the west side of the river, a few miles downriver from St. Paul. A trader visiting in 1849 reported that an Indian house at Kaposia had 200 tons of hay put up and almost 5,000 bushels of corn harvested. In 1850 the Indians had 65 acres of land under cultivation and harvested 30 bushels of corn per acre.

The Kaposia chiefs, all of whom were known by the name of Little Crow, were a family dynasty that passed leadership down from father to son through successive generations. (The English gave them the name of "Little Crow" because their ceremonial costume contained the skin and wings of a crow.) The first recorded Little Crow, who fought with the English in Canada during the American Revolution, was *Ta O-Ya-Te Du-Ta* (His Red Nation or People). The second (or possibly third) Little Crow was *Ce-Tan Wa-Ku-Wa Ma-Ni* (He Who Walks Pursuing a Hawk). This Little Crow signed the treaty of 1805 and died around 1827. His son was Little Crow IV who had the Dakota name of *Wa-Kin-Yan Tan-Ka* (Big Thunder).

Big Thunder signed the treaties of 1830 and 1837 and was accidentally shot in 1845 by his own rifle when it slid off the back of a wagon while he was walking behind it. Big Thunder saw the gun begin to slide, grabbed it by the barrel and it discharged. He was 43 years old and had 22 children by his six wives. At Big Thunder's death his son, Little Crow V, took the name of his ancestor, *Ta O-Ya-Te Du-Ta,* and assumed the leadership of his people.

Despite the encroachment of white settlers, Little Crow's community of Mdewakanton Sioux was gracious and generous to its neighbors. Little Crow V invited the Presbyterian missionary, Dr. Thomas Williamson, to move to Kaposia. Williamson, in turn, arranged for a young teacher to come to the territory. Harriet Bishop arrived at Kaposia on the steamer *Lynx* and on July 18, 1847, two Indian women in a dugout ferried her across the river to St. Paul.

Bishop's first view of St. Paul struck her as "a cheerless prospect. . . .

A few log huts composed the town, three families the American population. With one of these (the J.R. Irvine household) a home was offered
me. Theirs was . . . the only [dwelling] of respectable size, containing
three rooms and an attic." Though Bishop may have felt discouraged at
her first view of St. Paul, she exuded confidence to others. Contempo-
raries described her as "angular, positive, determined, such a woman as
is necessary for frontier life . . . tall, with a good figure; a bright expressive face; earnest and decided in manners and quick in speech." Little
Crow V deserves credit, along with Williamson, for bringing Bishop,
the first teacher, to the Minnesota Territory.

Father Galtier stayed in St. Paul for only three years. When he was
transferred to Iowa Father Augustin Ravoux succeeded him. In 1847
Ravoux extended the rear of Galtier's chapel about 45 feet and added a
small bell tower to house a bell salvaged from the *Argo*, a steamboat that
had sunk in the Mississippi. In 1851 when the diocese of St. Paul was
established, Joseph Cretin was named bishop and he designated the
humble log church as the cathedral of the diocese.

Then the building's luck ran out. When the little chapel began to
fall apart workmen numbered the logs and carried them up St. Anthony
Hill to the site that had been purchased for St. Joseph's Academy. The
plan was to rebuild the chapel and preserve it as a monument. Unfortunately, the planners failed to tell the workmen of their intentions. To the
laborers the historic logs looked like so much firewood and they burned
them to make their coffee and warm their hands. Only two fragments
survived and were made into gavels, one for the Cathedral and the other
for the Minnesota Historical Society. These, too, disappeared.

Ellen Rice Hollinshead, who had come to St. Paul from Vermont
with her brothers Edmund (a future Mayor) and Henry (a future Senator), described the village as it looked in the summer of 1849. "St. Paul
contained between two and three hundred inhabitants. In fact, Third
Street was St. Paul. There were very few buildings beyond it. On the
corner of Jackson and Third streets was a hotel built of hewn logs,
which was kept by J.W. Bass. Governor Ramsey's gubernatorial mansion was a small, frame house on Third and Robert. The parlor was his
office, reception and living room all in one. . . . St. Paul's church, built
of logs, stood where the Catholic block now stands. On the opposite
side of the street lived James M. Goodhue and family. The house in
which he lived was used for a dwelling and printing office and there was
published the first paper in the territory of Minnesota.

"On Market and Third stood a small log hut, covered with bark, which had been used for a blacksmith shop. The floor was mud and the benches were driven in the wall. In this building Miss Harriet E. Bishop taught school. . . . On Third Street, above Market, were two cottages occupied by H. M. and Edmund Rice. In the yard, connected with H. M. Rice's house, was a small log cabin in which Nathan Myrick lived while he was erecting his house on the corner of Chestnut and Fort.

"The Rev. E. D. Neill first preached in the log school house. During the summer he built a small lecture room on Fourth and Market. . . . In this lecture room he and his wife lived until the new house was finished. In the rear end of this room was the parlor, bedroom and kitchen, all in one, and the front was occupied by the pulpit and the benches of the congregation.

"There were three general stores, numerous saloons, the American House, a few offices and that was nearly all there was of St. Paul at that time. On the lower levee was a warehouse, kept by Louis Robert. On the upper levee, at the foot of Hill Street, were two warehouses, one of which was used for the goods of the North American Fur Company and in the other was stored the merchandise of the steamboats. Every arrival of a steamboat created excitement. One could see men standing on the bank of the river watching anxiously for its coming. In November the last boat arrived and departed and after that we were comparatively shut out from the world."

When not "shut out from the world" St. Paul was growing. E.D. Hopkins wrote to her parents from St. Paul in 1851, "There are people from all parts of the world here and still they come in hundreds on every boat. Rent is very high. Just across the street is a family that came on the boat a few days since who rather than pay so high rent got some boards and made a temporary shanty until they build. From the appearance of their furniture, carpets and fixings, I presume they are rich." The hunting was also good. "Here are the prairie chickens, ducks and pigeons in any number you like. Hit three ducks with one shot the other day. There have been about a hundred thousand ducks brought in this season and they are bringing in pickerel by two horse loads."

An English traveler who visited St. Paul in 1854 wrote of the town, "St. Paul is one of the hundred wonders of America. Here, five years ago, were only a few log huts; now there is a large and rapidly growing village of almost four thousand white people with handsome public buildings, good hotels, stores, malls, mechanics shops and every other element of prosperity. . . . The central portion of the village is upon a beautiful plateau, almost a hundred feet above the river; the remainder is chiefly near the water and already there is a strife for supremacy between the 'upper' and 'lower' towns."

Two flat areas, the deltas of streams flowing down from the plateau defined the upper and lower towns. Merchandise destined for shipment up the Minnesota River was unloaded at the Upper Landing, closer to Fort Snelling. Boats docking at the Lower Landing carried goods destined for St. Paul. Though the two locations were less than a mile apart, they competed fiercely for the steamboat landings—even, for a time, keeping two different times as if a dividing line of longitude crossed over the bluff separating the two patches of level ground.

The first recorded Jewish woman in St. Paul was Amelia Ullmann who arrived in 1855 to join her husband Joseph, a fur trader. When they were married in Europe, Amelia had promised to follow her husband "to the end of the world." She made good on her promise when she and her husband immigrated to America. "When we started up the river at noon on that bright May day, I did not think that the time to go to 'the end of the world' had come so soon," she lamented. She found the landing at St. Paul "leveled for a hundred feet or more and the swamp filled in with piles driven into the water at the edge to fasten the boat ropes. Stacks of merchandise were piled upon the riverbank and a crowd of people were lounging about awaiting the arrival of the boat. The boat's whistle was to St. Paul then as to most of the towns on the river, a signal for a general rush to the landing."

Two thriving and ambitious river towns sank their roots in the loamy soil of the Northwest. Separated by fifteen miles of rutted road, already strikingly different from each other in the manner in which they dealt with the challenge of the Upper Mississippi, St. Paul and St. Anthony—like gangly adolescents—looked around for room to grow.

MINNEAPOLIS

Residents of St. Anthony had always cast covetous eyes on the land across the river that belonged to the military reservation. If power could be generated from the falls on the east side of the river, they reasoned, why should not the same be done on the west? In the opinion of the settlers, a valuable natural resource of land and water was going to waste. Settlement by whites and subsequent growth of the city was being held back by the irrelevant detail that the land still belonged to the Indians.

The land on the west bank above the falls rises gently in uneven steps of five to twenty-five feet, gradually ascending for half a mile. The soldiers grazed their cows on the pasture leading one settler to quip that while Boston began with a cow-path, Minneapolis began as a cow pasture. Plympton had surveyed Pike's original purchase in 1839 but changes to the boundaries continued to be made. By 1852 officials had still not clearly established the lines and individuals began fording the river or crossing on the ice to stake out illegal claims on the land. In their attempt to outwit government officials they put together all sorts of devious schemes to pry the government mill and the lands around it away from the control of the fort.

Businessmen, doctors, lawyers, speculators all badgered army and government officials for permits to settle on the west bank. In an attempt to gain control of the government mill on the west bank, Henry Sibley and two partners, Kenneth MacKenzie, a St. Louis fur trader, and Adam Stuart, an officer who had been stationed at Fort Snelling, petitioned the government to release the mill to them. As Sibley wrote, "It would be the means of opening the Upper Mississippi to our enterprising lumber men who are at present excluded from the pine region in consequence of the falls remaining in possession of the government."

The quartermaster general of the army turned Sibley down pointing out that "the mills are situated in Indian country and that, although the United States may have had the right to construct and maintain them as necessary appendages to a military post, it is believed that the government cannot, consistently with our obligations to the Indians, sell or lease them out to individuals." The officer told Sibley what Sibley already knew, that the land and mills were on Indian land and could not be given away by the government.

While conscientious military men enforced the Indian treaties, politicians did not. In 1848 Robert Smith, a member of Congress from Illinois, used his political influence to gain permission from the War Department to move into a house by the government mill and hold a claim just below the falls, promising that he would "protect" the government mill. There was no indication that the mill was in jeopardy or needed protection, and Smith never lived on the site to fulfill his obligation as a protector of government property. Nevertheless, in 1849, he once more convinced the War Department that he was, indeed, living by the mill and as a result was given permission to claim additional property.

Smith's actions created a major rent in the wall around the military reservation and Franklin Steele wriggled through it. He convinced a friend and associate, Colonel John H. Stevens, to apply for a permit to operate a ferry at the falls. In exchange for his ferry services Stevens requested permission to claim 160 acres on the west bank above Smith's mill. The gambit worked and during the winter of 1849-50 Stevens built the first permanent home on the site of the future city of Minneapolis. The great land grab was underway. In 1852 Anson Northrup, who already owned a hotel in St. Anthony, claimed forty-eight acres next to Smith's, built a house and moved in. Charles Russell claimed twenty-six acres next to Northrup in 1854, moved in and began farming.

John Stevens had come to St. Anthony Falls in April 1849 from St. Paul with a group of ten individuals looking for a desirable location to settle. "Leaving St. Paul with no favorable impression of the Territory," he wrote, "we were divided in opinions which part of the country it would be best for us to examine. . . . Directing our attention to Fort Snelling we, for the first time, found that the land on the west side of the Mississippi was not opened to settlers, hence we left the forest and pursued our way to the Falls of St. Anthony" Stevens was impressed with the landscape. "As we journeyed from the forest the character of the country was beautiful beyond description. Not a solitary house except the old mill property was to be seen, an unbroken wilderness surrounded the site of Minneapolis. We saw a number of wolves start from their lairs and eagles . . ."

Only two of the colony, Stevens and J.P. Miller, ended up staying in Minnesota. As Stevens explained, "There were no sick—the doctor left in disgust. We had no children, the school-master went to another part. The farmers of the company did not like the east side of the Mississippi and they all went to California. Two of us determined to remain and I pitched my home on the west side of the Falls of St. Anthony, there to live." Living on the west side of the Falls was illegal and Stevens reported that he "struggled long for a permit to occupy the Reserve [military reservation]." Stevens' daughter was the first white child born in Minneapolis.

The rush to cross the river was like the bursting of a dam. Speculators and settlers gambled if they entered the restricted area, cultivated the land and established residences, the government would allow them to stay. Within months settlers who had once considered the Fort Snelling property to be a "useless and uncultivated blotch upon the finest portion of our Territory—a sort of military carbuncle," had taken up every acre of the land.

The government had lost control. In 1852 Sibley convinced Congress to remove 26,023 acres from the 34,000-acre military reservation and make them available for settlement. In 1855 the government granted preemption rights to the settlers. Seth Eastman came back to Fort Snelling in 1857 to survey and sell off the remainder of the military's land. Now that the Dakota had been moved to a reservation, the government no longer required a fort to assert its dominion. Eastman estimated the number of acres that remained and sold the whole lot to Franklin Steele for $90,000 or about $14 an acre.

The new village on the west bank needed a name. J. M. Goodhue thought the name "All Saints" was a good one (perhaps reflecting some competition with St. Paul) and Mary A. Scofield wrote letters for publications in the East, identifying them as coming from the town of "All Saints." At the first "claim meeting" in 1851 the name of "Lowell" was adopted. This name did not please Dr. A. E. Ames, Anson Northrup and several others who then suggested the English name of "Albion." That name, too, failed to gain approval. Then Charles Hoag, a pioneer farmer and schoolteacher, put together the Dakota word for water, "minneha" and the Greek word for city, "polis" and came up with Minnehapolis.

The name was not popular with some, but George D. Bowman, the editor of the *St. Anthony Express* liked the name and championed it in his newspaper on November 12, 1852. "By all means . . . adopt this beautiful and exceedingly appropriate title and do not longer suffer abroad from connection with the meaningless and outlandish name of "All Saints," he wrote. In time "all finally swallowed it." At a meeting at Colonel Stevens' house in December the matter was settled. The "h" was dropped from the spelling and the name Minneapolis was adopted for the town. They filed a plat for the town in 1855. Authorization for the municipal government came in 1856 but the citizens did not hold an election until 1858.

The villagers took other steps to organize their community. They held the first U.S. Court session on August 20, 1849, in the old government mill on the west side of the river. Judge Bradley B. Meeker presided and Franklin Steele was foreman of the grand jury. The two men waited for two days for some business to be presented. When nothing was, they declared the court adjourned and went home. They organized the University of Minnesota in 1851 with a federal land grant of

46,080 acres. Steele was chair of the twelve-member Board of Regents and pledged $500 to the new institution. Hennepin County was created in Stevens' home in 1852. Calvin A. Tuttle took over the old government mill on the west side of the river and advertised in the May 31, 1851 issue of the *St. Anthony Express* that "the undersigned is now in readiness for grinding Corn, Rye, Oats, Peas, Buckwheat and whatever else needs grinding including Salt."

Builders opened a suspension bridge on January 23, 1855, that spanned the west channel of the Mississippi from Nicollet Island to the Minneapolis side of the river and connected to one that had already been built from the east. It was the first bridge to span the Mississippi River. Although the bridge opened in January, the first team did not drive across until July fourth. A wooden sign on the bridge warned: "Heavily loaded teams keep 100 feet apart when crossing this bridge. Caution: $10 fine for riding or driving faster than a walk. Visitors are requested not to deface woodwork or paint with knives or pencils. Toll: Foot passengers 5 cents. Horse, mare or mule with or without rider, 15 cents. Two horse,

Two buggies wait near the Minneapolis suspension bridge, circa 1865. The photograph was taken by Beal's Art Gallery and printed as a carte de visite. Courtesy of the Minnesota Historical Society.

two mule or ox teams loaded or unloaded 25 cents. Single horse carriage 25 cents. Cow or ox 10 cents and sheep or swine 02 cents."

The toll keeper on the suspension bridge was Captain John Tapper, one of the best known individuals in the two communities. A visitor paid his five cents to cross on the bridge from St. Anthony to Minneapolis. When he returned Tapper charged the man another five cents. "But I paid once," the man protested. "Do I have to pay to go back?" "Young man," replied Tapper, "There is no going back in this country." Measured by population growth, Tapper was correct. By 1855 the town of St. Anthony on the east bank of the river boasted a population of nearly 3,000 and Minneapolis contained 1,000.

The residents of both communities were principally New Englanders with many coming from the State of Maine. Despite the fact that St. Anthony and Minneapolis were thriving, daily life was hard. The wife of Isaac Atwater wrote of her life in the West, "Although St. Anthony was a dull little town, still we had many diversions. One bright day something wonderful happened. By the weekly mail a huge parcel came out from which emerged 'David Copperfield.' 'Dickens' new novel has come' flew from mouth to mouth. It went the rounds and by the time the ice went out the book was literally torn to rags . . . The river was everything in those days. Our year was divided into two seasons, 'when the river was closed' and 'when the ice went out.' How happy we were when we heard the steamboat whistle at St. Paul in the spring. It meant renewed communication with the outside world. What did we have to eat? Salt pork. One grew to loathe the sight of it. No eggs, almost no milk. But we had fine vegetables raised in our gardens."

Utilizing the power from the falls, mills grew up on both sides of the river. At first the mills at St. Anthony were the larger. Then the mills spread to both sides of the river led by such farsighted and aggressive businessmen like Cadwallader Washburn and Charles Pillsbury. By the 1860's the leaders of both cities realized that the competition was not with each other but with the burgeoning commercial center at the head of navigation on the Mississippi. St. Paul, by 1870, boasted a population of 20,030 and was growing. Though it took a dozen years to convince the electorate, Minneapolis and St. Anthony, in 1872, merged their two communities into one. Both were flour milling towns. In 1870 Minneapolis produced more than 200,000 barrels of flour. Only 14 years later the city was the world's leading producer of flour. By 1890 Minneapolis was producing seven million barrels annually and the total swelled to

20,443,000 barrels of flour in 1915. The milling, first of lumber and then of wheat, produced a remarkable growth spurt in Minneapolis. Between 1880 and 1890 the city's population grew by 350 percent.

There were now two cities, Minneapolis and St. Paul, maturing rapidly at the upper reach of the Mississippi. Both were dependent on the river. One relied on the river for transportation, making it the commercial center. The other relied on the falls of the river for power, making it the milling city. The two communities were to become as different from each other as were the ways in which they used the river that flowed between them.

NOTES

James M. Goodhue's poem appeared in his newspaper *The Minnesota Pioneer,* as a New Year's Greeting on January 1, 1850. The story of Major Plympton's claim appears as Appendix 4 in the first volume of William Watts Folwell's *A History of Minnesota* (1921). Other sources for this chapter are Lucy Leavenworth Wilder Morris, editor, *Old Rail Fence Corners* (1976); Lucile M. Kane, *The Falls of St. Anthony: The Waterfall that Built Minneapolis* (1987); and the Fall 1991 issue of *Ramsey County History* (26: 3) which includes articles by Patrick R. Martin, "Forgotten Pioneer, Abraham Perry and His Flock"; Ronald M. Hubbs, "Who WAS 'Pig's Eye' Parrant, Anyway?"; and Virginia Brainard Kunz, "150th Anniversary of the Naming of St. Paul: Rush to Settlement—1840 to 1880." Father Galtier's chapel is shown and described in J. Fletcher Williams's *A History of the City of Saint Paul and of the Country of Ramsey, Minnesota* (1876) in a chapter for the year 1841. Ellen Rice Hollinshead's memories are found in papers preserved by her family. E. D. Hopkins' letter is in the collections of the Minnesota Historical Society. *The St. Anthony Express* published a *Historical Sketch of St. Anthony and Minneapolis from their First Settlement to November 1855* (1855). Other sources are Ruth Thompson, *The Twin Towns at the Falls of St. Anthony* (1926); John W. Reps, *Cities of the Mississippi* (1994); and for flour milling data, David B. Danbom, "Flour Power," *Minnesota History* (Spring/Summer 2003). Also see Linda Mack Schloff, *"And Prairie Dogs Weren't Kosher"* (1996) for the story of Amelia Ullmann.

CHAPTER 12

Life on the Steamboats

The explosive growth of the cities at the head of navigation led to an equally explosive growth of the steamboat industry. In 1844 forty-five steamboats made the trip to St. Paul in one season. In 1868 a record 1,068 steamboats docked at the landings in St. Paul. Steamboats were the advanced transportation technology of the time; their captains and pilots the lords of the river. Every boy wanted to become a steamboat captain.

Through a process of trial and error river pilots and captains gained a personal knowledge of the river that was uncanny. They memorized every detail of a stretch of the river, the shadows cast by a bank of trees at dusk, the ever-changing shape of the channel, the look of the water as it reacted to winds and flooding. Experienced captains catalogued in their minds thousands of landmarks along the river bank; a hill, bluff, grove of trees, stretch of brush, the location of creeks and sloughs that allowed them to guide their boats day or night over a river filled with hidden obstructions.

Every season the river was different. The Mississippi was constantly tearing at its banks, cutting new bends, building new points, and depositing new sandbars. Some bars were of sand and gravel, others of rock. Some were permanent; others shifted and reformed with every heavy rain. There were reefs, shoals, rocks, sunken boats and the hazards of storms that came up with sudden ferocity on the Lake Pepin stretch of the river. Pilots learned to tell, from the color and texture of the water, much of what lay beneath it.

Weaving back and forth from one bank to the other, the channel formed a river within a river. The channel was not static, but changed with the level of the water. When the water level was high, the channel was almost as wide as the river. When the water level was low, the channel could be narrower than the width of a large steamboat. Pilots going downstream kept their boats in the center of the channel, edging to the outside of the bends to take advantage of the depth of the channel and the faster current. Then, at a point sensed more than seen by the pilot, he swung the boat diagonally across the river to stay in the channel as, invisible at the surface, it swept across the river. Pilots going upstream kept their boats in the shallow and relatively slack water along the inside of the bends rather than run against the full force of the current. By tacking back and forth in counter-direction to the channel pilots learned to avoid the current when it was against them and thus save time and fuel.

There were two kinds of snags that pilots and captains dreaded. One, called a "sawyer," was a tree along the bank that had fallen into the water and lay horizontal just below the surface, swaying up and down with the current. The other type, called a "planter" was a tree that had fallen into the river and become embedded at an angle in the bottom. Its blunt branches lay just under the surface of the water, poised like a lance to pierce the fragile hull of any boat unlucky enough to hit them. It was this kind of snag that sank the *New Orleans,* one of the first steamboats on the Mississippi. Crews on the riverboats were ingenious when making

The steamboat *Quincey* struck a sandbar near Trempealeau on July 12, 1906. Salvage workers, sightseers, and a photographer named Gunderson all came to view the wreck. When salvaged and re-floated, the steamboat was renamed the *J. S.* Courtesy of Gregory Page.

repairs. More than one hole in the hull of the steamer, caused by a collision with a snag or rock, was temporarily patched by tying a mattress or a slab of bacon over the hole.

Mark Twain loved the river. To him it was "the great Mississippi, the majestic, the magnificent Mississippi, rolling its mile-wide tide along, shining in the sun." Charles Dickens felt otherwise. Writing in *American Notes* of the river at Cairo, Illinois, he called it "the hateful Mississippi circling and eddying before it, and turning off upon its southern course, a slimy monster, hideous to behold; a hotbed of disease, an ugly sepulchre, a grave uncheered by any gleam of promise. . . . An enormous ditch, sometimes two or three miles wide, running liquid mud, six miles

Steamboat lines offered fine dining to their excursion passengers, as this menu of the *Quincey*, printed on the back of a postcard, demonstrates. Courtesy of Gregory Page.

an hour, its strong and frothy current choked and obstructed everywhere by huge logs and whole forest trees . . . ."

Boiler explosions were a constant hazard. Mark Twain's brother, Henry Clemens, was a clerk on the steamboat *Pennsylvania* when four of the eight boilers exploded. Clemens was thrown from the boat into the water and, not realizing how seriously he had been injured, swam back to help in the rescue work before dying himself.

Riverboat captains, competing with each other on the river or try-ing to keep to a schedule, overtaxed the capacity of their engines. In 1858 the *Galena* entered Lake Pepin at full speed with stokers piling on fuel as fast as they could. One passenger compared the smokestacks to "volca-noes emitting showers of sparks." As the boat approached the Red Wing levee flames suddenly engulfed the boat's superstructure. Rescuers hastily threw a gangway to the dock but some passengers jumped over-board and five drowned. The boat burned to the waterline and the charred hull sank.

THE SEA WING DISASTER

The sinking of the *Sea Wing* during a summer storm on Lake Pepin on July 13, 1890, was the greatest steamboat disaster on the Upper Missis-sippi. The 109 ton boat, based in Diamond Bluff, Wisconsin, was on a Sunday excursion from Diamond Bluff to Lake City, Minnesota. The boat towed a barge for dancing and Captain David Niles Wethern had hired a small band to provide music for the excursion. After picking up passengers from Trenton on the Wisconsin side and at Red Wing, Min-nesota, the *Sea Wing* proceeded on to Lake City where thirteen compa-nies of the Minnesota National Guard's First Regiment were encamped.

The weather that Sunday had been hot and humid and the sky was dark and threatening when, at 8 P.M., Captain Wethern headed his *Sea Wing*, carrying approximately 215 passengers, north toward home. He had no way of knowing that, earlier in the day, funnel clouds had up-rooted trees and demolished cottages north of St. Paul and that within a few minutes barns would be blowing down at Red Wing. The *Sea Wing* had steamed five miles up Lake Pepin when it encountered the full force of the storm. Captain Wethern headed for Maiden Rock, hoping to steer his boat under the shelter of the bluff, but when he saw the squall ap-proaching, he turned his vessel toward the Minnesota shore to meet the wind head on. The women and children took refuge from the storm in the main cabin and when the top-heavy boat went over, they were trapped. Ninety-eight individuals lost their lives in the *Sea Wing* disaster, including the captain's wife Nellie and their son Perley. The small communities of Diamond Bluff and Trenton each lost ten individuals. Most of those who died came from Red Wing where five thousand mourners attended a memorial service. The greatest loss, overwhelming to the survivors, was of young women and children.

Other sinkings had less tragic consequences. A boat loaded with, among other things, asparagus seeds, hit a snag near Lake Pepin and sank. The seeds drifted to shore, took root and provided an asparagus crop that grew for years along Bogus Creek and between the villages of Pepin and Stockholm in Wisconsin.

STATE OF MINNESOTA, } ss.
  COUNTY OF GOODHUE,

Coroner's report to the Clerk of the District Court of Goodhue County, State of Minnesota, regarding the death of John Shifler of Red Wing Minn. *in the disaster on Lake Pepin July 13, A. D. 1890. After making investigation I found the following facts:*

That said John Shifler *went on the Steamer Sea Wing at* Red Wing *to go with the excursion party to Lake City and back on the 13th day of* July, *A. D. 1890, and on* his *return left Lake City about 8 o'clock in the afternoon of said day* for Red Wing *and after coming up the Lake about four miles a violent storm arose and capsized the boat leaving said* John Shifler *in the Lake without any means by which* he *could save* himself *from drowning. The above* John Shifler *was about* 45 *years of age.* in the morning of July 14th *A. D. 1890* his *body was found in Lake Pepin and brought to Red Wing* on Steamer Howard and delivered to Keyser for burial.

There being no sign on his *body of any violence, or any reason to believe or suspect any foul play, I therefore decided that no inquest was necessary and that* he *came to* his *death by drowning, from being thrown into the Lake when the steamer capsized on July 13, A. D. 1890, and so report.*

  Dated Red Wing, Minn., July 24, 1890.

                John E Kyllo
                Coroner of Goodhue County, Minn.

When the steamboat *Sea Wing* capsized in Lake Pepin on the Mississippi River on July 13, 1890, the Goodhue County coroner decided to use a printed form to record the numerous deaths by drowning under identical circumstances. Courtesy of the Minnesota Historical Society.

STEAMBOATS AND LECLAIRE

Pilots became experts on dangerous stretches of the river and sold their services to riverboat captains. Boats went through the hazardous fifteen mile stretch of rapids above Rock Island only in daylight and many took aboard a special pilot at LeClaire, Iowa, to steer the boat safely through to Davenport. Often several steamers would be tied up at LeClaire, waiting their turn to go down the rapids. Most of the pilots lived at LeClaire and after piloting a boat through the rapids, they dropped off at Davenport where they picked up another job, guiding boats through the rapids upriver. Davenport was the location of the "Green Tree Hotel," a magnificent elm in whose shade out-of-work boatmen gathered waiting for hire on the passing steamboats. A similar elm stood at LeClaire until 1964 when it succumbed to Dutch Elm disease at the age of 225 years. A section of the tree is preserved in the Buffalo Bill Museum at LeClaire.

> *"LeClaire, the home of the big green tree,*
> *Welcomes you," is the sign you see,*
> *When on the highway you motor down,*
> *And enter this quaint little Iowa town.*
> *It was in the shade of this big elm tree,*
> *That 'Buffalo Bill' learned his ABC. . . .*

Captain Philip Suiter arrived in LeClaire in 1856. For over one hundred years Suiter, three of his sons, two grandsons and two great-grandsons served as river pilots or captains. S.W. Van Sant, who became a governor of Minnesota, built his raft boats at LeClaire. *The Lone Star*, a steam powered wooden towboat at LeClaire set the record for the boat in the longest continuous service. The craft began service as a packet boat in 1869 and continued for 99 years. When it was retired in 1968 it was the last operating steam sternwheeler towboat on the Mississippi River.

The early steamboats had bells that were the pride of their captains. Some weighed as much as 800 pounds, were elaborately decorated and were masterpieces of bell making. To give the bells a clear, melodious tone their makers added silver to the mix of metal before they were cast. Some boat captains personally contributed as many as 500 silver dollars to be melted down for their ship's bell. When a boat was leaving a landing a deck hand would toll the bell slowly several times. Three quick rings on the bell were a signal to the crewmembers to stand by their posts. After 1845 steam whistles replaced the musical bells on the boats and many churches along the river received gifts of used steamboat bells.

When the steam whistle became standard on the boats a code developed among steamboat captains which was invariably followed. The right of way belonged to the boat going downriver but the captain of the boat coming upriver decided which side, either to the left or to the right, was the one to take in passing. One whistle indicated the right-hand direction was preferred, two blasts meant left. Blasts on the whistles, repeating the signal, were blown to signify assent. If the captain of a descending boat thought the course proposed by the boat coming upriver was unwise, he would sound three short, agitated blasts of his whistle. This would be followed by a repetition of the signal by the other boat, to indicate understanding, and the dialogue—via steam whistle—would start all over again. Steamboat whistles were loud and penetrating and, if the wind was in the right direction, they could be heard for miles. People living on the river took pride in being able to recognize individual boats by the tones of their bells and whistles.

A boat chant that shore residents heard on still summer nights was the call of the deckhands who measured the water depth with sounding poles. The poles were from twelve to twenty feet long, divided into one-foot marks with various colors of paint. The deckhand stood on the lower deck to measure the depth of the water. He relayed the message to a man stationed on the upper deck who, in turn called it out to the pilot above. Crewmen called out "NINE FEET, nine feet; TWELVE FEET, twelve feet; TEN FEET, ten feet," in rhythmic shouts and responses until the boat rounded a bend in the river and the voices faded away.

When they used lead lines to mark the depths pieces of flannel and leather were woven into the rope so the leadsman could recognize the depth as the rope slipped through his hands in the darkness. A single piece of leather on the line marked a six foot depth, leather split into two thongs indicated the twelve foot depth (Mark Twain) and leather split into three thongs, the Mark Three depth.

River men developed their own specialized vocabulary of the river. A *levee* was a place where a steamboat landed. A *slough* was the body of water in back of an island and separate from the main channel. The *texas* was the house on the roof that contained the captain's stateroom, the *jackstaff* was the flagstaff at the bow, *roosters* were deck hands, *floaters* were the hands on a raft, *old man* was the captain and *towing* meant pushing not pulling.

The two most skilled men on the boats were the pilot and the engineer, though many captains were also skilled pilots. Under the captain was the mate, the lowest paid officer on the boat. The mate was in charge of the deck hands and the loading and unloading of cargo. On most boats the mate was the shouting, cursing gang boss who ruled by brute strength and the vituperative nature of his vocabulary.

Local people celebrated the captains whose names and feats were known in every town up and down the river. One of the most colorful of the captains was Daniel Smith Harris, one of five Harris brothers, all of whom were noted for their steamboats. Daniel Harris came to Galena in 1823 and worked in the lead mines until 1836 when he became a steamboat captain and owner. His first boats were the *Pre-Emption, Frontier, Relief, Otter, Senator, Sutler* and the famous *War Eagle*. In 1857 he built the *Grey Eagle*, at a cost of $63,000, considered by many to be the fastest and finest steamer on the river. The boat measured 250 feet long, weighed 673 tons and every man on the river was in love with her.

The *Grey Eagle* was the sweetest thing in the way of a steamboat that man ever looked upon. Long, lean, as graceful as a grey hound, white as snow, except her chimneys ornamented with what were called 'petticoat tops' hanging about five feet from the tops of the chimneys, ornaments peculiar to that line of boats. Her jackstaff was six feet high, beautifully taped with white halyards, a pink and white nighthawk half way up. Above that a weather vane and on top of that a golden-feathered rooster who sat on his lofty perch as majestically as an eagle on his mountain top, swaying and bending in the breezes with a movement as graceful as that of a bird swinging and pecking at the dewdrops in a rose.

Traffic on the river was subject to summer droughts that lowered the level of water to only a few feet deep, floods in the spring that widened the river by miles and freeze-ups in winter. Between 1849 and 1866 ice prevented boats from reaching St. Paul on an average of 143 days a year. Lake Pepin was a particularly exasperating bottleneck because it thawed later than the rest of the river. The river would be open both below and above Lake Pepin while the lake stretch would still be frozen solid. In the spring of each year, before Lake Pepin thawed, shippers arranged to have their freight unloaded at Read's Landing below Lake Pepin, hauled by team to Wacouta at the head of the lake, and reloaded on another steamboat for transportation on to St. Paul.

The winter of 1856-57 was an especially cold one and, as so often happened, the Upper Mississippi, both above and below Lake Pepin, had melted while Pepin itself remained frozen. By April 29, twenty-two steamboats with 1,500 impatient passengers from as far away as Cincinnati and Pittsburgh waited at the foot of Lake Pepin for the ice to break up. A few boat captains tried butting the prows of their boats against the wall of ice without success.

In their eagerness to get to St. Paul, several hundred passengers got off the boats at Wabasha and set off on foot to walk the approximately twenty miles to Red Wing at the head of Lake Pepin. Here other riverboats met them and took them on to St. Paul. The first boat arrived on April 16, its decks jammed with passengers who had slept on the crowded decks using their carpetbags for pillows.

When the ice finally broke up below Lake Pepin, the boats raced to get to St. Paul. To be the first boat of the season to arrive carried a year's worth of free dockage as well as prestige. The whole town celebrated when the first boat arrived and captains organized dances that night on the winning boat. Captain Daniel Smith Harris on the *War Eagle* was in the lead when, just below St. Paul, a hapless deck hand fell overboard. Harris slowed to put out a rescue boat and the *Galena*, captained by Will Laughton, pulled ahead, arriving in St. Paul at 2 A.M. on May 1, fifteen minutes ahead of the *War Eagle*.

Harris had been first in other years. His was the first boat to St. Paul on April 9, 1849, when he brought word that the bill for the organization of Minnesota Territory had become law. During the fifteen years from 1844 to 1858, Harris won the coveted laurel seven times. Though the average date for the arrival of the first boat was April 13, in 1858 Harris, in the *Grey Eagle*, arrived in St. Paul on March 25, the earliest arrival then on record.

RELAYING THE QUEEN'S MESSAGE

Despite his frequent successes, Captain Harris could not accept losing any race. He was captaining the *Grey Eagle* in 1858 when operators flashed the first overseas telegraphic message, a greeting from Queen Victoria to President James Buchanan, sent under the ocean by the Atlantic Cable. Only two telegraph lines came into the Upper Mississippi region at the time, one to Dunleith (near Galena) where Harris was loading his boat and the other at Prairie du Chien, 61 miles upriver where the *Itasca*, under Captain David Whitten was also taking on cargo. Both boats left for St. Paul at 6 P.M.

Harris resolved that he would be the first to bring the news of the Queen's message to St. Paul. Since his boat was 61 miles further from St.

Paul than Whitten's, he piled on all the steam he could to move his boat upriver. The *Itasca* captain, not realizing that Harris was in a race with him, took his time, stopping at every landing, unloading cargo and taking on new shipments. He chatted on the docks with friends and agents.

Meanwhile Harris in his *Grey Eagle* stopped at only the major landings. Instead of pulling in to deliver the mail at the towns along the way he stationed a deck hand at the rail, steered his boat close to the levee and had his crewman heave the mail onto the dock. The *Grey Eagle* overtook the *Itasca* a few miles below St. Paul. When the startled Whitten saw the black smoke pouring from the stacks of the *Grey Eagle* he instantly understood what was happening. Harris had been adding barrels of pitch to his fires to keep them blazing fiercely.

Whitten stoked his own boilers and the race was on. The two boats churned the water as they raced prow to prow for St. Paul. Harris stationed a crewmember at the bow of his boat with the Queen's message tied to a piece of coal. When they approached the wharf, the man threw it to a worker on shore. The *Grey Eagle* beat the *Itasca* by a boat length. She had traveled the 290 miles from Dunleith to St. Paul in 18 hours, at a speed of 16 1/9 miles per hour going upstream. That is how the news of the Queen's message to the President was delivered to St. Paul.

Some steamboat races ended in disaster. John Hay, who served as Secretary of State and Ambassador to England, wrote a ballad about a common river tragedy, the blowing up of a steamboat during a race. "Jim Bludso of the Prairie Belle" (1878) was based on a true incident:

> *Wall, no! I can't tell whar he lives,*
> *Because he don't live, you see;*
> *Leastways, he's got out of the habit*
> *Of livin' like you and me.*
> *Whar have you been for the last three year*
> *That you haven't heard folks tell*
> *How Jimmy Bludso passed in his checks*
> *The night of the Prairie Belle?*
>
> *He weren't no saint,—them engineers*
> *Is all pretty much alike,—*
> *One wife in Natchez-under-the-Hill*
> *And another one here, in Pike;*
> *A keerless man in his talk was Jim,*
> *And an awkward hand in a row,*

But he never flunked, and he never lied,——
I reckon he never knowed how.

And this was all the religion he had,——
To treat his engine well;
Never be passed on the river;
To mind the pilot's bell;
And if ever the Prairie Belle took fire,——
A thousand times he swore
He'd hold her nozzle agin the bank
Till the last soul got ashore.

All boats has their day on the Mississip',
And her day come at last,——
The Movastar was a better boat,
But the Belle she wouldn't be passed.
And so she come tearin' along that night——
The oldest craft on the line——
With a nigger squat on her safety-valve
And her furnace crammed, rosin and pine.

The fire bust out as she clared the bar,
And burnt a hole in the night,
And quick as a flash she turned, and made
For that willer-bank on the right.
There was runnin' and cussin', but Jim yelled out,
Over all the infernal roar,
"I'll hold her nozzle agin the bank
Till the last galoot's ashore."

Through the hot, black breath of the burnin' boat
Jim Bludso's voice was heard,
And they all had trust in his cussedness,
And knowed he would keep his word.
And, sure's you're born, they all got off
Afore the smokestacks fell,
And Bludso's ghost went up alone
In the smoke of the Prairie Belle.

He weren't no saint, but at jedgment
I'd run my chance with Jim,
'Longside of some pious gentlemen
That wouldn't shook hands with him.
He seen his duty, a dead-sure thing,
And went for it thar and then;
And Christ ain't a going to be too hard
On a man that died for men.

While the *Grey Eagle* was considered one of the grandest steam-boats on the Upper Mississippi, the *Key City* was believed by many to be a close second. The exploits of her captain became legend, particularly after he ran the boat through forty miles of river curves without a rud-der. The *Key City* was coming down the river from Trempealeau, Wis-consin, in a fog when she hit something in the river that tore off the rudder. The captain stopped the boat and fished the rudder out of the water but his crew could not hang it back on the boat because the iron fittings had been damaged.

Despite not having a rudder, Pilot Bill Tibbals backed the *Key City* out of Trempealeau and headed her down the river. On its forty mile run it passed a rival steamboat, threaded its way through two crooked sloughs, criss-crossed the river several times to follow the channel and made two landings. Landing a steamboat that is headed downriver is a complicated maneuver. The captain must first pass the landing; then make a sweeping semi-circle in mid-stream to come up on the dock with the bow pointing upriver.

On another occasion the *Key City* was steaming lazily upriver through Lake Pepin, towing a heavily loaded barge, when the steamboat *Messenger* came up behind and passed her by. Captain Worden, of the *Key City*, might have accepted being passed except that when the *Messenger* did so she blew her whistle in derision, raised her flag and her passengers and crew shouted and cheered as they passed. This was too much.

Worden immediately sent some men onto the barge he was towing with instructions to cut it adrift in the river. Ordering his firemen to sift rosin in with the firewood and to stoke the boilers Worden took off in pursuit of the *Messenger*, itself a fast and powerful boat. Soon the chim-neys of both boats were red hot. Men with hoses stood at the ready on the roofs and boiler decks of the two boats to put out fires if neces-sary. At first slowly, then rapidly, the *Key City* overtook the *Messenger*.

When she was well ahead the *Key City* ran across the bow of her rival, circled back down the river and picked up the barge she had left floating in the river.

The *Key City* gained distinction in 1859 when, on April 20, she was the first boat to make it through the ice to St. Paul. At 8 o'clock in the morning, when the townspeople saw the smoke of a steamboat approaching around the bend in the river, "a stream of humanity poured down Jackson and Robert streets. A cannon was discharged to honor the occasion." The symbol of an Upper Mississippi River champion boat was a push-broom with a three-foot wide brush. Boats deemed champions, such as the *Key City*, proudly carried such a broom raised above the roof of their pilothouses.

In what may have been a reaction to the lawless nature of the frontier and river towns in particular, some riverboat captains strictly observed the Sabbath. Captain Orrin Smith was devout and always tied up his boat by midnight on a Saturday and, if there were no minister aboard, conducted Sunday services for the passengers and crew himself. Others did the same. Commodore William F. Davidson was one of the biggest boat owners on the Upper Mississippi and also one of the most pious. He did not permit gambling or dancing on any of his boats. One of his captains, however, was not so devout.

One Sunday Captain Laughton, commanding Commodore Davidson's *Alexander Mitchell*, allowed a few of his passengers to dance the Virginia Reel in the main cabin. When the dance ended, Laughton went to bed while the boat continued on downriver. About three o'clock in the morning a tornado struck the *Alexander Mitchell* tearing off both chimneys, the roof of the pilot house and a piece of the hurricane deck. The first mate was blown off the boat and when he was pulled back aboard, the commodore chided him, "That's what comes of dancing."

Davidson always conducted Sunday morning services on his boat. A listener remembered Davidson's prayer for the poor. "And, oh Lord, bless the poor. Give to every poor family a barrel of pork, a barrel of flour, a barrel of sugar, a barrel of salt, a barrel of pepper." Davidson hesitated a moment and then blurted out, "Hell no! That's too much pepper."

Not all the steamboat captains were devout. Traveling as they did, many had girl friends in towns up and down the river. A local lyric described a familiar situation:

I am a wandering steamboatman
And far away from home;
I fell in love with a pretty gal,
And she in love with me.

She took me to her parlor
And cooled me with her fan
She whispered in her mother's ear,
"I love the steamboatman."

The steamboats had individuality and personal characteristics much as did their pilots and captains. Some boats almost steered themselves, others were reluctant to respond to the wheel, and had to be forcefully held on course. A boat designed to be fast sometimes turned out to be sluggish on the water. The *Key City* and the *Itasca* were twin boats with the same dimensions and powered by identical engines. Yet the *Key City* invariably ran from one to three miles faster per hour than her twin.

DEATH OF THE GREY EAGLE

As Mark Twain movingly chronicled, mystique surrounded the lives of Mississippi River pilots. In love with the ever-changing river, matching their wits against the gods of weather and chance, possessors of a unique capability, contentious, competitive and independent, river pilots were romantic heroes. Piloting a boat was more than a job—it was a calling. The love they felt for their boats rivaled the affection they held for people.

In May 1861, Captain Daniel Smith Harris, at the wheel of his beloved *Grey Eagle*, left LeClaire at the head of the dangerous fifteen-mile stretch of the Rock Island rapids and started down the river. Just as he reached the Rock Island Bridge a sudden gust of wind hit the boat and drove her against a bridge abutment. The *Grey Eagle* sank in less than five minutes with the loss of several lives. The last man left on the wreck was Captain Harris. The *texas* was above water and rescuers found Harris going aimlessly about the upper deck picking up pieces. Broken-hearted over the disaster and the loss of his beautiful steamer, Harris retired to his home in Galena and, though he lived for many years after the accident, never piloted a riverboat again. Years later the once beautiful pilothouse of the *Grey Eagle* was discovered on a front lawn, serving as a summerhouse.

Considered as one of the handsomest and swiftest steamboats on the Upper Mississippi, the *Grey Eagle* was the pride of its captain, Daniel Smith Harris. This rare envelope from the *Grey Eagle* was mailed between 1857 and 1861. Courtesy of Floyd Risvold.

THE FASHIONABLE TOUR

Despite the hazards of river travel tourists in search of adventure and the romance of the American west, flocked to the Mississippi.

Charles Lanman, canoeing down the river in 1847, wrote of the scenery:

> The Mississippi between the Upper Rapids and the Lefever River, which leads you to Galena, is characterized by an extensive range of fantastic bluffs and isolated rocks. Covered as they are with vines and mosses, they present the appearance of ancient ruins and it requires no great stretch of the imagination to discover towns and turrets of ancient castles, fortress walls that have been partly battered down and solitary pillars rising in gloomy grandeur, as if to preach a lesson to the passing traveler upon the ravages of time. This same kind of singular beauty ornaments the river in the vicinity of Dubuque and extends as far as Prairie du Chien. As you ascend, the bluffs become more lofty and imposing. On the summit of one of the most beautiful bluffs is a small cabin and a large wooden cross where the French trader and miner Dubuque was buried, according to his own request, in a coffin made of solid lead.

To the visitors from the East, the Mississippi from Dubuque and Galena north to the mouth of the St. Croix bore a remarkable resemblance to the Hudson River Valley near the palisades. The hills of the driftless area are like the hills children draw, great lumps rising abruptly 300 feet or more from the plain. Heavily wooded, studded with sudden rock outcrops, these hills should have their own special name as do the deep ravines and steep-walled valleys, called coulees, which run between them.

In the mid-1830s the noted American artist, George Catlin, with his wife took a steamboat up the Mississippi to St. Paul. Catlin was born in Philadelphia in 1796 and was trained in the law but what he loved was painting. His special subjects were Indians. Between 1829 and 1837 Catlin traveled extensively in the west making 600 Indian sketches. Catlin exhibited this "Indian Gallery" in Europe and on the east coast, gaining him an international reputation.

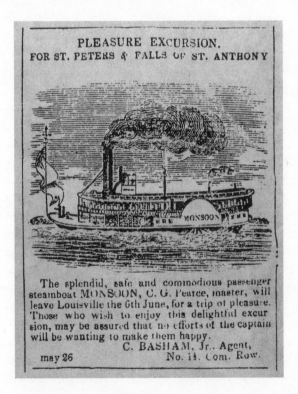

Travel advertisement from the *Louisville Journal* (June 4, 1840). Courtesy of Minnesota Historical Society.

Catlin was enchanted with the views of the Mississippi between Prairie du Chien and Fort Snelling and he sketched the Falls of St. Anthony, Maiden Rock, the Winona hills, Capoli Peak at McGregor and scenes of Fort Snelling. Catlin called on Potosa, Julien Dubuque's widow, and painted a scene of his grave. "The Upper Mississippi . . . must be approached to be appreciated," he wrote. "Until he reaches Prairie du Chien and from that place until he arrives at Lake Pepin every reach and turn in the river presents to his eye a more immense and magnificent scene of grandeur and beauty."

Catlin wrote with enthusiasm about the magnificent bluffs lining the river and urged easterners to take a "fashionable tour" of the Upper Mississippi. "All that can be seen on the Mississippi below St. Louis, or for several hundred miles above it, gives no hint or clue to the magnificence of the scenes which are continually opening to the eye of the traveler and riveting him to the deck of the steamer, through sunshine, lightning or rain, from the mouth of the Wisconsin to the Falls of St. Anthony."

After spending several days visiting at Fort Snelling, Catlin sent his wife back down the river on a steamboat while he followed more slowly with two companions in a canoe so he could sketch the scenery. Catlin's paintings and descriptions of the river between Fort Snelling and Prairie du Chien attracted attention in the East, and soon the steamboats were carrying passengers who were neither immigrants nor speculators. They were tourists.

The boat captains were quick to respond to the needs of this new class of passenger by putting together special excursion cruises that ushered in the Golden Age of steamboats. Gone were the corn-husk mattresses and signs stating that gentlemen were forbidden to lie down in berths with their boots on or whittle on the furniture. Captain Throckmorton advertised spring mattresses. He gave titles (Judge, General, and Esquire) to his passengers if they did not already have one and introduced them ceremoniously and with champagne to the officers at Fort Snelling. Captains hired chefs, hung crystal chandeliers, put down thick carpeting and laid tables with shining silver and sparkling cut glass. In 1858 more than a thousand steamboats docked at the Port of St. Paul.

A few amenities were lacking. One passenger wrote to a friend of her riverboat experience. "One must learn to dispense with milk on one's voyage in the West. I can manage to swallow coffee without milk but it is almost impossible for me to take tea without it. I made a little complaint about it at tea last evening. 'Well,' said a Colonel Baxter, an

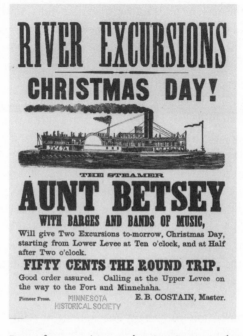

Poster for excursions on the *Aunt Betsey* on the Mississippi River from St. Paul to Fort Snelling and Minnehaha Falls, circa 1860. Courtesy of the Minnesota Historical Society.

excellent man sitting opposite to me, 'we frequently did not taste milk for many weeks during the Mexican campaign.' 'Oh,' said I, 'but then you had glory to console yourselves with. But here on a steamboat without glory and without milk, it is too much.' This morning we had plenty of milk for breakfast."

On the excursion trips tourists could enjoy the scenery and the accommodations without being jostled by bedraggled immigrants on the last leg of their two-month-long journey from Europe. There were still times, however, when genteel tourists were jammed on the boat with hundreds of deck passengers, smelly livestock and cargo that occupied every available space. A passenger from England wrote of his trip in October 1847, on the *Red Wing:*

> First class passengers occupy the cabins on top of the deck where there is plenty of fresh air and the balcony enables one to take a little exercise without getting dirty. But if one ventures

down on the deck he finds the most terrible filth, mud, stagnant water and a most offensive odor everywhere. In the washroom, which all the men use in common, there is a huge towel which is suspended over a wooden roller. One must lay aside all instinct of cleanliness when one enters this place.

The walls, the ceiling, the beds, all are uniformly painted white. The only sign of luxury in the men's parlor is that the tables and parts of the floor are left uncovered so that the men can indulge to their hearts content in their favorite pastime of unrelenting, merciless spitting. Their operations generally center about two stoves where they sit as silent as statues, each one chewing his tobacco. A further convenience for this occupation of theirs is found in a hole in the floor which is so large that a lady could easily get her foot caught in it. To avoid such a calamity, the carpet has been cut away around the hole so that everyone can see and avoid it.

In the competition for passengers captains provided music. They found that a calliope added personality to a boat as did a "cabin orchestra" of a half dozen Blacks who could play stringed instruments and sing. Steamboat pilot George Merrick wrote that word got around about which boats had the best musicians. One of the boats on which Merrick served had a sextet of black firemen whose duty was to stand on the capstan and sing as the boat pulled into a levee. The leader, Sam Marshall, "who had a voice of rare sweetness and power" improvised the lines and the other five replied in a chorus of responses:

> De Captain stands on de upper deck;
>   (Ah ha-a-a- ah! Oh ho-o-o- ho!)
> You nebber see 'nudder such gentleman, I 'spec;
>   (Ah ha-a-a-ah, Oh ho-o-o-ho!)
>
> De pilot he twisses he big roun' wheel;
>   (Ah ha-a-a- ah, Oh ho-o-o-ho!)
> He sings, and his whissels, and he dance Virginia reel,
>   (Ah ha-a-a-ah, Oh ho-o-o-ho).
>
> 'Gineer in the engin' room listenn' fo' de bell;
>   (Ah ha-a-a-ah, Oh ho-o-o-ho,)

He boun' to beat dat oder boat or bus' 'em up to...heb'n,
(Ah ha-a-a-ah, Oh ho-o-o-ho).

Other songs they sang haunted Merrick for their intimations of suffering and heartbreak:

De night is dark, de day is long
And we are far from home,
Weep, my brudders, weep!

De night is past, de long day done,
An' we are going home,
Shout, my brudders, shout!

For a brief period following the Civil War the streamboats were fitted out with extraordinary elegance. The ladies' cabins featured carpets and mirrors, the dining rooms served food that rivaled that served in eastern hotels and passengers promenaded the decks in their best

Interior corridor of the steamboat *J. G. Parke*, circa 1900. Courtesy of Floyd Risvold.

clothes. The captains put aside their pilots' caps for silk top hats and wore diamond studded, ruffled shirts and kid gloves.

The ostentation of the boats and the river captains did not go unnoticed. A story soon made the rounds that at a rural landing a lanky man astride a mule hailed the crew of one of the elegant steamboats and asked to speak to the captain. Crewmembers tried to put the man off but he would not be dissuaded. Finally, with some annoyance, the captain came out on deck and asked what the man wanted with him.

"Good afternoon, Captain, the man replied. " I just wanted to know if my mule can take a drink out of your water."

Passengers who rode on the decks of the steamboats did not enjoy the comforts of the cabin passengers. Crewmen treated deck passengers much like freight and expected them to find their own accommodations on or around the piles of boxes, barrels and stacks of cord wood piled in the cargo area. Lower decks were partially open to the weather and deck passengers suffered from exposure to rain, wind and cold. Captains provided only one stove for a boatload of desk passengers to cook their food and gave little or no attention to cleanliness. Boat owners expected the deck passengers to bring their own food and when the boats were delayed the travelers' supplies were soon exhausted. Immigrants from Europe, already worn out from their long journey, often fell ill on the boats.

The best that deck passengers could hope for was a spot on a dirty, splintered deck, the boat's cargo of bales and cartons their only furniture. Because they were in the working area of the boat, deck passengers often got in the way of deck hands and aroused their ire. "Deck passengers were stowed like hogs on the lower deck of the steamer where they were made to feel all the degradation of poverty in the brutal and disgraceful treatment they received from the petty officers belonging to the boat," a German deck passenger advised. "Whoever is not obliged to save a few dollars should avoid this Trojan belly into which the poor are packed like herring, giving up all comfort."

Charles Babcock saw his first Mississippi River steamboat in 1854 (as part of the Grand Excursion) and called it a "queer looking affair to a green Yankee. The hull is little less than a sharp pointed scow while the upper works, two or three stories high, look in some respects like an Indian pagoda. Their hulls, if hulls they can be called, are shallow and much resemble an elongated tea saucer. The bottoms are flat and draw but little water—no more than a common scow. The furnace, boiler and engines are all within this shallow enclosure." Babcock added that "the saloons are very splendid but I cannot say as much for the staterooms, which are too contracted. They have each two berths, one above the other. In these state rooms there is no room for a writing table or even a wash stand and hardly room for dressing."

The fashionable tours were mainly an early summer business before the water level dropped. In 1837 the number of fashionable tourists exceeded the number of immigrants on the boats. In early June 1856 Nathan Parker came to St. Paul on the *Northern Belle*. It was a boat filled to capacity, Parker wrote in his *Minnesota Handbook for 1856-7* (1857). "Staterooms were entirely out of the question, and bunks upon the floor or seats at the table were at a premium."

An advertisement in Dubuque offered, "Pleasure Excursion. From Dubuque to St. Peters and the Falls of St. Anthony. Passenger Steamer *WAR EAGLE* D.S. Harris, Master. Will leave for the above and intermediate Ports on Friday the 27th inst, At 10 o'clock A.M. The *War Eagle* is a new and Splendid Boat and will be two weeks making the trip. Capt. Harris intends to make a pleasure excursion in reality and will stop at all places of curiosity or amusement as long as the passengers may desire. A Band of Music will be on Board. Strangers and Travelers will have a fine opportunity of visiting one of the most beautiful and romantic countries in the world. For Freight or Passage, apply on Board."

Travelers on the fashionable tours wrote critical comments about the towns they visited. Of Dubuque, one writer commented in 1848, "Dubuque, we must say, looks slightly slack about the feet and ankles. There is about many of the houses a margin of clutter where all should be clean." The writer noted approvingly that, "We saw no hogs about town." The same writer called Davenport, Iowa, and Rock Island, Illinois, "two bright eyes looking out from the wilderness," and had a dire forecast. "Moline, just below, is a prosperous town. But the three towns lie too thick in a bed. Two of the three will wake up some morning strangled by the strongest."

Riverboat captains often acted heroically. In 1854 fourteen-year-old Alidon Amidon fell from the steamer *Nominee* into the river. Throwing off his coat, Captain William H. Laughton dove into the river after the boy. He swam almost a mile with the boy in tow before his crew pulled him to safety onto the boat. The passengers took up a collection of gold and silver to reward the captain but he refused it. They then gave the money to the grateful parents with instructions to use it to buy the captain a gift.

On Christmas Day of the next year a silver pitcher arrived at Captain Laughton's Galena home. The pitcher was from Tiffany's in New York. On one side was engraved the story of the saving of Alidon Amidon and a picture of the *Nominee*. On the other was a sketch of Laughton bringing the boy out of the water. The Amidon family immigrated to Minnesota where Alidon was later killed in the Dakota War of 1862. During his career, Captain Laughton saved eleven people from drowning in the Mississippi River.

One stop on the fashionable, upriver country tour was the village of Frontenac. General Israel Garrard and his brother Lewis established the town in the early 1850's for the sole purpose of catering to aristocratic visitors. All the best boats, the *War Eagle, Rock Island, City of Milwaukee, Minnesota*—as many as six a day—stopped at Frontenac. The Garrards were determined to keep all signs of commerce out of their fiefdom and permitted only one store near the large riverfront hotel. All other businesses were forced to locate several miles inland. Rates at the Frontenac Hotel in the 1870's were $3 a day or $2 a day for the season, which ran from June 15 through October 1. Children and servants stayed for half price.

THE PANORAMAS

The popularity of a distinctive form of nineteenth century entertainment called "panoramas" spurred further interest in the Upper Mississippi. A panorama was a painted canvas, over twelve feet high and thousands of feet long, that an operator rolled from one spool to another while a lecturer, often the painter himself, narrated the scenes unfolding before the spectators. Panoramas offered a mix of history, travel and news. While they were shown in ordinary theaters, both St. Paul and Minneapolis had for a time special round panorama buildings. Artists painted at least four panoramas of the Mississippi River, three of the Upper Mississippi. Two others which survive deal with the Sioux Uprising.

John Banvard claimed that his panorama of the Mississippi below St. Louis was three miles long. Through a backstage contraption, he produced what appeared to be real smoke and steam spewing out of the pipes of the painted steamers as the canvas unrolled. Charles Dickens and Henry Longfellow saw Banvard's canvas and so popular was the spectacle that Queen Victoria ordered Banvard to give a command performance in Windsor Castle. His run in London lasted twenty months and the attendance was over 600,000. So many people thronged to see Banvard's painting in Boston and New York that promoters scheduled special excursion trains to bring people to the theater.

Henry Lewis's panorama, now lost, is known through sketches and his journal. Lewis was a self-taught artist of considerable skill who was born in England in 1819 and eventually settled in St. Louis. Lewis made trips to the Upper Mississippi in 1846, 1847 and 1848. The last trip was on the *Senator,* captained by Daniel Smith Harris. When the *Senator* docked at Galena, Henry Sibley boarded to return to his American Fur Company trading post at Mendota and Lewis and Sibley became friends. Lewis wrote of the landscape in his journal, "As I looked I felt how hopeless art was to convey the soul of such a scene as this and as the poet wishes for the pencil of the artist so did I for the power of description to tell of the thousand thoughts fast crowding each other from my mind." Clearly, Lewis was impressed with the scenery.

At Dubuque the boat stopped to take on a farmer with his wagon and eight head of oxen. As Lewis wrote of the incident, "He [the farmer] stepped quietly aboard and asked the captain what he would

Artist John Banvard points out details in his Mississippi River panorama to Queen Victoria and her family at Windsor Castle, circa 1850. Courtesy of the Minnesota Historical Society.

charge to take him to the falls of the St. Croix as if it were an everyday matter. In a few minutes we had his oxen aboard, his wagon unloaded and taken to pieces and stowed away and the bell rang for a start. We had got to about the middle of the river when one of the oxen, objecting en toto to this mode of traveling, broke his rope and jumped overboard, making for the shore. This happened to be bluff so that he could not get out and after a good deal of maneuvering we managed to catch him again and got him aboard."

Lewis spent several days at Fort Snelling where he met and became friends with a fellow artist, Seth Eastman. While at the fort Lewis bought two Indian canoes and fastened them together leaving a four-foot space between. He boarded over the space and the middle sections of the canoes, creating a platform eight feet wide by ten feet long. Over this he built a roof and hung temporary walls of canvas to protect against wind and rain. Inside the shelter he constructed various compartments to hold books, sketch pads, provisions and a tent. When it was completed, Lewis and two companions set off down the Mississippi, making sketches and camping at night. The simple craft, christened "Minnehaha," worked remarkably well. To go ashore they threw off a rock tied to a rope. Lewis wrote of the boat, "She floated downstream quietly and safely, never rocking, so that there was no difficulty in making sketches on board."

Lewis did have problems with the mosquitoes. He wrote, "We hailed with pleasure at a beautiful looking spot about half past seven where we concluded we would encamp. But, oh, how appearances in nature do sometimes deceive. . . . We had hardly landed when we were attacked by hundreds. The fire, after it was made, attracted thousands and we ate our supper attended by the attentions of millions, until fairly driven into our tent and under our bar where we thought we should have some little peace. But bars were no bar to them and we had scarcely got under it when whiz, whiz, hum, hum, you would have thought yourself in a hive of bees. . . It was dreadful after the fatigue and heat of the day thus to be annoyed . . . We got no sleep that night and were fairly driven away without our breakfast for it was impossible to eat it even if we cooked it." Despite the problems of the insects the trip was a success and Lewis considered those days on the river "as among the happiest of our entire lives."

The first thirty paintings of Lewis's 1,325 yard-long Mississippi River panorama —some of which were made from sketches supplied by

Eastman—are supposed to have shown the area from Dubuque north to Fort Snelling. Lewis's painting of the Falls of St. Anthony shows a broad stretch of falls and rapids with large chunks of stone that had broken off and fallen into the water. Two islands are pictured in the middle of the falls.

Both Banvard and Lewis spent years painting their panoramas. Lewis moved to Dusseldorf where he published a book of sketches and diary entries of his canoe trip down the Mississippi. There he served as a U.S. Consular Agent.

Toward the end of his life in 1901, Lewis sold several of his painting depicting St. Paul, Fort Snelling, Fort Crawford at Prairie du Chien, Fort Armstrong at Rock Island and the Falls of St. Anthony to T. B. Walker, the Minneapolis lumberman. Walker's heirs presented some of the paintings to the Minneapolis Public Library and the Minnesota Historical Society. The Minneapolis Institute of Arts owns another of Lewis's paintings. The artist died in 1904.

Through their panoramas, Lewis and Banvard popularized the Mississippi, turning it into a wonder of the world. Tens of thousands of people watched transfixed as scenes of the great river unrolled before them."Mississippi" became among the first words school children learned to spell and they gleefully recited it to each other, rushing through the repetitions of the "s'es" and "p's". Others sang the ditty:

> *M-I-S-S-I-S-S*
> *-I-P-P-I-*
> *It used to be so hard to spell,*
> *It used to make me cry.*

The panoramas of Lewis and Banvard elevated a river that had been known only to fur traders, pioneers and fashionable tourists into a geographic feature of mythic proportions. And when these early moving pictures lost their appeal John Greenleaf Whittier would write in "The Panorama" (1856):

> *My task is done.*
> *The Showman and his show,*
> *Themselves but shadows,*
> *Into shadows go.*

THE RIVERBOAT GAMBLERS

Professional gamblers rode the Upper River boats but they did not strive for the high stakes that were common on boats further south. Passengers on their way to St. Paul were not wealthy plantation owners and the gamblers were not excessively greedy, seemingly satisfied to take in two or three hundred dollars a week. The men all knew each other, recognized each other's turf and were careful not to intrude on each other's territory. Groups of two or three gamblers often worked the boats together. All were consummate actors. They never came on board together, never gave a flicker of recognition when they saw each other, had elegant manners and were often introduced to each other by their intended victims. They only pretended to be heavy drinkers. Most of the time they drank water or tea colored to resemble whiskey. When they started playing they cheerfully lost large sums of money to each other, drawing their victims ever closer into the web of deceit.

Riverboat gamblers were able to control the game and win because they worked with marked cards that were stored with the bartender in the boat's bar. The marking consisted of a process called "stripping." Gamblers shaved a tiny fraction of the edge of the face cards off the middle, an alteration undetectable to a player not alert to the practice. When they had shaved the cards, they re-wrapped them, sealed the packages and returned them to the bar.

With the connivance of the boat's bartender, gambler Bill Mullen would take a gross of cards to his stateroom and spend hours trimming, re-wrapping and sealing the decks of cards. No matter how many times a worried player might call to the bartender for a new deck of cards, the only cards he would be given would be another deck of marked ones. When the victims had been relieved of their money, one of the gamblers would get off the boat at Winona, another at Prescott or Hastings while the third would continue on to St. Paul. The three would then reunite on a trip down river and resume the search for more victims.

THE ECONOMICS OF THE STEAMBOATS

Between 1849 and 1862 steamboats made fortunes for many of their owners. For almost a decade there were not enough boats to carry all the people who wanted to come to the farmers' and lumbermen's paradise of Iowa, Illinois, Minnesota and Wisconsin. By 1857 there were 125 steamboats registered in St. Paul alone. A typical sternwheel boat measuring 200 feet long by 30 feet wide with three large iron boilers cost from $25,000 to $30,000 depending on how elaborately it was finished. A boat of this size could accommodate 200 passengers in cabins and at least 100 more in second class, which meant riding on the deck. The boat itself weighed 200 tons and carried from 300 to 350 tons of cargo.

Passenger fares ranged from $12 to $16 for cabin passage from Galena to St. Paul. Deck passengers paid half of that. Since demand for passage was high captains often charged whatever they could get. More than one man paid full cabin fare only to learn, once he was on the boat, that he was expected to give up his room to the ladies and sleep on the deck. The freight rate from Galena to St. Paul was $1.50 per hundred pounds and proportionately less for shorter distances.

Since there was less demand for passage downstream, the fares were less. Cabin passengers could make the trip for $8. It also cost the captain less to run his boat downstream on a current flowing at a steady four

This bill of lading notes the cost of passage on the *Sucker State* for Dan McLean from Stillwater to Dubuque on July 25, 1869, and the costs to transport his possessions. The *Sucker State* was built in Pittsburgh in 1860. It burned and was abandoned in the Alton Slough in 1872. Courtesy of Floyd Risvold.

miles per hour. The cargo on the return downriver trip consisted of wheat, potatoes, corn, horses, mules and the furs and buffalo robes from the northern plains delivered via the Red River trails. Moving upriver were cargoes of apples at $1.50 a barrel and barrels of whiskey which sold for $1.10 to $1.75 a gallon. A favorite activity among the crew on the boats was to loosen the metal hoops on a barrel of whiskey, bore a small hole, siphon some of the liquid off, plug the hole and drive the metal hoop back down over the plug. More than one barrel of whiskey arrived at St. Paul mysteriously empty.

If a captain made four trips a month to St. Paul he could count on a net profit of over $11,000. Typical net earning for a season would be $56,300 with many captains earning far more. During the boom period of the 1850's the profits from one round trip were often enough to pay for the boat. While some captains paid for their boats in a few months, there were risks. Some unlucky captains wrecked their boats on their maiden trips and few boats were insured. For those steamboats that did survive fire, sandbars, snags and collisions, the life expectancy was still only five years.

THE PACKET BOATS

The first steamboats left port whenever they had a load to take up or downriver. As passenger traffic assumed more importance the boats began to schedule regular runs. Boats that ran on a schedule were called "packet boats." In 1847 one boat began advertising regular service between Galena, St. Peter's, Fort Snelling and Stillwater. By 1849 the boat was making weekly runs between Galena and St. Paul for a cabin fare of $6 upstream and $5 downstream. Fares dropped when more boats began scheduling regular runs. By the early 1860's five steamboat companies operated packet boats and competition reduced passenger fares between Winona and St. Paul to $1 and freight on wheat to St. Louis to ten cents a bushel.

It quickly became apparent that boat captains would profit by joining together to form packet boat companies. Galena resident Captain Daniel Smith Harris of the *Grey Eagle* organized the Galena, Dunleith and Minnesota Packet Company that soon had agents in towns up and down the river. Captain James Worden, of the *Key City*, was from the rival community of Dubuque. Worden and Harris not only competed with their steamboats, their two communities were fierce competitors.

Worden was unhappy that Dubuque had been left out of the name of Harris's packet boat company. To retaliate Worden founded a rival company of his own, calling it the Dubuque, Sinconsi and Minnesota Packet Line. After a year or two the two companies merged into the Galena, Dubuque, Dunleith and Minnesota Packet Company. Now names of both towns were in the title and everyone was happy.

It was inevitable that the boat owners would develop a monopoly. The Galena, Dubuque, Dunleith and Minnesota Packet Company controlled all the shipping between Galena and Dubuque wholesale houses and, soon, all the freight business from Dunleith and the Prairie du Chien railroads. Agents of the packet boat company rode the railroad cars and sold boat tickets to the unsuspecting passengers who planned to continue their journeys by boat on the Mississippi. What the passengers did not know when they bought their tickets from the friendly agents on the train was that the tickets were good only on the Galena, Dubuque, Dunleith and Minnesota Packet Boat Company boats.

The leading riverboat captains had extraordinary power and influence. In the early 1850's Captain Daniel Smith Harris became angry at an enterprise in La Crosse and refused to let his boats stop at the town. This might have meant an economic disaster so the two Davidson brothers, Peyton and William F., who owned a sawmill in La Crosse, added a foundry and began building steamboats of their own. The Davidson brothers were good boat builders and by the middle 1850's had made La Crosse the largest boatworks north of St. Louis. Due to its location, halfway between Dubuque and St. Paul, La Crosse, in 1857, had 1569 boat landings in a single season while St. Paul had 711. More steamboat captains lived in La Crosse than in any city north of St. Louis.

THE LAMPLIGHTERS

With steamboats running both day and night on the river, the Department of Commerce and Labor hired lamplighters to mark the navigation channel in St. Paul and other major ports with kerosene lanterns. The instructions for the keepers of the lights were precise and strict. "The lights must be lighted by sunset and kept burning until sunrise, then extinguished. Clean, trim and fill the lantern daily. Use a feather or soft pine stick to clean the burner. Polish the glass. Ignorance will not be considered an excuse for inefficiency. The steamboat *Lily* is the lighttender of this district. When the tender's signal is heard, keepers will be in readiness to receive oil and supplies, return empty cans and give an account of the oil and supplies that may be on hand. Keepers must report to the inspector at once whenever they fail to light their lights from any cause whatever stating their reasons for not lighting."

The job paid $10 a month per light. There was a waiting list for the positions and the jobs were passed down in the same family for generations. A few lamplighters were women and they were among the best, not allowing a speck or smear to dim the quality of their lights. Jane Muckle Robinson, of South St. Paul, kept the river channel between Dayton's Bluff and the stockyards lighted for thirty-six consecutive years. Beginning in 1885, Robinson rowed her boat into the river every night and morning, through rain and snow, without fail, during the navigation season, to tend four lights. The daughter of Irish immigrants, Robinson, a sturdy, broad-shouldered woman, rowed over 50,000 miles in her heavy rowboat. She married and had children, one of whom took over the lamp lighting task when Jane retired. Charlie Maguire, former National Park Service singing ranger, wrote a ballad, "Light the River," about Jane Robinson:

> *Rowing on the water*
> *Pulling on the oar*
> *Jane Robinson "post light keeper"*
> *Along the Mississippi River shore.*
> *Rowing on the water*
> *To shine a light*
> *On "Big Muddy" for all who study*
> *His tarnished silver highway through the night.*
>
> *(Refrain)*
> *"Light the River*
> *Show your light until the break of day*
> *Now Jane, light the river*
> *Then we'll be on our way."*
>
> *Rowing on the water*
> *Spring-flood to fall*
> *Four lights showing whether clear or blowing*
> *From Dayton's Bluff to South Saint Paul*
> *Rowing on the water*

River woman, Jane
Bend your back in service to the brightest, purest
Government specified clear, white, flame.

Rowing on the water. Pulling on the oar—
Old Man River is sneaking off
To join the shadows on the shore.
Rowing on the water. Light the river, Jane
Before the fireflies shine in the evening time—
Before the sun goes down and leaves us blind
Before the stars come out into the sky
This is what the pilots say,
"Before a snag-log catches our poor boats,
Before a sandbar lifts us too high to float,
Before the river grabs us by the throat.
Light the river, Jane."

The steamboats brought not only commerce to the river towns, they brought culture as well. Itinerant musicians, actors and artists traveled the river to bring their artistry to the towns. Even small towns had an opera house where traveling artists performed. Showboats tied up to the levees and played to enthusiastic audiences.

Steamboats brought tourists, immigrants, circuses and theaters to river towns. *French's New Sensation* was one of five showboats, operated by a husband and wife team. They were both thespians and river pilots, and began bringing drama to the River in 1878. This photograph is circa 1895. Courtesy of Floyd Risvold.

The complexity of the steamboats, their adaptation to the peculiar requirements of river trade and their cultural and economic influence made them a major achievement of America's early industrial age. The river was the cable that tied the farmers, the businessmen and traders into the life of the nation. No one believed that connection could ever be broken. By 1848 the steamboats were so deeply embedded in the economic and social life of the Upper Mississippi that they were able to mount an effective (but ultimately losing) challenge to the new transportation technology looming distantly on the eastern horizon—the iron horses of the railroads.

NOTES

Mark Twain's love song to the Mississippi is found in the fourth chapter of *Life on the Mississippi*, just after he recalls wanting to be a circus clown or pirate when he grows up, before returning to his greatest ambition: to be a steamboatman. Frederick L. Johnson recounted the Red Wing steamboat tragedy in *The Sea Wing Disaster* (1990). Anthony Phillip Londroche's poem, "The Home of the Big Green Tree" was published in his *I AM Mississippi* (1954). Sources on steamboats and their culture are Mildred Hartsough, *From Canoe to Steel Barge on the Upper Mississippi* (1934); Charles E. Brown, *Old Man River. Upper Mississippi Steamboating Days; Stories, Tales of Old Time Steamboats and Steamboatmen* (1940); Frank Fugina, *Lore and Lure of the Upper Mississippi River* (1945); and Frederick Wonden, *Racing for the Broom* (1986). John Hay's poem has often been included in anthologies such as John T. Flanagan, editor, *America is West* (1945). See B. A. Botkin, *A Treasury of Mississippi River Folklore* (1955) for the "Wandering Steamboatman" poem and other stories.

George Catlin's comments appear in his *Letters and Notes on the Manners, Customs and Condition of the North American Indians* (1857). Catlin's paintings have often been exhibited in Europe and America. 445 of them belong to the Smithsonian Institution and many were included in a Washington D.C. exhibition in 2002-2003.

Charles Lanman's account is *A Summer in the Wilderness* (1847). The story of a trip on the *Red Wing* in 1847 is from a letter in the collection of the Dubuque County Historical Society. The songs remembered by George Byron Merrick are in his *Old Times on the Upper Mississippi* (2001, reprint). Charles Babcock's story is in "Rails West. The Rock Island Excursion of 1854 as Reported by Charles F. Babcock," *Minnesota History* 3: 4 (Winter 1954). Willoughby Babcock reported travelers' comments in "Steamboat Travel on the Upper Mississippi in 1849," *Minnesota History* 7: 1 (March 1926). See also William J. Petersen, *Steamboating on the Upper Mississippi* (1968). Theodore Blegen analyzed both the tour and such additional attractions as panoramas in "The 'Fashionable Tour' on the Upper Mississippi," *Minnesota History* 20 (December 1939). On Henry Lewis, see Bertha Heilbron, editor, *Making a Motion Picture in 1848. Henry Lewis' Journal of a*

Canoe Voyage from the Falls of St. Anthony to St. Louis (1936). In 1967 the Minnesota Historical Society published Lewis's book, *The Valley of the Mississippi*, also edited by Bertha L. Heilbron.

Charlie Maguire, former singing Park Ranger for the Mississippi National River and Recreation Area of the National Park Service, has composed over 800 songs. He has become well known through his ten years of appearances on Garrison Keillor's "Prairie Home Companion" radio program. The ballad is used with his permission.

CHAPTER 13

Rafting the White Pine

Furs were the first commercial cargo carried on the Upper Mississippi River. By 1837 the fur trade had declined and was replaced by lead from the mines of Dubuque and Galena. When lead ceased to be the principal cargo on the river, the transportation of both wheat and people filled the boats and barges until the new age, the age of lumber, burst upon the northern territory.

White pine forests flourished wherever 25 to 35 inches of rainfall fell per year. The forest stretching across the northern Midwest from Michigan to Minnesota was the greatest stand of pine in the world. A forest the size of New England was located at the heads of big Midwest rivers that seemed to have been foreordained by providence to float logs. The trees stopped abruptly within forty miles of prairie country.

At one time white pine covered 38,000,000 acres, almost 70% of the total land area of Minnesota. One acre of white pine in Carlton County yielded 94,000 board feet of lumber. (Yields of 25,000 square feet were more common due to waste.) White pine was light in weight, strong, easy to cut. Buildings made of white pine, if the wood were protected from moisture, lasted hundreds of years. The demand for white pine to build the cities of the Midwest and the barns and homes of newly arrived farmers was insatiable.

At the peak of the cutting of the white pine 140,000 lumberjacks toiled in the winter forests of the Upper Midwest. It was dangerous, cold work. Workdays began in the dark and ended in the dark. Men stacked logs in great piles on the banks of frozen rivers or on the ice. When spring came, they shoved the logs into the water to float down to places like Boeuf Slough where they were sorted by owner and formed into rafts for delivery to a mill. Few of the logs went any further south than St. Louis. Pine logs ranged from 36 to 48 inches in diameter. Some logs were hollow and occasionally workers found large catfish in them when they were sawed into lumber. The fish had worked their way into the hollow spaces but, because of their fins, could not back themselves out.

The men who organized the cutting of the pine forests were, for the most part, from Maine and other New England states. Their parents were farmers and most of the men were born between 1810 and 1850. Their education was limited to elementary school. Many had worked on stores and farms in their youth, had been full time wage-earners from the time they were sixteen. Most started in the lumber business while still in their twenties. They were hard-working, frugal, capable, with simple personal traits. It was said of lumberman P. M. Musser, "He cannot bear to see anything go to waste. If he sees a board broken without good cause, or a shingle or lath thrown into the wood pile, which should have been utilized, there is where he gets worked up."

The lumbermen formed partnerships, many of them representing family groups. There were the Laird and Nortons of Winona, the Rusts of Eau Claire, the Mussers of Muscatine and the Wintons of Minneapolis. It was Frederick Weyerhaeuser, a man of integrity and strong leadership skills, who eventually achieved a loose hegemony over a large group of associates.

The young Weyerhaeuser moved to Rock Island in 1856 where he earned one dollar a day working on a construction gang for the railroad. Within a few months he had found a job as a clerk for a small sawmill called the Mead, Smith and Marsh Mill where he recorded lumber as it was cut and sold. One day some buyers came to the mill and, since no one else was around, Weyerhaeuser waited on them and made the sale. The mill owners were impressed with the young man's initiative and soon put him in charge of the struggling mill.

The panic of 1857 forced the mill into bankruptcy. Out of a job, Weyerhaeuser began dealing in lumber on his own. Since there was almost no currency in circulation his first transactions were barters. He exchanged cut lumber from the mill for hogs, horses, oxen and eggs. These he traded for logs from the rafters on the banks of the river. He took the logs to the mill, sawed them into lumber and started the process all over again. As he explained it, "This country produce I retraded to the rafters for logs or to the merchants for stoves, tin ware and logging kits, often carrying through the whole transaction by pure barter and to my great astonishment I made $3,000 in the first nine months and in the second year, $5,000."

By 1860 Weyerhaeuser was eager to acquire his own sawmill. He approached his brother-in-law, Frederick Carl August Denkmann, and suggested a business partnership. At first Denkmann was not interested. Denkmann was a machinist who had been bitten by gold fever and planned to go off to the gold fields in Colorado. At the time Weyerhaeuser approached him, Denkmann was busily constructing a wagon in which to make the trip west.

Weyerhaeuser pointed out that he had made $8,000 in two years in the lumber business. He urged Denkmann to join him in buying the distressed Mead, Smith and Marsh Mill where, just three years before, Weyerhaeuser had been hired as a clerk. Denkmann eventually agreed and the two men went into business together, buying the mill and turning it into the cornerstone of their lumber empire. The year was 1860. Weyerhaeuser was 26 and Denkmann was 39 years old.

Weyerhaeuser had made a wise choice in Denkmann. While Weyerhaeuser was the strategist and dealmaker, the Denkmanns were the engineers who kept the machinery running. A family member remembered that "E. P. Denkmann worked in the mill nights and Sundays, if necessary, so it would run uninterruptedly through the working days when the crew was present. When short of funds to buy bolts he shaped spikes to do the work. If in the morning the 5 A.M. whistle was weak, he'd be out at once to look into the trouble and it was a waste of time to send to him to say that breakfast was ready—and waiting—and getting cold. He worked at repair until the defect was cured if at all possible."

The lumbermen migrated as the trees were cut. Most moved three or more times, from Michigan to Wisconsin and Minnesota, then on to the Pacific Northwest. The Upper Mississippi men disparaged the Chicago lumbermen for putting on airs, wearing silk hats and patent leather shoes. Lumbermen of the Upper Mississippi wore mackinaw jackets and were up at dawn shaking hands with their workers. They were shrewd traders who also exhibited a great deal of common sense. Their politics were Republican and most were content to "say nothing and saw wood." They were willing to start small and work hard funding their businesses with only a small amount of capital. Of humble origins, the skills the men had developed in farming and working in small mills were sufficient for them to enter and then dominate the lumber industry.

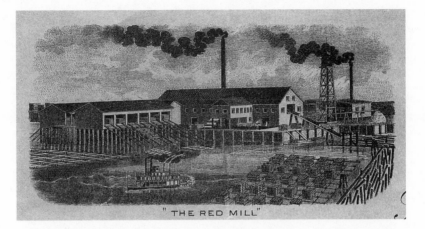

" THE RED MILL"

Letterhead of the Hershey Lumber Company, Stillwater, Minnesota, 1903. The firm's specialty, white pine lumber, is shown stacked and ready to be transported downriver on the St. Croix to the Mississippi, by the waiting steamboat. Engraved by Brown, Treacy & Co., St. Paul. Courtesy of Pogo Press, Incorporated.

The key to the success of the lumber industry was transportation—moving the timber from the forests to the mills, where it was sawed into lumber, and then shipped on to customers. The only way lumber could be moved was by water. For lumbering to be successful, someone would have to figure out how to move large quantities of logs down the river to the mills and markets

The first rafts of white pine to come down the Mississippi River were of cut lumber because the lumbermen were not sure how to corral whole logs to make the trip. The problem was solved in 1843 when the water rose on the St. Croix River overflowing a log boom that had been holding back 400,000 feet of logs—the entire winter's work of cutting. When the river breached the boom the logs went tumbling down the St. Croix and on into the Mississippi. The owners of the logs watched in dismay, certain that there was no way that they could get them back. The logs, along with the winter's work, would have been lost if a determined man named Stephen B. Hanks, a cousin of Abraham Lincoln, had not seen an opportunity.

Hanks was a farmer who had driven a herd of cows from Illinois to a Wisconsin lumber camp to feed the lumbermen. After selling his cows, he had worked at the camp during the winter and had planned to go back to his farm when the logs broke loose. Using some of the money he had made from selling his cows, Hanks bought the runaway logs from the owners at a low price and, accompanied by some friends, raced down the river after the floating logs. Hanks and his friends managed to find the logs, corral them into a backwater and tie them together into a 600-foot raft. Thirty days later Hanks safely piloted the raft to a mill in St. Louis, turning such a tidy profit that he gave up farming and went into business floating log rafts down the Mississippi. Hanks's experience did not go unnoticed. Sawmills were soon springing up all along the river to capture the logs rafted down from the Minnesota and Wisconsin pineries.

Opportunities were everywhere. Sawmills were simple and cheap to build. John Knapp inherited $1,000 when he was twenty-one and, forming a partnership, bought a half interest in a small sawmill. Thirty years later, in 1878, Knapp, Stout and Company of Menomonie, Wisconsin, was the largest lumbering establishment in the nation.

Sidney S. Grannis came to the Upper Mississippi in 1856 from Vermont looking for a place to set up a sawmill. His first visit was to the Falls of St. Anthony. "The village was on the same side of the river, with a bridge of sawmills, on the very brow of the falls where the logs ran in on the upper side and the lumber ran out onto a platform below and was carted off on sluices some ways below to be rafted. Minneapolis was a myth," he reported in a letter.

Not finding what he wanted at St. Anthony, Grannis went on to other lumbering towns—Stillwater, Taylor's Falls, Prescott, Hastings. Still not satisfied, he visited Red Wing where, at the end of Bluff Street and extending from La Grange to Levee Street, he noted a rock ledge about twenty-five feet above high water. By cutting it down fifteen feet and throwing the rock into the river he believed that he could build a solid foundation next to the water that would be a prime site for a sawmill.

Grannis enumerated to his partners the advantages of the location. "One, all logs from the vast pineries above, going to a down river market, must pass this point; two, [there is] deep water for booming logs; three, near proximity to the steamboat landing at the foot of Potter street where everybody came; four, the splendid farming country, for an indefinite distance back, that must, at no distant day, be supplied from the river with lumber." Satisfied with his analysis, Grannis bought the site for $750.

Locating the machinery to equip a sawmill at the frontier community of Red Wing presented Grannis with a major problem. St. Paul had none of the equipment that he needed. Grannis ordered his smokestacks from a company in Dubuque, his circular saws from Chicago and the boilers and heavy castings from Binghamton, New York. By April 20, 1857, Grannis was back on the Mississippi going upriver with his workers and the machinery and equipment for his new sawmill.

"When we arrived at Read's Landing, at the foot of Lake Pepin," he wrote, "we found some 24 steamers, all waiting for the ice to break up and let them through. The weather was cold and very rainy. Board was $1.25 per day. Our boat determined to return and we had to change to another and some of our crew determined to go around the lake on foot—thirty miles. Teams were running to take passengers. Women and luggage might ride but the men had to walk and carry a rail to pry the coach (lumber wagon) out of the mire."

The mishaps continued. The mud was ankle deep. The steamboat *Hamburg* on which some of his workers had elected to wait out the thaw moved upriver too soon and was crushed in the ice at a point later called Hamburg Point. No one was killed and his workers eventually made their way to Red Wing. Later in the season Grannis made the trip back to Read's Landing and found someone to haul his ten trunks of supplies.

A national financial collapse caused additional problems. Grannis's note with his Binghamton supplier came due and he had to borrow money at 5% a month to meet his obligation. Financial panics devastated many. In Red Wing owners of city lots on which taxes of as little as $2.50 were due were forced to forfeit them. John Anderson was forced to exchange his 160-acre farm for three horses in a tax forfeiture proceeding. Despite all of the difficulties, Grannis sawed his first log on July 20, 1857.

After Hanks demonstrated that logs could be assembled into rafts for the journey down the river, the logging companies followed his example. They assembled great rafts of logs and equipped them with long bladed oars to guide the rafts around bends in the river. The oars, or sweeps, were forty-five-foot long tamarack poles fitted with huge pine blades, fourteen inches wide and three inches thick. The oars balanced on pivots. With a strong man on each of the twelve oars, directed by a pilot who gave his signals with a whistle, the rafts could navigate the twists and turns of the river. One blast on the whistle meant pull to the right; two blasts meant pull to the left. Most rafts were sixteen feet wide and four hundred feet long. To construct the rafts, workers placed the logs in rows, side by side, butt to butt, and held them together with sixteen foot long poles laid across the tops of the logs and fastened with hickory lockdowns and wood plugs.

The pilots of the rafts were highly skilled and colorful. They wore French calfskin boots, black cashmere trousers, finely knitted red flannel shirts, large black silk neckties tied in a square knot and wide-brimmed black or white hats. Every worker on the river wanted to ship with a skilled pilot such as Hanks who could bring his raft down the river safely. Pilots earned high wages for that time and lumbermen hired them for their knowledge of the river and their ability to manage a motley crew of men.

The crew of twelve oarsmen, a cook, a helper and the pilot lived on the raft in little shanties, kept low because of the wind, and cooked their meals in a pail on a pile of sand in the middle of the raft. When it was windy they erected a rough screen to protect the cook and his efforts. Crew members, who earned $35 for the trip down the river and fare for the trip back, ate their meals from a rough board table nearby. At night they tied the raft up to a bank.

Food on the rafts was monotonous and the crews often scavenged for additional supplies. One crew had taken a fat two-year-old heifer from a farmer's field one morning, dressed it and laid it under a piece of canvas in the center of the raft when the irate farmer spotted the raft in the river, rowed out to it and came aboard. The crew members crouched at the corners of the raft and the pilot sat with his elbows on his knees, his head down, his eyes downcast. The pilot greeted the upset farmer by telling him he was glad to see him.

"Why?" asked the puzzled farmer, caught off-guard. The pilot pointed to the canvas in the center of his raft. "See that white t'ing down there? Smallpox. It's one of my best men, the cook. Will you help me take him ashore and bury him?" The farmer backed off, nearly falling in the river in his haste to get away.

To go over rapids the rafts had to be split in two—called "double-tripping." Half the raft went through first and then the pilot and crew doubled back for the other half. When both sections were past the rapids they tied the two sections of the raft back together again. Some of the rafts were stolen. Thieves floated rafts up sloughs, sank them with sandbags and re-floated them when their owners stopped looking for them. They stole many of the highest quality white pine logs in this way, cut them into cordwood and sold them for $2.50 a cord to be used as firewood. If a log raft were moored overnight without a watchman guarding it, it was likely to be missing in the morning. Wildcat sawmills bought stolen logs. One such mill near North McGregor ran short of logs during a period of low water. Employees took advantage of moonless nights to row out to rafts stranded on sandbars and cut loose strings of logs.

The only way to get the lumber out of the woods was by the rivers and the Upper Mississippi was a difficult river on which to pilot a floating leviathan of a raft. The twists and turns were continuous. The only straight stretch, through Lake Pepin, was 22 miles long, walled in by cliffs and hills and either had too much wind or not enough. The upper rapids, beginning at LeClaire, Iowa, were fifteen miles long with a fall of twenty feet. At the bottom lay the big and sometimes bare Rock Island. Pilots had to depend on having just the right wind and enough water flowing over the rocks for their rafts to make it safely through.

Until the middle 1860's strong men manning oars guided all the rafts of both logs and cut lumber down the river. By 1857, 3,000 men were engaged in lumbering in Wisconsin on a log crop valued at $4,000,000,000. Every twig and chip and log of it floated to the mills on the great river. In 1864, loggers sent ten rafts of logs, manned by two hundred men, south from Stillwater on ten successive days.

Stephen Hanks, the farmer who piloted the first lumber raft down the Mississippi from the St. Croix River in 1843, was bringing four rafts of logs tied together down the river when he had a mishap. In high water on the Mississippi Hanks lost control of his raft. Three of the rafts broke up and the logs floated away. Hanks later found the logs scattered all over a farmer's cornfield. The rafter was responsible for the logs until they were delivered to the mill.

The damage caused by Hanks' runaway rafts of logs plus the loss of the logs themselves amounted to $10,000. To pay for it, Hanks reported that he "turned over all my money and property to make good the loss." It could have been the end of his career on the river but it was not. Hanks went on to pilot steamboats and become a famous pilot on the Upper Mississippi. Hanks charged $3.50 for each thousand feet of logs rafted. He carried a thousand laths for twenty-five cents and shingles at the same rate.

A log raft pilot called "Pappy" and his crew took a large raft of logs down the Mississippi. Pappy's wife, Betsy, came along to cook for the crew and worked from a small tent set up in the middle of the raft out of the way of the 40 foot sweeps. Just below Fountain City, Wisconsin, at a bend in the river, the log raft struck the point of an island and split in two. One half of the raft went down the back channel chute and the other half, with Betsy on it, went down the main channel. Fortunately the two halves along with the stray logs that had been knocked loose met in the river below the island. The crew snagged the half of the raft with Betsy riding on it, put the halves back together again and continued without further incident on to the mill. Thereafter, the back channel was known as "Pappy's Chute" and the other section, "Betsy's Slough."

The captains of the packet boats found sharing the river with the log rafts a problem. Slow-moving rafts going down stream often clogged the river channel. If a raft broke up, the derelict logs left floating in the river were a serious hazard to the boats. Some packet boat captains so hated the sight of a raft that they let their steamboats get out of control and ram a raft, breaking it up. The raft crews retaliated by firing on the boats from shore. A shooting took place at Read's Landing and a crewman was badly beaten at Hastings. Captain W.H. Laughton of the packet boat *Galena* mounted a small cannon on the deck of his boat with a man standing ready with a hot iron to fire it off. Angry rafters never molested his boat.

Some raft pilots were a wild bunch. Whiskey Jack of the Wisconsin River was a giant of a man, over seven feet tall and had prodigious strength. He and his crew were heavy drinkers and when word came down the river that Whiskey Jack and his men were coming through taverns laid in extra supplies of "forty-rod" and "tanglefoot." If there were any kind of a celebration going on, such as a wedding, Jack and his men joined in the festivities—often staying for days. When his men had sobered up, Jack made up the lost time by rigging a sail on his raft and taking shortcuts, bumping over islands and sandbars, often reaching his destination before his arrival was anticipated.

THE BOEUF SLOUGH WAR

In the 1860's Frederick Weyerhaeuser along with the owners of other lumber companies began buying up large stands of white pine along the Chippewa River in Wisconsin. As the logs were cut workers marked each company's symbol on the ends of the logs and floated them down to log booms near Eau Claire and Chippewa Falls. At the booms, jammed with tens of thousands of logs from many lumber companies, workers sorted out each company's logs, formed them into rafts, and launched them down the Chippewa into the Mississippi.

Effective as the Chippewa River booms were, there was a better location for a boom. This was on a strip of backwater called Boeuf Slough that ran parallel to the Chippewa and emptied into the Mississippi about twelve miles below the mouth of the Chippewa River. Boeuf Slough was a beautiful, calm waterway, protected from currents and winds, making it an ideal location for the storing and sorting of logs.

Around 1865 lumbermen in Eau Claire discovered, to their alarm, that timber speculators were buying up forested lands on the Chippewa to supply their mills downriver. The Eau Claire lumbermen clearly understood the strategic importance of the location of Boeuf Slough. To a large extent, whoever controlled the Slough, controlled the best place to sort and store logs before they went down the Mississippi River.

The Eau Claire lumbermen quietly began buying up the land around Boeuf Slough and obtained a franchise from the State of Wisconsin to develop it. This action was not lost on the outside timber interests who also understood the strategic importance of the Slough and, in 1867 they organized their own company with the all-inclusive name of "The Boeuf Slough Manufacturing, Booming, Log Driving and Transportation Company." The Boeuf Slough Company promptly built a boom at the entrance to the Slough. The Eau Claire lumbermen retaliated by filing suit and tearing down the boom. The Boeuf Slough Company then went to the Wisconsin legislature and lobbied for a charter that would give it the same rights to the Slough as the Eau Claire group had obtained.

Lobbyists for both sides engaged in questionable tactics as they battled it out in Madison. Then, through a complicated legislative maneuver, the Boeuf Slough Company gained the upper hand. Toward the end of the 1868 legislative session a Portage City Gas and Light Company bill was passed with a rider stating that every individual who owned part of a franchise had an equal right to fulfill the charter of that franchise. One of the partners in the Eau Claire lumbermen's franchise was an individual named James H. Bacon. Bacon had been convinced to turn on his partners and cooperate with the Boeuf Slough Company. Using Bacon's name and under the rights of his franchise, the Boeuf Slough company rebuilt its boom and started up its logging enterprise once again.

The outraged Eau Claire group retaliated by holding back as many of the logs as they could behind their booms just north of Eau Claire and letting only a minimum number float on down to the slough. When

Boeuf Slough Company officials protested, the Eau Claire lumbermen insisted they did not have time to do the necessary sorting of the logs. In the spring of 1869 the dispute came to a head when a logjam of 150,000,000 board feet of logs piled up behind the Union Lumber Company boom above Chippewa Falls. The Chippewa River, from the bottom to thirty feet above the surface of the water, was completely jammed with logs for a distance of fifteen miles.

Although the 1870 Wisconsin legislature had authorized the free use of Boeuf Slough by all outside logging interests, the Eau Claire group remained confident, believing it had won. The withholding of logs had driven the Boeuf Slough Company into bankruptcy. Before the Eau Claire lumbermen could celebrate their victory, Frederick Weyerhaeuser stepped into the picture. He had been a minor partner in the Boeuf Slough Company but now he had a new and better idea. The system by which each company logged and marked its own logs, only to have to sort them out at the boom, was costly, wasteful and time consuming. When several companies logged and operated sawmills in the same area there were huge jams at the booms and much confusion over which logs belonged to which company.

Weyerhaeuser called a meeting of his rivals, the owners of seventeen of the Upper Mississippi mills, including the Dimick & Gould, Keator & Wilson of Moline and the Schricker & Mueller Mill of Davenport, at the Briggs House in Chicago in 1870. At the meeting Weyerhaeuser convinced the competing sawmill owners to pool their resources, buy land and timber along the Chippewa together, use one brand, make one unified drive downriver to the mills and, at the end, take out logs proportionate to their shares in the company. This would end the lengthy sorting of logs at Eau Claire and Chippewa Falls. The owners agreed and organized the Mississippi River Boom and Logging Company.

With the capital Weyerhaeuser and his partners raised, they bought out the bankrupt Boeuf Slough Manufacturing, Booming, Log Driving and Transportation Company and incorporated it into their Mississippi River Boom and Logging Company. This gave Weyerhaeuser control of the large holding pen of Boeuf Slough. The struggle over access to timber, known as the Boeuf Slough War, went on for ten more years but Weyerhaeuser, who was president of the new company, and the secretary, Thomas Irving, eventually succeeded in getting it resolved.

Weyerhaeuser brought good management and capital to what had been a hodge-podge of local businesses and in the process turned logging into a major interstate industry. Weyerhaeuser held the position of president of the Mississippi River Boom and Logging Company for 40 years, owning more acres of standing timber than any other single American. One member of the consortium of lumber companies involved in the business said of Weyerhaeuser, "Whatever he thought best to be done they fully concurred in, and all through the life of the enterprise his genius for controlling men and making them feel that they were safe in trusting him and following him made operations on the river easy and successful."

In 1885, 1887 and 1889 the company's output was 545,000,000 feet of logs per year. During the 1880's 87 raftboats departed with rafts per week, making Alma and Boeuf Slough one of the busiest river ports in the world. During the peak year of 1890, mills in Davenport, Moline and Rock Island employed 2,000 men and sawed 213,629,000 board feet of lumber.

By the late 1880's the Mississippi River Boom and Logging Company had become the major financial power on the Upper Mississippi. In 1889 deposits of sand at the head of Boeuf Slough, along with unusually low water in the river, blocked the opening of the slough. The company asked the U.S. Army Corps of Engineers to dredge open the blocked opening and the Corps refused. In defiance of the Corps, a Logging Company foreman blew up the government dam at the head of West Newton Slough. Then, without the permission of the Corps, the logging company moved its entire sorting and rafting operation across the Mississippi from Boeuf Slough to West Newton Slough, about eight miles downstream.

This change in location meant that up to 500 million feet of logs were floated, every year, directly across the busy navigation channel of the Mississippi to West Newton Slough. Steamboat captains immediately complained about the hazards caused by loose logs in the river. Major Alexander Mackenzie of the Rock Island Corps of Engineers informed the logging company that it could not block the main channel and that floating loose logs across the Mississippi "has caused much inconvenience, damage, danger and delay to steamboat navigation." What to do? The Mississippi River Logging Company was obviously breaking the law. The government could prosecute but the $1,000 fine proscribed by law was like a mosquito bite to the huge logging company.

When the Secretary of War asked for Mackenzie's concurrence in an injunction to stop the lumber company's actions, Mackenzie waffled. His office was in Rock Island, the same town as Weyerhaeuser's headquarters. Rather than enforce the law, Mackenzie decided to let the various interests using the river fight it out among themselves. He could see that members of Congress from states bordering the Mississippi Valley believed the floating of logs to be a form of river transportation—and transportation, in their minds, was the purpose of the river.

Steamboat pilots who suffered damages from collisions with loose logs in the river could, Mackenzie rationalized, file suit. Some did and won their claims. But resentment grew at the U.S. Army Corps of Engineers' failure to act in the face of the powerful logging company's unlawful movement of logs across the river. The Logging Company continued to send its timbers across the river to West Newton Slough until 1905 when the company closed the slough because the northern forests had been exhausted. That same year Mackenzie was promoted to the position of Chief of Engineers of the Corps.

In a period of only a few years, lumbermen rafted hundreds of millions of feet of pine down the Mississippi. Logging led to the growth of Prescott, at the mouth of the St. Croix and to the boom years at Alma and at Read's Landing, across the Mississippi from the mouth of the Chippewa River. Alma, at the mouth of Boeuf Slough, had a population of 731 in 1880 and 1525 by 1885. It took 600 men to operate the slough during the summer when they assembled the logs into rafts.

THE RAFT BOATS

The first rafts floated down the river at 2.5 to 4 miles per hour, moved along by the river's current and guided by strong men wielding oars. Innovative steamboat captains thought they could do better and in 1869 the era of the raft boats began. The first boat to shove a raft downriver was the *Union*, a small sidewheeler owned by George Winans. Winans towed a raft (he called it "towing" but in reality it was pushing) of logs from Read's Landing to Winona where the raft continued under manpower to Dubuque and the Knapp, Stout and Company mill. LeClaire boat-builder Captain S.R. Van Sant, at the request of Weyerhaeuser, built the first steamboat especially designed to push a lumber raft. Weyerhaeuser, himself, rode the raft as it was pushed downstream.

The Van Sants were a boat building family and Van Sant's great-grandfather had fitted out boats for the American Revolution. The family moved to Winona in 1884 to be near the rafting business and Van Sant went to work for Weyerhaeuser. Van Sant also had a contract with the Musser Lumber Company of Muscatine, Iowa, to bring logs down the river. The contract lasted for 35 years and earned the Van Sants $1,000,000 for towing logs. Van Sant, who later became governor of Minnesota, and his company ran more logs and lumber to market down the Mississippi than any other single company. The volume of logs was overwhelming. As much as 1.6 percent of all the white pine west of the Appalachians may have been in the Chippewa River valley alone. From 1867 to 1905 as many as 600,000,000 logs (11,365,875,930 feet) passed through the great log boom at Boeuf Slough.

After Van Sant built his log-rafting steamer at LeClaire during the winter of 1869 and proved that it would work, more than 70 raft boats began operating on the Upper Mississippi. Sternwheelers pushing rafts down river made far better time than when the rafts were propelled by the current alone. This innovation also led to the construction of larger and larger rafts. A large lumber raft pushed by a steamboat was comparable, in surface area, to the flight deck of an aircraft carrier. They built the rafts in sections, called "cribs" (heavy frames measuring 16 by 32 feet) that held the lumber tightly in place.

Workers piled from ten to twenty-four layers of lumber on a crib in a kind of open-face lumber sandwich and then tied the cribs together to make up the rafts. A Mississippi raft held from 120 to 200 cribs. Workers at Read's Landing assembled the logs from the Chippewa River into the great rafts. The use of raft boats reduced the delivery time of logs to St. Louis by one half. By 1892, a hundred towboats, valued at $750,000 were rafting logs down the Upper Mississippi. Annual receipts of wood products at St. Louis in the 1880's averaged over a quarter-million tons.

A raft boat required a double crew of two pilots, two engineers, two or four firemen, two ash-haulers and two watchmen. Half were on duty at a time. The men stood six-hour watches, changing at breakfast, dinner and supper and at midnight. The "call the watch" shout was the signal to wake up the sleeping pilot, engineer and fireman to go on duty. Broad-chested Irish, Scotch and Scandinavian men, rugged and full of spirit, manned the raft boats. They wore white broad-brimmed felt hats, cotton shirts that were never closed at the neck and cotton trousers, the legs of which were tucked into the tops of high boots.

Skippers used smaller steamboats attached crosswise at the front end of the raft to help steer while a large boat pushed from the rear. On a signal from the pilot of the raft boat the smaller boat at the front ran its engine either forward or backward. This would swing the forward end of the raft to either starboard or port to guide the raft around bends, between sandbars and through the narrow passages under drawbridges. Captain George Winans fastened the sternwheeler *Satellite* in front of a raft measuring 275 feet wide by 1,450 feet long, containing 44 cribs, and carrying 2,250,000 board feet of logs. The larger boat *Julia* pushed the raft, whose surface area was approximately ten acres, downstream. Winans made it to St. Louis from Read's Landing in twelve days.

CAPTAIN HEERMAN AND THE TORNADO

Each captain of a raft boat was responsible for delivering the logs on his raft to the mill. Captain E.E. Heerman was towing a log raft with his steamboat *Minnietta* from Boeuf Slough to Burlington, Iowa, in July 1874, when he reached a place cursed by raftsmen—the bridge over the river at Clinton. To get past the bridge he had to divide his raft into two parts. Tying one half of the raft between two piers of the bridge he took the first half under the bridge. Leaving it floating in the river Heerman went back for the other half of the raft. He had just gotten the second half past the bridge, caught up with the floating first half and was busy tying the two back together when he looked up and saw the black funnel of a tornado bearing down on him.

Heerman's nine-year-old son was along for the trip. Heerman shouted for the boy to run for a device on the raft called the "snubbing works." The snubbing works was a platform of securely fastened logs topped with huge cleats used to tie the raft up to shore. The captain told his son to lie down and hold tight to the cleats. Heerman was fairly sure that part of the raft would hold together and the boy, though he would certainly get soaked in the downpour of rain, would be safe.

With the raft reconnected together and his son holding fast to the cleat on the snubbing works, Heerman ran for the empty pilothouse. When the full force of the storm struck, the boat keeled so far over to starboard that Heerman was standing on the walls of the pilothouse. The door was stuck fast and he could not open it. Forcing open a window, he straddled the sill and shouted down the speaking tube to the engineer, asking him to stick by his post. "I'll stick all right," called back the engineer. "But this boat's done fur. The water's up to the sheet iron on the boiler."

Contrary to the engineer's expectations, the boat survived but the raft was broken into pieces. Heerman found his son and the crew huddled, cold, wet and frightened, on the one piece that was left of the raft, the fragment of 40 logs which contained the snubbing works. The rest of the logs appeared to be "scattered all over the state of Illinois." The demoralized crew members announced to the captain that they would not be persuaded to hunt down the missing logs.

Wisely Heerman did not argue. Instead he ordered the cook to prepare a scrumptious dinner with chicken and pie. Once the crew members were warm, dry and fed, they changed their minds and agreed to help the captain retrieve the lost logs. Some were found floating down the river but most were entangled in brush. For eight days the men pulled logs out of cornfields, thickets, briars, from sandbars and islands. To dislodge the logs the men worked with hooks amid thorns and brush. Before long their clothes were in tatters. By the time all of the logs had been retrieved, the crew was almost naked.

The men put together enough garments to decently clothe one man. Accompanied by the captain wrapped in a sheet the two ventured on foot to a small river village. The captain stayed out of sight while his crewman bought him a suit of the only clothes available. They were far too small for the tall captain. Four inches of leg showed between the end of the trousers and the captain's shoe tops. Wearing this garb Captain Heerman delivered the raft to the mill at Burlington with only three logs missing.

In 1901 Knapp, Stout & Company sent downriver a raft with 9,153,000 board feet of lumber and a million board feet of shingles and lath piled on top. The longest *log* raft came down the river in 1896 pushed by Captain O.E. McGonley with his steamer *F.C.A. Denkmann*. The raft was 275 feet wide and 1550 feet long.

By 1890 it was clear to Weyerhaeuser that the lumber was running out. He moved to St. Paul to be closer to his lumber operations that were already moving west. On November 18, 1905, he closed his mill in Rock Island. As the last log was pulled from the river for the mill, Charles Russell, a literate longtime raft-man reflected that, "In the literature of waste, this is our *Iliad*."

Few, other than Weyerhaeuser, could imagine that the lumber would ever be exhausted. The "rapacious romp" through an American resource had wiped out the great stands of white pine. The assault on the pine forests had been ruthless. Sixty to seventy percent of the timber that was cut was wasted, left to dry out on the forest floor where it became the kindling for disastrous fires. One Wisconsin fire killed more

than a thousand people and ravaged a million acres. Logging on the
Chippewa ended in 1905 after 25,365,875,950 board feet were rafted out.
Logging on the St. Croix ended in 1914 with 12,444,286,720 feet of lumber removed. The magnificent stands of white pine were gone and with
them went the rafting years on the Mississippi. The vast forests of the
north had been spent.

Reflecting on the role of the Corps of Engineers in the lumber industry, Corps historian Raymond Merritt wrote, "It is evident that the
lumber industry enjoyed an unrestrained exploitation of the bountiful
forests. . . . The Corps became an active agent in river management *after*
large lumber corporations had already jammed the rivers with logs. . . .
District engineers became concerned about the arrogant assumptions of
timber syndicates that they could wantonly control the nation's waterways. . . . Conflict between populist concepts of the free use of the nation's waterways and the growing power of large corporations resulted
in numerous controversies. The Corps of Engineers became a regulatory agent, as a result, between the opposing factions."

The issue of how the river should be used, raised by Mary Gibbs
when she dared put her hand on the sluice-gate lever at Itasca, was still
unresolved. For the timber industry the answer was clear and unequivo-
cal. The river existed to float logs to the mill.

The last great raft of sawed lumber went down the river in 1915
with the *Ottumwa Belle* at the stern and *Pathfinder* at the bow. The lumber in the raft was sawed at Hudson, Wisconsin, and was delivered to

Steamboat towing a raft of logs under the Wabasha bridge in St. Paul, circa 1900.
Courtesy of the Minnesota Historical Society.

Fort Madison, Iowa. The raft measured 128 feet wide and 1150 feet long and contained five million feet of lumber. When the raft reached Albany, Illinois, the captain stopped, tied up at the dock, and went in search of the retired Captain Hanks. The elderly man came aboard the boat, took over the wheel in the pilot house and brought the raft down as far as Davenport. Hanks rode the first lumber raft on the Mississippi and he piloted the last. Stephen B. Hanks died two years later, just two days short of his ninety-sixth birthday.

NOTES

Material on the lumber era on the Upper Mississippi is found in Agnes Larson, *History of the White Pine Industry in Minnesota* (1940). Frederick William Kohlmeyer, "Northern Pine Lumbermen. A Study in Origins and Migrations," *Journal of Economic History* 16 (1956); John Hauberg, *Weyerhauser and Denkmann* (1955); the John Hauberg Papers at the Rock Island County Historical Society (Moline, Illinois); S. S. Grannis, "Incidents in the Early Days of Red Wing," at the Goodhue County Historical Society (Red Wing); Lydia Hedin, Jean M. Chesley, John P. Anderson, and Louisa A. Sargent, *Alexander P. Anderson 1862-1943* (1997); Walter P. Blair, *A Raft Pilot's Log. A History of the Great Rafting Industry on the Upper Mississippi 1840-1915* (1930); and Richard G. Lillard, "Timber King," *The Pacific Spectator* 1 (Winter 1947). On the log rafts see Louis C. Hunter, *Steamboats on the Western Rivers* (1949); for Captain Heerman's story see Charles Edward Russell, *A-Rafting on the Mississipp'* (1928); and Edward Mueller, *Upper Mississippi River Rafting Steamboats* (1995).

CHAPTER 14

The Grand Excursion

Steamboat captains were the storied heroes of the Upper Mississippi and their boats were the marvels of the region. Believing themselves secure in their dominance of transportation and shipping on the river, few captains could imagine a threat to their authority. Nevertheless, a challenge was coming. While folk in the West still looked to their rivers as the primary highways on which to move people and goods, many in the East turned to a new transportation technology—the railroads.

At first, not recognizing the deadly nature of their competition, steamboat owners hailed the railroads as partners. They posted agents on the cars to sell steamboat tickets; off-loaded freight from trains to boats. Though business briefly boomed, it was a false spring. The magical boats were the doomed dinosaurs of transportation and the upstart railroads, while rickety and prone to breakdowns, were the harbingers of a new age.

The railroads' primary problems were those of cost. They were expensive to build. A United States Senator from Illinois, Stephen A. Douglas, who wanted the railroads to extend a line from Chicago through his state of Illinois to the Mississippi, solved the financial problem. Douglas's three-step plan was for Congress to turn over public land to the states which, in turn, would give it to the railroads. The railroads could sell the land and use the money to lay track and buy cars. Douglas asked that the Illinois Central Railroad Company be given alternate sections of land on each side of the railroad right of way, six miles deep. In return for this gift, the railroads were to give seven percent of their gross revenues to the state and transport troops and property of the government without charge.

The law passed on September 20, 1850. In the first land grant made to a railroad, the Illinois Central received 2,595,133 acres of land on which it realized a profit of twenty million dollars. (The government was to give away between 150,000,000 and 160,000,000 acres of land to railroads during the next twenty-two years, making the construction of the lines to the Pacific Coast possible long before there were enough people in the western states to justify a railroad.)

An advertisement in east coast newspapers announced, "Homes for the Industrious in the Garden State of the West. The Illinois Central Railroad Company have (sic) for Sale 1,200,000 acres of rich farming lands in tracts of forty acres and upward, on Long Credit and Low Prices." Land in Illinois sold for $6 to $25 per acre depending on its location. The railroad required buyers to pay a year's interest at 6% in advance and to pay for their land within seven years. At the end of five years half the property was expected to be fenced and under cultivation. Douglas's scheme of giving public land to the railroads to spur their development worked exceedingly well and by 1853 the iron horses were poised to move to the Mississippi.

A committee of Davenport business leaders headed by George Davenport and Antoine LeClaire was actively enticing those iron horses toward their section of the river. The men, who met regularly at Davenport's island home in the river, were convinced that the best route to the West for the railroad to follow led through their communities of Rock Island and Davenport. Two weeks before his death in 1845, Colonel Davenport hosted a meeting of railroad investors, including Antoine LeClaire, at his home. The men raised capital and on February 27, 1847, the company received a charter from the General Assembly of the State of Illinois to establish the Rock Island and LaSalle Rail Road Company. They planned to build the line from Rock Island east to the Illinois River at the terminus of the Illinois and Michigan Canal. With the money in hand, they went in search of a contractor to build their railroad.

Henry Farnham, of the firm of Farnham and Sheffield, had just completed the building of the Michigan Southern railroad into Chicago from the East when the delegation from Rock Island met with him at a Chicago hotel. Farnham listened to the proposition of the men from Davenport. He agreed to be the contractor for their railroad only if they would build it all the way to Chicago through Joliet, Ottawa and LaSalle. There was no future, he told the committee, in building a small rail link between two waterways. When Farnham offered to help raise additional money in the East to pay for the extra miles of track, the committee agreed. The charter from the State of Illinois was amended to include Chicago and work began on the railroad.

At 5 P.M. on February 22, 1854, George Washington's birthday, a decorated locomotive pulled six bright yellow coaches into the Chicago and Rock Island Railroad passenger building at Rock Island. Crowds had gathered throughout the day for a great "Rail Road Festival" and they were not disappointed. Bands played, artillery fired into the air. People surged into the cars as the startled passengers left their seats. Crowds of people, many of whom had never seen so much as a picture of a train, climbed onto the engine and over the roofs of the cab and the coaches. The implications of this new invention, now in Rock Island, were overwhelming. The arrival of the railroad was not simply the extension of a rail line but the marriage of the East to the West. Rock Island celebrated nothing less than a joining together of two sections of the country.

Guests of the Chicago and Rock Island Rail-Road were invited for a truly Grand Excursion by train and steamboat from Chicago to St. Paul and return. Courtesy of the St. Paul Riverfront Corporation.

The first toast of the evening called February 22nd "the espousal day of the Mississippi River and the Atlantic Ocean." Henry Farnham had the same imagery in his mind. He declared to the flag-waving crowd, "Today we witness the nuptials of the Atlantic with the Father of Waters." He added, "Tomorrow the people of Rock Island can go to New York, the entire distance by railroad, and within the space of 42 hours." The year before a trip to Chicago alone had taken two weeks by wagon. To the isolated residents of river towns and the farming hinterland of Minnesota the arrival of the railroads seemed as miraculous as the landing of a comet.

The railroad to the Mississippi had been nine years in the making—embroiled in the national struggle pitting forces advocating north-south transportation against those urging an east-west movement. It was a contest between the old paths of migration versus the new; between the slower, cheaper transportation by water and the faster but more expensive movement of people and goods by rail. Even those who favored east-west rail routes were divided. Southerners wanted a route through New Orleans to San Diego. Northerners wanted the line to run through Chicago to San Francisco. St. Louis and Chicago were pitted against each other in an intense rivalry. Citizens of Rock Island and Davenport supported the Chicago route as their two towns lay directly in the line of the northern route and, moreover, were located at the narrowest point in the channel of the Mississippi.

The extension of a railroad line to the Mississippi River at Rock Island was a momentous event. The entire country took note of the achievement. To properly celebrate the arrival of the first railroad to the bank of the river, Farnham and other investors in the railroad conceived of a monumental "Grand Excursion." The investors in the railroad "were full (sic) aware of the general ignorance that prevailed in the East with regard to the West." Farnham resolved to invite eastern friends "not only over the line of the new road but also up the Mississippi River to St. Paul in order that they might see with their own eyes the resources of the New West."

The Excursion would not only take the railroad's guests from wherever they lived to the terminus of the line at the Mississippi, but also upriver to St. Paul and the headwaters of navigation of the great river. Visitors could see for themselves the beauty and the economic potential of the vast, unsettled Northwest Territory. The trip would be the epitome of the Fashionable Tour to the Falls of St. Anthony.

As the *Galena Jeffersonian* explained the trip, "The Rock Island Railroad Company foots all the bills. It is in the programme to take each guest at his own house, whether in New York, Boston or Maine, and after having feasted, feted and excursioned him, to return him safe, sound and in good order and well conditioned to the shadow of his own vine and fig tree, wholly at the company's expense. The entertainment as a whole is a conception worthy of Farnham & Sheffield, the builders of C. & R. I. Road and we doubt not that under their care, it will be long remembered as the most magnificent festival of the age."

Invitations were issued to hundreds of the leading citizens in the East and hundreds accepted. Leading the celebrants was Millard Fillmore, who had just completed his single term as President. He was not nominated for a second term and had been out of office for only a few months when he joined the Grand Excursion. Fillmore may have had personal reasons for making the trip as well. His brother, Charles, had come to St. Paul in 1852 where he was engaged in real estate speculation.

As many as 1500 people accepted Farnham's invitation to make the journey and he distributed free railroad passes on nine eastern railroads, including the New York Central, the Great Western, the Erie and Cleveland, and the Hudson River railroads. Organizers instructed the guests to gather at Chicago and be prepared to depart on the Chicago and Rock Island Railroad on June 5, 1854. John H. Kinzie headed the reception committee at the Tremont Hotel in Chicago.

The guest list was impressive. Besides Fillmore and his twenty-two-year-old daughter Mary Abigail, there was Samuel J. Tilden, a governor of New York who almost became a United States president; the Harvard historian George Bancroft; Francis P. Blair of Maryland and his son Francis P. Blair, Jr.; Ninian Edwards, former governor of Illinois; Edward Bates of Missouri who would later serve as attorney general in Lincoln's cabinet; Judge Joel Parker from Harvard; A.C. Twining, Leonard Bacon, Eleazer Thompson and the eminent scientist Benjamin Silliman, all from Yale; and Henry Hubbard from Dartmouth College.

Every metropolitan newspaper of any note sent writers on the Excursion. Charles A. Dana was there from the *New York Tribune*, Hiram Fuller represented the *New York Mirror*, Epes Sargent the *Boston Transcript*, Charles Hudson the *Boston Atlas*, Charles Hale the *Boston Advertiser*, Thurlow Weed the *Albany Evening Journal*, William Schoiler the *Cincinnati Gazette*, W.C. Prime the New York *Journal of Commerce*, C. Cather Flint the *Chicago Tribune* and Charles F. Babcock the *New Haven Palladium*.

Altogether, fifty newspaper editors made the trip. The *Chicago Tribune* referred to the group of excursionists as "the most brilliant [party] ever assembled in the West, an ex-president, statesmen, historians, diplomats, poets and the best editorial talent in the country." As the *Galena Jeffersonian* explained to its readers, "the object of the excursion, on the part of its projectors, is not so much pleasure merely, as a desire to make a thousand more or less men of capital and influence acquainted with the enchanting beauty, the boundless resources and the unexampled prosperity of the Great West."

Early on the morning of June 5 the throng of excursionists met at the Chicago railway station to board two trains of nine coaches each. Farnham had ordered the cars decorated with flowers, flags and streamers and they departed from Chicago to the salutes of serenading bands and booming cannon. Though there were numerous stops along the way to acknowledge the welcoming crowds, to make speeches, and for a lunch at Sheffield, the trains covered the 181 miles to Rock Island by 4 P.M. where five steamboats awaited the travelers. The *New York Times* reported, "We arrived at Rock Island amid the firing of cannon, the waving of flags, and the acclamation of the multitude. A banner on the Rock Island depot was inscribed 'The Mississippi and the Atlantic shake hands.'" Most of Rock Island's 4,500 residents were at the depot to welcome the visitors.

Here Farnham's carefully prepared organization ran into some difficulties. When they began to match steamship cabin assignments with the passengers they found many more people than anticipated or invited. Moreover, organizers had assigned husbands and wives to different boats; some had even lost their tickets. Quickly additional boats were chartered: the *Jenny Lind*, and probably the *Black Hawk*. Lacking berths, about three hundred travelers turned back to Chicago leaving 1,200 eager to board the boats and sail upriver to St. Paul. The boats crossed the river to Davenport where speakers regaled the guests, followed by fireworks from Fort Armstrong and a "sumptuous feast" that diners claimed rivaled anything offered by the best hotels of the East.

The boats carrying the Grand Excursion party were the *Golden Era*, captained by Hiram Bersie; the *G.W. Spar-Hawk*, under Captain Montreville Green; the *Lady Franklin*, with Captain Legrand Morehouse; the *Galena* with Captain D.B. Morehouse; and the *War Eagle*, under the command of Captain Daniel Smith Harris. (The *Jenny Lind* and possibly a seventh boat, the *Black Hawk*, made the trip only to Galena.)

Catherine M. Sedgwick, writing for *Putnam's Magazine*, reported that the boats left Rock Island and Davenport with more fireworks from Fort Armstrong as well as the ringing of bells and sounding of whistles. Captain Harris in the *War Eagle* led the procession while the *Golden Era*, with the former president on board, brought up the rear.

Charles Babcock, who had planned to go only as far as Rock Island and then drop out of the Excursion, reflected the prevailing opinion of the Northwest. When he learned that ladies at St. Anthony Falls were preparing a picnic for the visitors he changed his mind. "Think of that," he wrote. "Ladies at St. Anthony's Falls where I had anticipated seeing only Indians, bear, catamounts and other like citizens of a primeval forest!"

"None of that happy company," wrote Catherine Sedgwick of the departure, "will ever forget the moment when our fine steamers, their bows wreathed with prairie flowers, left, one after the other, their moorings at Rock Island and sailed, like birds by their own song, lighted by the moon and saluted by gay fireworks from the Old Fort."

Around midnight of the first night on the river a violent thunderstorm aroused the passengers. This made resting particularly difficult for the many young men who had not been assigned berths and slept on mattresses on the cabin floors. Since the mattresses could not be put down until after midnight and had to be removed before 5 A.M. in the morning for the stewards to prepare breakfast, the men got very little sleep. The young men sleeping on the floor were awakened "by the novel method of a waiter coming along and pulling each sleeper by his big toe," the *New York Times* writer noted. "The queerness of the operation atoned for its unpleasantness," he added.

Morning found the boats near the mouth of the Fever River— renamed the Galena in 1853. The *War Eagle* led the file of boats up the river to a tumultuous welcome from the residents of Galena. The passengers disembarked and proud citizens led them on a tour of the lead mines and then to a picnic in the woods. Charles Dana reported that "Wines of Ohio and of France stood upon the board. . . and glasses were drained to the health and prosperity of Galena and its citizens." Dana added that "total abstinence is not the rule of the Mississippi Valley, everybody feeling it to be a sort of duty to temper the limestone water of the country with a little brandy or other equally ardent corrective."

Leaving Galena the boats reached Dubuque in the late afternoon. A heavy rain was falling but that did not discourage the residents of Dubuque from coming down to the levee to greet their visitors. Flags waved, cannons fired, and residents of Dubuque cheered. Nor did the rain deter ex-president Millard Fillmore, Professor B. Silliman of Yale University, George Bancroft and others from making lengthy speeches to the throng. Leaving Dubuque, the boats made a night passage to La Crosse where, while the boats took on wood the next morning, the passengers climbed the bluffs to get a better view of the countryside and Fillmore addressed the assembled citizens.

Babcock described the scenery. "Mountains, narrow plains, tangled forests and beautiful groves are sweeping by like a never ending panorama. [There are] perpendicular cliffs, rounded out in front so as to resemble the baronial castle with towers, turrets and battlements . . . During our progress up the river we met several immense rafts, some guided by five or six men, others by twice that number. They eat and sleep upon these rafts for weeks. They cheered our boats and swung their hats and one of them for the want of a piece of artillery, fired his rifle several times in the way of a salute. We are now in La Crosse, a thriving little settlement of several hundred inhabitants."

Dana, of the *New York Tribune,* confused Trempealeau with La Crosse and in his dispatch described La Crosse as "a wooding-place on the eastern shore with two or three frame houses." When the paper published his description thirteen outraged citizens of La Crosse wrote to the editor of the *Tribune* pointing out that La Crosse had forty subscribers to the *Tribune* and that "there are in the place two church edifices, one courthouse, fifteen stores and groceries, four taverns, one steam mill . . . two bakeries, two tin shops. . . one United States Land Office. . . and about two hundred frame buildings, including some possessing at least a fair amount of architectural beauty."

The continual need for wood to power the steamboats gave the passengers opportunity to go ashore at Monteville, Prescott and Trempealeau, Wisconsin. At Trempealeau, on June 7, Mary Abigail Fillmore borrowed a horse from one of the townspeople and rode to the top of a nearby bluff. The view, she later said, was the finest she had ever seen. She could see for miles up and down the river and she could not understand how the pilots found their way through the myriad channels and islands, all seemingly alike. When, from the summit, she waved her white handkerchief to the boats below they responded with loud salutes from their steam whistles.

While the Grand Excursion gave the politicians and editors an opportunity to debate current politics—it also offered them a "Grand

Escape." During those days on the Upper Mississippi they were far from the acrimonious debates taking place in Washington and Philadelphia. The land along the Mississippi River appeared to extend forever, its resources inexhaustible, the possibilities for the young nation unlimited.

America was in a period of the greatest growth and prosperity the country had yet experienced. The United States held a permanent frontage on the Pacific making it a neighbor to the Orient. Miners were flocking to the mineral-laden mountains of Colorado, Oregon would soon join the Union and California was on track to become one of the wealthiest of the States. Looking out over the crystal waters of the river, the wooded hills and fertile prairies, the travelers found it impossible not to be optimistic about the future. How, they asked themselves, could disaster descend on so magnificent a scene and country?

Travelers on the Grand Excursion ate well. Chefs prepared meats and vegetables in one kitchen and pastry and desserts in another. They purchased fish, game and vegetables in towns along the way. Cooks picked up two bushels of speckled trout during the stop at Trempealeau and purchased dozens of lambs and pigs from local farmers. Charles Babcock described the meals on the *Golden Era*. "We have had oysters and lobsters daily, though two thousand miles from the sea. These, of course, were brought in sealed cans. Hens, turkeys and ducks have given their last squeak every morning. Two cows on the lower deck furnish us with fresh milk twice a day. The dessert consists of all kinds of fruits, nuts, cakes, confection ices and other things too numerous to mention. Such is our daily fare. Then there are meats for supper, with tea and coffee with toast, cold bread, warm bread, Indian bread, biscuits, rolls, etc."

An anonymous writer noted that while "the table is abundant, butterknives and sugar-tongs are not among its luxuries." He added, "Those who know how to overlook these little deficiencies cannot hope anywhere to behold nature in such multiform loveliness and grandeur as on the waters of the Mississippi between Rock Island and St. Paul."

The *New York Times* writer was astonished to discover dramatic hills and bluffs where he had expected to see prairie along the river. "Perhaps you have beheld such sublimity in dreams, but surely never in daylight waking elsewhere in this wonderful world. Over one hundred and fifty miles of unimaginable fairy-land, genie-land, and world of visions, have we passed during the last twenty-four hours. . . Throw away your guide books, heed not the statement of travelers; deal not with seekers after and retailers of the picturesque; believe no man, but see for yourself the Mississippi River above Dubuque."

When the boats reached Lake Pepin around 10 P.M. the captains lashed four of the five boats together and proceeded upstream under a full moon. Sedgwick was impressed at the precision of the maneuver. "At a given signal by the leading boat, which had been previously agreed upon between the captains, all prepared to come alongside and lash the whole four abreast. The engines of the *Galena* were stopped and by the time the others reached her, she was resting motionless upon the surface of the calm, current-less water. The coming together and making fast was done with such skill and precision that, although the motion of the three hind-most boats was not entirely stopped, yet they came up so gently and easily that not so much as the least perceptible jarring or friction was created in the execution of the design. Thus the four moved through the lake, offering an opportunity of a general exchange of intercourse between the company, and affording a scene of grandeur and pleasing excitement which perhaps the waters of Lake Pepin will not again behold for many a day." Sedgwick reported that the remainder of the night was spent in "dancing, music, flirtations, et cetera."

On the morning of June 8 the residents of St. Paul awoke to a dramatic sight. Five steamboats were coming around the bend in the river all abreast as if in a line of battle. The *Galena Jeffersonian* reported, "The *War Eagle* in advance, the boats came near together in the channel and with head toward shore, tarried a few minutes to form a line, and then with streamers flying, with a gay crowd on deck responding with a will to the cheers of those who lined the shores, they floated slowly to land."

The passengers were excited to be arriving in St. Paul. *The Daily Democrat* recorded that "those on board gave vent to their enthusiasm by repeated cheers, which were answered from the levee and bluffs, and amid the clash of instruments, the roar of escaping steam, the huzzas of the great gathering, the gay appearance of the boats," the crafts glided to the levee.

The *Daily Tribune* writer described the arrival. "Two full bands of music were on board, both of which struck up lively airs as the boats neared the landing. This, with the rays of the bright June sun which broke forth in all his glory . . . the animation of the company on board the boats and the enthusiasm of the assembled hundreds on shore . . . produced a scene of excitement which St. Paul has never before witnessed and perhaps will not again for many years."

While the residents of St. Paul had good reason to be excited they were also dismayed at the sight of the five boats advancing on the city. The steamers had arrived a day early. St. Paul officials had expected the

Grand Excursion to arrive on June 9 and preparations were well underway to entertain the guests. A ball had been organized at the Capitol and tickets sold for $5 that would admit one gentleman and two ladies. Six gentlemen had been assigned as floor managers, and another six designated to escort the guests as they made their way from the boats to the Capitol.

The citizens of St. Paul had been requested to "tender the use of their carriages and wagons at the disposal of the guests on Friday morning." On Thursday, June 7, the Common Council of St. Paul had passed a resolution calling on every citizen of St. Paul "to do all in his power to render the sojourn of the guests of the Chicago and Rock Island R.R. Co. among us pleasant and agreeable; and that all are called upon to do something toward establishing the good name of our infant city for warm hearted, generous hospitality."

When they saw the approaching steamboats, members of St. Paul's reception committee put aside the plans they had made to entertain their distinguished guests and rushed to make new ones. Five boatloads of guests, 1,200 in all, had arrived a day early and the town of 6,000 struggled to cope. Civic leaders scrambled to reschedule the reception and ball. Down at the boat landing excited visitors, aware that they had but a few hours before their boats would depart back south, clamored to visit the Falls of St. Anthony. Owners of wagons and carriages saw an economic opportunity and were quick to take advantage of it. They offered to rent, some at outrageous prices, anything that moved to take the eager tourists to St. Anthony Falls, Fort Snelling, Fountain Cave and Minnehaha Falls.

Three prominent New York editors rode precariously on a one-horse water cart. The editor of the *Galena Jeffersonian* wrote, "Here was a governor bestride a sorry Rozinante of which even the Great Don would have been ashamed; here a U.S. Senator, acting the part of footman, stood bolt upright in the baggage boot of a coach, holding on by the iron rail surrounding the top; here the historian of whom the country is justly proud, squatted on his haunches on the top of a crazy van, unmindful of everything but himself, his book, his hat and spectacles. . . there a beautiful specimen of the feminine gender seated over the hind axle of a lumber wagon."

Historian Bancroft's unmindfulness almost led to his injury. He was searching through the pockets of his coat when he lost his balance and toppled from the top of his carriage into the road. For a moment his fellow passengers feared he had been run over by the wheels, but Bancroft got to his feet, dusted himself off and climbed back on board.

One of the party, a Colonel Johnson, brought with him a vial of water from the Atlantic. At the Falls of St. Anthony he made a speech and then, with appropriate ceremony and to the cheers of the party, mingled the water with that of the Mississippi. Members of the party clambered over the rocks and onto the massive logs that high water had wedged among them. The editor of the *New York Times* stepped onto a log that promptly rolled over, dumping him into the river. The editor was quickly pulled out, wet and chilled but uninjured.

From the Falls of St. Anthony, some of the travelers went on to visit Fort Snelling. The editor of the *Chicago Democratic Press* described the Fort for his readers. "Fort Snelling, situated on the bluff at the confluence of the Minnesota and Mississippi, is very striking and picturesque in its appearance. Its frowning battlements and air of solidity and strength impresses the beholder and calls up visions of old towers and castles upon the Rhine. We stood upon its ramparts when the boats came up from St. Paul and as they rounded to the shore and took position, side by side, one after another, the flag of our country was saluted with cheers long and loud." Participants in the Grand Excursion must have been hoarse from all the cheering.

Not all writers were forgiving toward St. Paul over the mix-up in dates. A *New York Times* reporter, identified only as "W," observed, "At Galena, at Dubuque, at every place we touched during this, our . . . expedition, the people received us gladly. With firing of cannon they received us—but they fired no cannon at St. Paul. With garlands of evergreen and flaunting banners they received us—but there were no garlands or banners at St. Paul. With vehicles, free of charge, to take us into the interior, they received us, giving us champagne, but at St. Paul there was no champagne."

The *Times* writer went on to complain about the charges levied for transportation to the falls and for having been charged 50 cents for chewing tobacco. "A buggy to carry two persons to the falls of St. Anthony, eight miles distant, one hour and a half mean time, $10. Those charges were a great sin, which will be chronicled against Minnesota cormorants throughout the United States . . . "A drinking friend," he wrote, "requiring some brandy (to counteract the effects of the Mississippi water) having a half dollar in his pocket, placed it innocently on the bar-counter and beheld it swallowed up by the till, or money-drawer, which yielded back not so much as a half-dime."

The writer's sense of outrage getting the better of him, he declared, "St. Paul . . . stands alone, unrivalled, un-approached, as the greediest place on all this Western Continent. . . . The same system of extortion pervades every business proceeding. The land is fertile but very far behind the Illinois prairie land which you can buy—the best of it—for $10 an acre. Within three miles of St. Paul inferior land is valued at from $75 to $100 an acre."

The editors of the *St. Paul Daily* News stoutly defended their community. They pointed out that "preparations had been made by the citizens to pay all the livery bills but the hurried manner in which the guests came upon us prevented any sort of arrangement or system which had been laid out by the committee." The editor of the St. Paul *Daily Democrat* could not restrain his indignation over the insult to the city. "We conversed with a large number of the most respectable visitors," he wrote "and one and all expressed their satisfaction and delight at the reception they met with in St. Paul."

Warming to his topic, he imagined a different reception for "W." "We regret too that a good conveyance in the shape of one of our small scrub oaks, cut down and the branches trimmed off with a sharp axe, could not have met him [the *Times* writer] at the landing, where Benson with one end on his shoulder and Willoughby the other, he might have been placed astraddle with all due form and ceremony and conveyed to his appropriate quarters in a small building we have back of the courthouse. We regret all this, but should he come again, we will endeavor to furnish him with such a ride and he shall not complain of the price."

The editor of the *Chicago Democratic Press* showed more understanding of St. Paul's situation. He wrote, "The fleet of boats arrived here this morning at half past 9 A.M. The town was taken by surprise, no one expecting us till Friday. Arrangements were in preparation to receive us at the Capitol in a befitting manner, but now everything was thrown in confusion. The party left the boats and every vehicle in St. Paul, even down to a water cart, was put in requisition to convey the visitors to St. Anthony. Hundreds visited the falls and were delighted with the rapid settlement of the country through which they passed, its charming landscapes and the grandeur of the scenery at and around St. Anthony. On the islands for a couple of hours the scene was animated and ever and anon amid the roar of waters would come up the sounds of gay conversation and the joyous laugh."

Another noted that "the genuine and unmistakable cordiality of [St. Paul's] welcome made amends for any lack of ceremonial appropriate to the occasion." The writer seemed relieved to have escaped the lengthy speeches. " It was *not* a matter of regret that the intended speeches, no doubt eloquent and apropos, were omitted for as soon as the boats landed, there was a general rush for carriages in which to visit the Falls of St. Anthony, Fort Snelling and the Cave."

The *New York Tribune* writer was also generous in his description. "The position of St. Paul as you approach the town from below is very admirable. The river bends there almost at right angles and the town stands on the north bank. Though but six years old, it already has 6,000 people and looks like a long civilized city. There are brick dwellings and stone warehouses, a brick capitol with stout, white pillars, a county court-house, a jail, several churches, a market, school-houses, a billiard-room, a ten-pin alley, dry goods stores, groceries, confectioners, and ice-cream-ers, a numerous array of those establishments to which the Maine law is especially hostile [saloons] and a glorious, boundless country behind."

Despite the unexpected early arrival of its guests, St. Paul rallied to produce a lavish dinner at the House of Representatives that evening followed by a reception and dance in the Supreme Court chambers. Women spent the day decorating the ballroom with evergreens and gar-lands and hung lace and damask curtains in the windows. "The blaze of the illumination [of the Capitol] was observable in many parts of the city and the citizens began to gather to attend the ball or to be lookers-on. The carriages bringing the guests from the boats arrived in quick succes-sion and before nine o'clock an assemblage was gathered within the walls of the Capitol such as was never before seen in this or any other place."

Territorial governor Willis A. Gorman and former congressional representative Henry Sibley welcomed the visitors. Fillmore thanked the citizens of St. Paul for their hospitality and Bancroft urged Minnesota to become "the North Star of the Union, shining forever in unquenchable luster." A band played on a raised platform in the second floor vestibule leading to the grand reception room. The hosts laid out "a great variety of delicacies, prepared with much taste" in an adjoining room. The steamboats' blowing of whistles signaling the revelers to return to the boats for a late departure cut short the festivities at 11 P.M. By midnight the boilers were hissing steam and the boats were underway, their pilots backing them away one by one from the levee, turning their bows slowly downriver.

The boats sailed back down the river at a steady clip of ten miles per hour. The passengers spent their time passing resolutions of apprecia-tion to Farnham and Sheffield for arranging the trip and taking up collections for gifts for the boat captains and officers. Both Captain Bersie of the *Golden Era* and Captain Morehouse of the *Lady Franklin* received silver pitchers, properly engraved. Passengers ordered an engraved cup of solid gold to be given to the six-month-old son of Henry Farnham, who was along for the trip. Presumably Farnham's wife was also on the boat though there is no mention of her presence.

The momentousness of the whirlwind, one-day visit obviously overwhelmed the residents of St. Paul. The Reverend Edward Duffield Neill, in a sermon titled "Railroads in the higher and religious aspect," preached to his Presbyterian congregation on the Sunday following the

Passengers on the Grand Excursion steamboats presented gifts to their captains. This elegant 12" tall silver pitcher, made by Eugene Jaccard of St. Louis, was given to Captain LeGrand Morehouse of the *Lady Franklin*. Courtesy of the Minneapolis Institute of Arts, the Fred R. Salisbury II Fund in honor of the 25th Anniversary of the Decorative Arts Council.

arrival of the Grand Excursion, foresaw the railroads being of great benefit to religion. In Neill's opinion "railroads would prove an antidote to bigotry," which prevailed in remote and sparse settlements. Transported by railroads an eloquent preacher might discourse on a certain Sunday in an Atlantic city, on the next in the Mississippi Valley, on the third on the mountain tops of Oregon and on the fourth on the Pacific Coast." Enthused by his topic, Neill exhorted his listeners saying, "A Pacific Railroad would be a voice in the wilderness saying 'Prepare ye the way of the Lord.' My hearers! Some of you have tickets that will lead you to hell. The car of death is hastening on . . . before it arrives we urge you to change that ticket."

Conspicuous in its absence from the commentaries by the participants in the Grand Excursion is any reference to the Indians. One looks in vain for an acknowledgement that Native Peoples were in evidence— that anyone was curious about them or was concerned about their fate. The majority of nineteenth century Americans believed that in a generation or two the Indians would disappear. Many preferred not to see the Indians at all. Indians were an artifact of the past and the participants in the Grand Excursion were focused on the future. By omitting references to the Indians (who must have been all about them during the Grand Excursion) participants revealed more about their attitudes toward Native Peoples than they might have been able to express through writing.

Up to the 1850's, as the *Chicago Tribune* declared, the Grand Excursion was "the most magnificent excursion, in every respect, which has ever taken place in America." The *Galena Jeffersonian* stated that "in its conception and execution it is the most magnificent fete ever given in this country or any other." It was certainly the most spectacular tourist event in pre-Civil War history. The total cost of the Grand Excursion was about $50,000 in 1854 dollars. The affair was a success on many levels. The editor of St. Paul's *Daily Pioneer* declared that, as a result of the Grand Excursion, "More will be known about Minnesota in the Eastern and Middle States within the next ninety days, through this instrumentality, than would otherwise have been in ten years."

The writings of the fifty editors who took the trip introduced East Coast readers to a previously little known region. Even the most sophisticated and jaded among the writers professed themselves astonished at the dramatic scenery along the river. All declared themselves impressed with the industry of the residents and the abundance of the natural resources.

For their part, residents of the Upper Mississippi felt a smug pride that they, on the often-disdained frontier, had thrown a party that dazzled and impressed the severest, most sophisticated critics in the nation. If Farnham's purpose in organizing the trip was to open the eyes of industrialists of the East to the wealth of the West, he was successful. The population of Minnesota in 1850 was 6,077. In just ten years it jumped to 172,023—a 28-fold increase. In the same period Wisconsin went from 305,391 to 775,881; Iowa from 191,214 to 674,913 and Illinois from 851,470 to 1,711,951. Much of the impetus for the explosive growth of these states was the Grand Excursion of 1854. Immigrants, capital and enterprises began to flow into the region. The publicity surrounding the Grand Excursion led to a population boom that quickly moved Minnesota Territory past the level required for admission as a state of the Union. As a result of its increased population, in 1858, four years after the Grand Excursion, Minnesota achieved statehood.

Mark Vander Schaaf, a St. Paul historian who first suggested the recreation of the Grand Excursion in a report to the St. Paul Riverfront Corporation in 1997, likens that event to the California Gold Rush. "Beginning in 1848, the Gold Rush opened the Far West to an influx of settlement and led to California becoming the 31st state in 1850. Six years after the Gold Rush began, the Grand Excursion opened the Far North to an influx of settlement and led to Minnesota becoming the 32nd state in 1858." Vander Schaaf's idea gained additional support at the River of Dreams Conference in 1998. Organized under the title of the Grand Excursion the re-creation became a reality in early summer 2004.

The Grand Excursion had political consequences that reverberated far beyond its impact on the economic development of the Northwest. Throughout the 1840's the U.S. Congress had carefully maintained the balance of power between the North and the South by admitting a northern free state to the Union only when it could be matched with a southern slave state. The rush of population to the north following the Grand Excursion upset that balance, unmistakably identifying the Northwest—from Minnesota to Northern California—as the area about to experience dynamic growth. That trend was reinforced when Oregon came into the Union in 1859, only a year after Minnesota. The trigger of the Grand Excursion set in motion events that overturned the carefully cultivated balance of power among the states as economic development, like water seeking its outlet, shifted to the northern sector.

The immediate result of the linking of the Atlantic with the Mississippi by the railroads was to increase traffic on the Mississippi. The completion of the Illinois Central to Dunleith, Illinois, (now East Dubuque) gave an additional impetus to immigration. The direct railroad link between the East Coast and the Mississippi River not only increased access to the area for settlers, it lowered costs. From April 12 to July 5 of 1856, 812 families consisting of 4,504 people crossed on the ferry from the railroad terminal at Dunleith to Dubuque. The amount of public domain land sold at the Dubuque Land Office during approximately that same period was 1,610,363 acres.

Each train brought hundreds of immigrants to the shores of the river and off-loaded them on the banks. A decade later they were still coming. A party of 250 Norwegians arrived at Dunleith in June 1866 and took passage on the *Jennie Baldwin*. The Dubuque *Herald* commented in a story, "Emigrants by the Car Load—Twelve carloads of German emigrants came in Tuesday bound for some point up the river and being too late for the boats they were compelled to lie over." Some boats had space for 300 cabin passengers and another 300 on the exposed deck. Passengers often slept two-deep on the decks. The land rush was on and no hardship was too great to reach the promised lands of the Upper Mississippi.

THE PILGRIMS

No group among the waves of immigrants from Central Europe, Italy and the Scandinavian countries had a more harrowing trip to Minnesota than a raft load of seventy-six Black men, women and children that a river steamer towed to St. Paul. When the Civil War ended, emancipation of the slaves came slowly on the frontier. Robert Hickman, a man of exceptional physical strength and a keen mind, was born into slavery in Boone County, Missouri, on New Year's Day, 1831. Hickman's owner taught him to read and write and Hickman became a local preacher, though without formal training or ordination.

One account of his departure from Missouri states that in the spring of 1863 Hickman engineered the escape of his wife and two children, who resided on another plantation, as well as 72 of his followers. Under Hickman's direction the fleeing slaves, who called themselves "pilgrims," built a crude raft, and set sail for freedom. The raft, with its human cargo, floated down the Missouri into the Mississippi and was drifting south when it was spotted by the steamboat *Northerner* which promptly took it in tow.

It is possible that Hickman and his party were recently freed slaves, called by the Northern Army "contrabands." Because so many men were fighting in the Civil War, the Twin Cities area was experiencing a labor shortage. The St. Paul and Galena Packet Boat Company sent boats as far south as St. Louis to gather recently freed slaves for work as deck hands and farm laborers. Henry Sibley had requested a load of "contrabands" to serve as mule drivers for his expedition against the Indians in 1863.

Whether Hickman and his followers were indeed on a river raft floating south when they were discovered by the Captain of the *Northerner* or contrabands requested from the Union Army for their labor, the *Northerner* arrived in St. Paul towing a raft bearing 73 Black individuals including ten women and twenty-six children. If Sibley was expecting a raft-load of male mule-drivers, he was certainly surprised and, perhaps, disappointed.

When the *Northerner* arrived at the dock in St. Paul Irish dockworkers, fearing for their own jobs, rioted. The local police joined in and kept Hickman and his people from disembarking from the raft on the pretext they were paupers without any means of support. Unable to land the raft in St. Paul, the *Northerner* towed it to Mendota across the river where the refugees found shelter. Within a few weeks they moved back to St. Paul where they found work. A church later formally ordained Hickman who went on to found the Pilgrim Baptist Church of St. Paul.

Former National Park Ranger Charlie Maguire has commemorated Hickman's Pilgrim voyage with a song:

> *Reverend Hickman's hands were those of a working man*
> *Swinging a hammer and splitting rail by the light of day*
> *Reverend Hickman's hands were those of a preaching man*
> *At night they built a boat to take the pilgrims away.*

> *(chorus)*
> *Oh Pilgrim, Run to the river, Run to the river,*
> *Run to the river! The river in prayer, Oh Pilgrim*
> *Run to the river, Run to the river! For Freedom! Freedom!*
> *Freedom waiting there.*

> *Reverend Hickman's hands were those of a fearless man*
> *When the cry went out they were long, long gone.*
> *Reverend Hickman's hands were those of a preaching man.*
> *No man, no woman, no child will ever get caught.*

Oh stories say they built a boat, Glory on the River!
Raft of logs, anything that floats, Glory on the River!
Jefferson City, they did go, Glory on the River!
Underground, underground railroad. Glory on the River!
War Eagle they hooked a ride, Glory on the River!
Towed or rode on the riverside, Glory on the River!
Up the Mississippi to St. Paul, Glory on the River
Founding Congregation on and all, Glory on the River!
Glory on the River, Glory on the River.

Reverend Hickman's hands were those of a riverman,
Down the wide Missouri, up the Mississippi too.
Reverend Hickman's hands were those of a preaching man.
And he guided on the Bible and the river to see him through!

In an 1896 speech to the Minnesota Historical Society, Captain Russell Blakely of the Minnesota Packet Boat Company, looked back on the Grand Excursion. "The success of this visit and the character of the people, especially the editors of the daily press of the country, did more than the best laid plan for advertising the country that has ever been made since. . . The great papers of the day and the magazines of the country were all full of the most laudatory literature in relation to the country, the scenery on the river and the pleasure and comfort of the journey. Good results came back to us in a thousand ways and for many years."

NOTES

On the Grand Excursion, see William J. Petersen, "The Rock Island Railroad Excursion of 1854," *Minnesota History* 15 (December 1934) and William J. Petersen, *Steamboating on the Upper Mississippi* (1937); Virginia Brainard Kunz, "The Grand Railroad Excursion of 1854—The Most Notable Event of the Year," *Ramsey County History* 30: 1 (Spring 1995). Two articles by Excursion participants are Catherine Sedgwick, "The Great Excursion to the Falls of St. Anthony," *Putnam's Magazine* 4 (1854), and Charles Babcock, "Rails West. The Rock Island Excursion as Reported by Charles F. Babcock," *Minnesota History* 34: 4 (Winter 1954). Reverend Edward Neill included an abstract of his sermon in his book, *The History of Minnesota* (1882).

Statistics for the Illinois Central are taken from "Iowa and the Illinois Central," *Illinois Central Magazine* (November 1927).

The story of Reverend Hickman and his followers is analyzed in David Vassar Taylor, "Pilgram's Progress: Black St. Paul and the Making of an Urban Ghetto, 1870–1930," Ph.D dissertation, University of Minnesota, 1977. Charlie Maguire's ballad, "Reverend Hickman's Hands," written while Maguire was a singing National Park Service Ranger, is used with permission.

CHAPTER 15

The Railroads

Two railroads reached the Mississippi from the East Coast in 1854, the first at Rock Island and the second at Alton, Illinois, across the river from St. Louis, Missouri. Railroad fever had been burning in parts of the west for a decade before the rails actually reached the banks of the Mississippi. A year before Farnham completed his Chicago and Rock Island railroad to the river Iowa businessmen had already incorporated a line called the Mississippi and Missouri railroad. The businessmen wanted to construct a railroad bridge over the Mississippi and then extend the rail line into Iowa's interior. It was obvious that a railroad bridge over the Mississippi should be the first priority.

While everyone agreed on the need to build a railroad bridge over the river, where that railroad bridge should be located was a matter of dispute. Chicago and St. Louis were in fierce competition to control the western transportation routes and the proposed Rock Island Bridge became an issue in that conflict. For a time the struggle between Chicago and St. Louis to control the trade of the West hung on a court's decision.

On June 31, 1854, the St. Louis *Intelligencer* reported that the City Council of St. Louis had resolved that " the free and uninterrupted navigation of the Mississippi river is deemed to be of essential and vital importance to the trade and commerce of the city of St. Louis and the erection of a bridge across the Mississippi river . . . at or near the town of Rock Island in the State of Illinois . . . will prove an obstruction to the free navigation of said river." The Council instructed the mayor "to procure the interference of the State of Missouri in preventing the erection of the said bridge by an application in the Supreme Court of the United States for a writ of injunction, restraining the building of the same."

The court never issued the writ of injunction and businessmen quickly incorporated the Railroad Bridge Company in Illinois on January 17, 1853. They named Henry Farnham president and chief engineer of construction. The charter empowered the company to "construct, maintain and operate a bridge in such manner as to leave unobstructed the navigation of the waterway and furnish a connection with all railroads in Illinois and Iowa which might have terminals at or near said bridge."

Designers drew up plans for a bridge and when they found that the west end of the bridge terminated in LeClaire's front yard in Davenport, LeClaire magnanimously deeded his land for the bridge. In the presence of an immense crowd at the groundbreaking ceremony to start construction of the bridge, LeClaire personally shoveled some of the dirt. A local reporter wrote that the crowd went wild with enthusiasm to see LeClaire take off his coat and go to work

ABRAHAM LINCOLN
AND THE RAILROAD BRIDGE

The first railroad bridge over the Mississippi River opened on April 21, 1856, crossing from Rock Island, Illinois to Davenport, Iowa. The wooden trestle bridge was 1,582 feet long, rested on five massive stone piers and stood 35 feet above the water. The swing-span that opened to let boats pass through was 285 feet long. The bridge was located just below the Rock Island rapids at a point many river men felt was deliberately chosen to interfere with navigation. The draw span sat at an angle to the current and when the river was high, violent maelstroms developed between the piers.

Completion of the bridge was a momentous event, a cause for celebration on both sides of the river. Speaking at the dedication LeClaire said, "The last link is now forged in the chain that connects Iowa and the great West with the states of the Atlantic seaboard. The iron band that will span our hemisphere has been welded at Davenport—one mighty barrier has been overcome."

When the first train crossed the span the governors of both states, the president of the railroad, and most of the population of Rock Island and Davenport were on hand to celebrate. Bands played and church bells rang. As a direct result of the railroad bridge over the Mississippi from Rock Island, the sleepy hamlet of Davenport, which had only been incorporated in 1851, became a boom town, its population swelling to 20,000 in less than four years.

Fifteen days after the first train crossed the bridge, on May 4, 1856, the side paddlewheel steamboat *Effie Afton,* after stopping at Davenport to let off passengers and freight, turned around and started upriver. The swing-span on the new railroad bridge opened, the *Effie Afton* passed through and continued up the Rock Island rapids. Then, without warning, the starboard paddlewheel shaft on the boat suddenly broke. Helpless, the *Effie Afton* drifted back down the river and crashed against the railroad bridge.

The wood-burning stove in the galley of the boat tipped over, the smokestacks fell and the *Effie Afton* caught fire. The burning boat ignited the wooden bridge. Three hundred panicked oxen on the deck of the *Effie Afton* leaped into the river. Hundreds of small boats rushed to the rescue but the *Effie Afton* burned to the water line and sank. No lives were lost but the first railroad bridge to cross the Mississippi River was badly damaged and it took a week to round up all the oxen.

The outraged captain of the *Effie Afton* who, like his fellow river men, believed bridges over the river were a threat to navigation, sued the railroad for damages. The captain sued not only for the loss of his boat, but to prevent the railroad from building any bridges across the Mississippi River. River men called the Rock Island Bridge "the most dangerous obstruction to navigation ever constructed on account of its being located over a chain of rocks producing boils and cross-currents which were difficult to keep a boat in." George Merrick called the bridge "that invention of Satan and the Rock Island Railroad. No better trap for catching steamboats could be imagined." River men contributed more than $20,000 to support the captain's suit.

Facing a substantial lawsuit, the principal railroad investors Henry Farnham, Norman Judd and Joseph Knox of Rock Island met at the Tremont Hotel in Chicago to decide what to do. Judd spoke. "There is only one man in this country who can take this case and win it and that is Abraham Lincoln." Farnham concurred. "Let's get him up here tomorrow." Lincoln traveled to Rock Island to see the situation first hand and immersed himself in the details of the case, studying the river flow and the currents until he had an impressive technical understanding of the problem.

Lincoln had long been a supporter of railroads, despite a personal conflict with railroad management. He had previously won a case for the

Alton and Sangamon railroad before the Illinois Supreme Court that was later cited as a precedent in twenty-five other cases. When Lincoln presented his bill for $2,000 the railroad refused to pay, saying he charged too much. Lincoln tore up the bill and wrote a new one for $5,000. When the railroad management again refused to pay, Lincoln sued the railroad and won his fee.

When the Rock Island Bridge case came to trial in federal court in Chicago Lincoln argued that one man has as good a right to cross a river as another has to sail up or down it. Lincoln asked if the means for crossing the river always had to be by canoe or ferryboat. "Were the products of the West forever destined to be carried to the banks of the river, unloaded from cars, loaded onto a boat for the crossing, unloaded and reloaded again to continue the journey east?" he asked. "Millions of dollars have been spent on navigable rivers yearly in removing obstacles from them and keeping their channels clear. Railroads, like navigable rivers, are great national highways and the rivers must yield so much of their vested rights as to permit bridges to be built across them to accommodate travel and commerce that naturally seek the railroads."

Using a model of a boat, Lincoln demonstrated to the jury how he believed the pilot had been incompetent in guiding his boat under the bridge. Lincoln closed by saying that the captain had to prove that the bridge was a material obstruction and that the boat had been managed with reasonable skill. "Difficulties going down stream will not do, for they were going up stream. Difficulties with barges in tow have nothing to do with the accident for they had no barges."

The jury couldn't agree, so the judge dismissed the case. Nevertheless, it was a victory for the railroads. Lincoln's argument that a man has as good a right to go across a river as another has to go up and down it exerted a powerful influence on the transportation system of the country. A subsequent suit eventually went all the way to the Supreme Court which, in 1872, decided for the bridge, a decision that precipitated bridge construction up and down the Mississippi. Lincoln is recognized as an early author of the American doctrine of bridges. The decision assured the eventual triumph of Chicago as a railroad center over its rival St. Louis.

Lincoln and his cousin, Stephen Hanks, strongly disagreed on the subject of bridges over the Mississippi. Hanks, together with other river pilots, staunchly opposed the building of railroad bridges across the river. Feelings between men who worked the railroads and those who sailed on the river ran high. In 1864 the Chicago and Northwestern railroad hired Hanks to take the *War Eagle* to Clinton and run it under the railroad bridge there to prove that the bridge was not a danger to navigation. Hanks successfully ran the boat back and forth under the bridge under various conditions, with and without barges. But when the railroad asked him to sign an affidavit to clear the railroad, he refused. The railroad then sent Hanks out to get other river pilots to sign statements to the effect that the bridge did not obstruct navigation. Not a single one would sign.

Hung jury or not, there was no doubt that the Rock Island Bridge was a hazard to navigation. Pilots called it the "Gate of Death." The *Grey Eagle* met her end at that bridge in May 1861. Of the 1,677 boats that passed under the bridge in 1857, fifty collided with the structure. Finally, in 1866, the Coast Guard formally declared the Rock Island Railroad Bridge a navigation hazard. An Act of Congress in 1872 appropriated the funds to build a new bridge a mile downriver from the lower end of the Rock Island Rapids and the first railroad bridge to cross the Mississippi was taken down.

The proliferating bridges (by 1887 fifteen railroad bridges crossed the Upper Mississippi alone) continued to present problems for steamboat captains but pigeons provided some unanticipated help. A pilot bringing a steamboat with barges in tow down the river needed to know far in advance if a railroad bridge span were open or closed in order to be able to slow down or stop. All communication between river pilots and the bridge tenders was by horns. River pilots were supposed to have priority over the trains, but the bridge tenders worked for the railroad and the significance of that was not lost on the steamboat captains.

When he was a mile from the bridge the steamboat captain would blow a blast on his whistle to announce his imminent arrival and to request that the bridge be opened. If the tender heard the boat's whistle he would blow one long reply to indicate that he was opening the bridge. If the boat were going to have to wait for a train to cross first, the tender would blow four short blasts on his horn. The horns from the bridge were not very loud, and if the wind were blowing in the wrong direction the boat captain would be unable to hear them. In this situation pigeons saved the day. Pigeons nested on the bridges. When the tender started to open the swing-span of the bridge 50 to 100 pigeons would take to the air. Seeing the birds, the captain would give a sigh of relief and ease his boat and tow down to the bridge.

The Illinois Central completed the route to Galena and continued it on to Dunleith, opposite Dubuque, Iowa, in 1859. The arrival of the railroad to Dunleith was a coup for Dubuque and revenge against Galena

214 - RIVER OF CONFLICT, RIVER OF DREAMS

for historic slights. Not content with the state's gift of public land, the railroad asked the town of Galena for additional free land for a terminal on the west side of the Fever River where the business district was located. The town fathers had paid little attention to the railroad, believing that the river would always dominate commercial transportation so they said "No" to the railroaders' request. That was a fatal decision for Galena for the terminal by passed the town and ended up at Dunleith across the Mississippi from Dubuque.

In 1860 a Dubuque paper poked fun at Galena and branded her an "inland-town," the worst possible insult, when the steamboat *W.L. Ewing* had been "unable to get up the Fever River on account of the mud." At a meeting of the Dubuque City Council a member proposed a resolution that the bed of the Fever River "be plowed up and potatoes planted." The resolution failed when someone in the council chamber observed that the bed of the Fever River was too dry, even for potatoes.

The chiding of Galena by members of the Dubuque City Council reflected the political dimension of the routing of railroad lines. The routes for the railroads were strongly influenced by lobbyists who sketched them out far from the locales they served. Dubuque booster General George Wallace Jones, a former senator from the Iowa and Wisconsin Territories who "knew everyone and was intimate with the president," negotiated the agreement that brought the railroad terminal to Dunleith. Through its ties to the well-connected Senator Jones, Dubuque wielded more political power in Washington than did Galena.

Jones influenced the decisions that led to the construction of the Dunleith and Prescott Railroad that ran up the river on the Illinois and Wisconsin side of the river. Where being bypassed by river steamers once sounded the death knell for a town, now being bypassed by the railroad guaranteed a community's decline. As a result of their differing decisions on the railroad, Galena faded while Dubuque, its rival across the river, thrived.

Andrew Carnegie was one of the bidders on the bridge to span the Mississippi from Dunleith to Dubuque. The industrialist, himself, drove to Iowa to compete for the business. "We found the river frozen and crossed it upon a sleigh drawn by four horses," he later wrote. "We found we were not the lowest bidder. Our chief rival was a bridge-building concern in Chicago, to which the board had decided to award the contract. I lingered and talked with some of the directors. They were delightfully ignorant of the merits of cast and wrought iron. We had always made the upper cord of the bridge of the latter while our rival's was made of cast iron. This furnished my test. I pictured the result of a steamer striking against the one and against the other. In the case of wrought iron it would probably only bend. In the case of the cast iron, it would certainly break and down would come the bridge."

Carnegie had chosen the right argument. A few days previously one of the directors had run his buggy against a cast iron lamppost and the post had fallen, breaking into pieces. He understood Carnegie's logic and convinced the other directors to award Carnegie the contract—after first making him match his rival's price.

Within a year of the completion of the railroad to the Mississippi in 1854, it had become apparent to even the most insular of village officials that the future of their towns no longer depended on the river but on the railroads. Where communities had once jockeyed for favorable positions on the Mississippi River—Winona had dumped a load of rock into the river to protect its steamboat landing—they now maneuvered to be connected to a railroad. Officials completed the first railroad in Iowa, the Mississippi and Missouri, at Davenport in 1855 making Iowa equal in railroad construction to Missouri. Then Iowa pulled ahead. The race was on—between states, regions and communities to see who could build railroads the fastest.

In Minnesota the feverish excitement over railroads coincided with the movement for statehood. The year before Congress voted to admit Minnesota to the Union the 1857 Land Grant Act allocated to the Territory of Minnesota six sections of land per mile of railroad as a bonus to stimulate its construction. (A subsequent act of Congress in 1864 granted four additional sections per mile.) Since it was illegal for a territory to vote aid to the railroads, members of the legislature, giddy with railroad enthusiasm, had to wait for statehood before taking action. As one writer described the excitement over railroads in Minnesota, "Being a repressed desire, it took especially virulent form when it was allowed to come to the surface."

As soon as Minnesota achieved statehood, railroad supporters convinced the state to pass, by a large popular vote, a constitutional amendment which provided for a state loan of $5,000,000 to the railroads, which were also benefiting from the Congressional land grant. The sale of state bonds financed the loan that was secured by a first mortgage on railroad property. The agreement called for $100,000 to be advanced for each ten miles of railroad roadway that the company graded and an additional $100,000 for each ten miles of track it laid.

What the railroad enthusiasts failed to take into account was the fact that Minnesota lacked credit, had no capital, had a small population base and was too far north to attract through lines. And then there was the disastrous Financial Panic of 1857. Despite these problems, men began to sell bonds and work on the railroad. Workers with teams of horses graded routes through the woods for a railroad. In most cases "grading" meant the driving of a few stakes in the ground and running a horse-drawn scraper over the surface where a future rail line might be built. Grading a ten-mile stretch was an easy way to earn $100,000. It was certainly far easier and less expensive than constructing an actual railroad line.

The railroad bubble burst after a year. The value of the bonds fell. Workers had graded two hundred miles of road but the only track in existence was a stretch of 1,400 feet used to store the one engine belonging to the Minnesota and Pacific Railroad line. The rapid failure of the loan brought about an equally rapid change in public attitudes. While everyone was still enthusiastic about railroads, most realized they had gone about their construction in the wrong way.

The constitutional amendment authorizing the loan was repealed in 1860 and the voters believed that was the end of the matter. No one made any provisions to pay off the outstanding bonds. For twenty years the holders of the now infamous railroad bonds tried to work out a settlement. In 1870 the state offered to trade the bonds for land but the bondholders refused. Eventually, in 1881, the state agreed to pay the principal and interest due on the bonds at the rate of 50 cents on the dollar.

JAMES J. HILL AND HIS RAILROAD

Despite the debacle of the bonds, the Minnesota and Pacific Railroad (later renamed the St. Paul and Pacific) opened for business in 1863, running the twelve miles from St. Paul to St. Anthony. The first locomotive in the state, named the *William Crooks* after the first construction engineer on the Minnesota and Pacific Railroad, pulled the train. One of those in the crowd watching the train on its initial run was a young man who had come to St. Paul as a teenager from Guelph, Ontario, in 1856. James Jerome Hill had intended to go west with the Red River ox carts, but he changed his plans when he discovered that the last convoy of carts had already left St. Paul for the season. Needing to support himself,

Hill took a job on the levee and worked as a clerk for the Dubuque Packet Company. It did not take long, working on the busy levee, for Hill to grasp the central role in the economy played by the shipment and transfer of goods on the river.

As Hill, who was about to found his own forwarding and warehouse business, watched the wood burning *William Crooks* chug out of St. Paul on its twelve-mile run to St. Anthony, he was certain he was looking at the transportation of the future. Carefully he watched the fortunes of the grandly named Minnesota and Pacific Railroad Company. Years earlier investors had floated a $13,800,000 bond issue to fund what was supposed to be a transcontinental line. However, they laid only 500 miles of mostly unusable track and corrupt contractors had siphoned off most of the money.

Two bondholders, Dutch venture capitalists, were left with "two streaks of rust and a right of way for their money." The financial panic of 1873 pushed the feeble railroad into bankruptcy and, in a complicated transaction, Hill and three associates paid off the bonds and acquired the stock of the company. Hill renamed the line the St. Paul, Minneapolis and Manitoba and immediately extended the line north to the Canadian border where it linked up with the Canadian Pacific Railroad. Two big wheat harvests followed—most of which rode to market through St. Paul on Hill's railroad.

Hill built a union railroad depot in St. Paul and Minneapolis wanted one too—as well as to be connected by rail to eastern markets. In December 1881 Hill, together with Minneapolis businessmen, organized the Minneapolis Union Railway Company to build a railroad bridge across the Mississippi from St. Paul to Minneapolis. The question was where to put it. The shorter, less expensive, route was above the falls but Hill's engineer, Charles Smith, feared that any major construction on the riverbed above the falls might cause their further destabilization.

Year after year the sandstone layer under the falls had eroded away. Memories of the 1869 collapse of a tunnel being dug between Nicollet and Hennepin Islands were still vivid. Millions of gallons of water had gushed through the tunnel taking large pieces of the two islands with them. With that disaster in mind and despite the fact it made the project far most costly, Hill decided to build a bridge diagonally across the river at a point below the falls. Hill and Smith sited the east end of the bridge just below the St. Anthony mill district and the west end 500 feet downstream from the Hennepin Avenue suspension bridge. The rail line over the bridge would end at a union depot to be located between Nicollet and Hennepin Avenues.

Hill's bridge over the Mississippi was unusual. Most railroad bridges were wobbly wooden affairs, built to last only a few years. Trains crept over them at the speed of a walk. By contrast, Hill planned a $650,000 monument, built to last for centuries. Skeptics called the bridge "Jim Hill's folly." Contractors used one hundred thousand tons of rock in the bridge. Hill was a stickler for quality. When he became dissatisfied with the stone being shipped to the bridge site by a Mankato quarry, he purchased the stone company. Construction went on year-round.

Workmen stood up to their waists in icy water to earn $1.25 a day. To cure the cement in sub-zero temperatures the contractor added eight quarts of salt into each barrel of cement and mixed it with hot water. The salt content prevented the cement from freezing and, once it had dried, the stone absorbed the salt. Hill's construction, the venerable Stone Arch Bridge, resembles a Roman aqueduct and is a masterpiece of bridge design. The two thousand-foot long bridge, with twenty-three arches, sweeps across the river on a diagonal directly in front of the falls. Completed in 1883, the bridge carried railroad traffic until 1978. Pedestrians and bicyclists are now the principal users of the bridge. (Its former destination, the Great Northern Depot, was demolished in 1978. A new Federal Reserve bank building stands where the depot once did.)

With his projects making money, Hill turned to his big dream— extending his railroad, now named the Great Northern, all the way to the Pacific. Hill was a meticulous planner. His railroad to the Pacific covered the shortest route and climbed the lowest grade over the mountains from St. Paul to the Pacific of any transcontinental railroad. In seven and a half months in 1887, 8,000 of Hill's men laid 643 miles of railroad track from Coulee, North Dakota, to Helena, Montana. Trains hauled every timber, tie and nail to the work site from Minnesota. In 1893 Hill completed the line across the continent to Seattle. Built without a land grant or any government assistance outside of Minnesota, the Great Northern was the only northern transcontinental railroad to avoid bankruptcy. With the exception of E. H. Harriman, no man controlled more railroads at the time than did James J. Hill.

When the Hill railroad reached the Pacific in January 1893, the celebration was not immediate. St. Paul, in fact, waited until June to host a celebration with a grand parade and the presentation of a silver punch bowl to Hill. A warehouse, a grain elevator and a map of the railroad lines appear on the bowl, while the *William Crooks* is on the punch ladle handle.

Rather than wait for the Mississippi to be bridged and the rails to reach them, groups of investors in communities along the river took matters in their own hands. They formed railroad companies, raised money however they could and surveyed possible routes for a railroad. Like the roots of a fast-growing, invasive plant the rail lines spread over the region. Overnight, every community wanted a railroad. Within four years of the first railroad's reaching the Mississippi seven others had been established. Between 1865 and 1869 builders constructed three railroad lines across the Mississippi into Iowa. By 1880 thirteen railroad bridges spanned the Upper River. The first locomotive to run within the state of Iowa was the *Antoine LeClaire*. Builders stamped LeClaire's name in gold under the cab window. On one side of the bronze sand box of the engine's boiler was a bust of LeClaire and on the other side, one of Pocahontas.

Once they had breached the barrier of the river, rail lines snaked north and south, up and down both sides of the river and crept west into the rich wheat-growing hinterlands. Farmers were quick to grasp the importance of the railroad in moving their crops to market. The growing of great quantities of grain in Iowa and Minnesota facilitated the growth of the railroads. The railroad promised year-round connections to other towns and to the great markets in the East. Gone would be the struggle to haul grain to a river terminal. Gone would be the long isolation of the dark northern winters. No longer would gleeful throngs gather on the levee to greet the first boat of spring, relieved at its arrival.

Instead of congregating on the levee to greet the boats, villagers now lingered at the railroad stations for the dramatic arrival of the trains. In 1871, during the third month of rail service to Red Wing, watchers at the station were perplexed when the engine pulled in without a single coach behind it. Where were the passengers? The engineer, when he looked back, was equally startled. Hastily reversing his locomotive, the engineer backed down the track and found the car, filled with its patiently waiting passengers, near Hastings.

Construction on the Winona and St. Peter Railroad began on December 9, 1862. A locomotive called *Old Tiger* pulled the first train of four flat cars, a passenger car and a baggage car along eleven miles of track to Stockton. The first train load of wheat arrived in Winona the next day. The car returned to Stockton loaded with lumber. By August

1870, workers had extended the line to Mankato and St. Peter, a distance of 139 miles.

The Winona and St. Peter line was built faster and further than any other railroad in Minnesota. Following the wheat farmers, it passed through New Ulm and crossed the Dakota border in 1872. The next year it reached Watertown, South Dakota, 324 miles from where it had started in Winona. At the same time the St. Paul and Sioux City line, owned by the Chicago, Milwaukee and St. Paul, began construction of a line from St. Paul south through the choice farm land of Central Minnesota reaching the Iowa border, 148 miles away, by 1869.

To connect the Winona and St. Peter line with the railroad on the eastern side of the Mississippi River, investors raised $250,000 to build a railroad bridge across the river at Winona. They completed the wooden trestle bridge on May 26, 1871. The next day, after a big community celebration, the first train was to cross. The train arrived at the river and stopped to wait for the bridge tender to come back from lunch and close the swing-span that had been left open for boats to pass. When the tender saw the train waiting, he ran to the riverbank, jumped into his rowboat and hurried to the bridge to close the span. He was excited. This was his first train. The man rowed to the swing-span, tied up his boat, climbed up on the bridge, stoked the fire in the boiler for power, got up steam and slowly swung the span closed. Then he signaled for the train to cross.

In his hurry, the tender forgot to re-couple the track. The locomotive made it across the bridge successfully but the flatbed cars, loaded with heavy quarry stone, snagged on the unaligned rails and plunged into the river, taking the entire swing-span and the unfortunate tender with them. It took a year to repair the bridge. In 1882, the Chicago Northwestern purchased the local railroad and replaced the wooden bridge with one made of steel. The Chicago Northwestern was one of four larger railroads out of Chicago (others were the Burlington, the Rock Island and the Illinois Central) that had all crossed the Mississippi by 1856. These better organized and financed companies gobbled up the many small, partially completed, short line enterprises.

NARROW GAUGE RAILROADS

For many small communities a narrow gauge railroad was the only way they could benefit from rail transportation. Prior to the Civil War no one had attempted to standardize the width of the tracks. Tracks varied in width from three feet six inches to six feet, though "standard gauge" soon came to be understood as four feet eight and a half inches wide while a "narrow gauge" was only three feet wide. It was a long time before the significance of having the track widths the same became apparent.

Communities built narrow gauge railroads because they cost less to build. The rails could be light, weighing only thirty pounds to the yard. The engine and the rolling stock could be lighter. Workmen could lay rails on poorly graded rights of way in much less time if a three-foot gauge line were built. The ultimate hope in the minds of the narrow gauge builders was that, in time, a standard railroad would acquire their narrow gauge line and widen it.

On December 16, 1867, a group of Dubuque, Iowa, businessmen incorporated the Dubuque and McGregor Railroad Company. In 1869 they changed the name to the Dubuque and Minnesota Railway and amended the articles of incorporation to enable an extension of the rails to Winona, Minnesota. This was the beginning of the River Road. By 1872 the Dubuque and Minnesota Railway had over one hundred miles of narrow gauge track hugging the western bank of the Mississippi from Dubuque to La Crescent, Minnesota.

It had become fashionable, in railroad circles, to include the name of the growing rail center at Chicago in the names of railroads in the hope that, someday, the company's rails might go there. So the name of the company was again changed, this time to the Chicago, Dubuque and Minnesota Railroad. The fact the railroad did not go anywhere near Chicago did not seem important. By 1880 the River Road, including all of its branches, contained 200 miles of track.

A few were not enthusiastic about the railroads, particularly when tracks crossed their land. The St. Paul and Chicago Railroad had begun construction on a line running south from St. Paul to connect the river communities when it ran into a problem in Red Wing. Civil War hero Colonel William Colvill objected to the amount of money the railroad had offered to pay for its right-of-way over land owned by Colvill's wife. When the dispute was not resolved to his satisfaction, Colvill quickly built a house squarely in the center of the area where the rails were to be laid.

When the astonished railroad crew arrived on the scene they were met by Red Wing's most famous war hero with a pistol in his belt, blocking their path in front of his new house. Workers for a railroad could not intimidate the man who had stood up to Robert E Lee and the Confederate army at Gettysburg. When the railroad officials' explanations and arguments failed to convince Colvill to retreat, the workers removed his belongings from his house and tore the structure down around him, piece by piece. Though he lost the argument, Colvill's dramatic gesture brought him some satisfaction. In the final settlement his wife received several hundred dollars more from the railroad than had been offered originally.

In building their lines, the railroads set up a tiered system of "bonuses" that they expected from each town through which the railroad passed. If a town did not pay, it risked being bypassed by the railroad. Since communities were aware of the importance of having a rail line through their town, most (unlike Galena) paid their assessment. Promoters of the St. Paul and Chicago railroad set their fees at $500,000 for Winona, $100,000 for Wabasha, $75,000 for Lake City, $40,000 for Hastings and $100,000 for St. Paul. Minneiska, Minnesota, was left out but the railroad assessed the small town of Read's Landing $10,000. Wabasha and Hastings did not pay the money but many communities did. The citizens of Read's Landing held an election to decide whether to pay the railroad assessment and it passed by fourteen votes. Opponents of the measure claimed that supporters of the measure had brought woodchoppers from across the river in Wisconsin to vote favorably on the matter.

The bank issued the bonds in 1877 with the first principal payment due in 1892. The bonds bore 7% interest payable to the First National Bank of St. Paul. The village of Read's Landing paid interest on its bonds until 1881 when it stopped because Read's Landing was shrinking. The state revoked the town's charter in 1896 because of its declining population. With the charter gone the village of Read's Landing legally ceased to exist. The buyers of the bonds sued and forced the county to pay which caused hard feelings among citizens in other towns who had to pay for the Read's Landing railroad bonds. The railroad went through Read's Landing, since there was no other place between the river and the bluff to lay the rails, but the village lost its depot and became a "signal stop" where the train stopped only when signaled.

The final blow to Read's Landing was the construction in 1882 of a railroad up the Chippewa Valley in Wisconsin connecting Eau Claire to the river towns by rail. No longer did boats stop at Read's Landing before continuing on their upriver journey. The decline of steamboat travel on the Mississippi ended the annual spring wait for breakup when a dozen or more boats loaded with impatient passengers waited at Read's. Soon Read's Landing became just another abandoned town. The traffic on the river, which had been its life-blood, ended and so did the community of Read's.

The Milwaukee and Mississippi (later known as the Chicago, Milwaukee and St. Paul) was the last of the major railroads to reach the river. It arrived in Madison, Wisconsin in 1854. From there it took three years to reach Prairie du Chien, opposite McGregor, Iowa, arriving on April 14, 1857.

St. Paul did not have a railroad until 1867. Before that time packet boats carried the tide of wheat flowing out of St. Paul to Prairie du Chien where it was put on trains destined for the lake port of Milwaukee. In 1865 the railroad built an elevator on the riverbank at Prairie du Chien with a capacity of 200,000 bushels and for years handled over 100 carloads of grain per day.

Advertising card for one of the railroads linking St. Paul and Chicago. Courtesy of Floyd Risvold.

The railroad arrived in La Crosse on August 23, 1858, connecting the city directly to New York by rail and fundamentally altering immigrant patterns from Europe. Instead of coming up river from New Orleans, as they had previously done, immigrants disembarked at New York and boarded trains for the west. The rail connection to La Crosse was a major factor in New York's replacing New Orleans as a significant immigrant port.

From 1858 until 1876, La Crosse had a railroad running directly to the banks of the Mississippi but no bridge to take trains across the river. The problem was solved by transporting trains across the Mississippi on steamboats. Workers laid tracks on barges and on the lower decks of steamboats. Engineers then ran the trains carefully down the riverbanks onto the boats. The *McGregor* was one of the steamboats that ferried trains across the river at La Crosse. During the winter tracks were laid on the surface of the frozen river and the trains crossed over on what they called "ice bridges."

THE DEATH OF THE WAR EAGLE

When the railroads first reached the river they served as feeders to the riverboats, and were not the deadly competitors they became later. The famous *War Eagle*, the boat owned by Captain Daniel Smith Harris that had led the Grand Excursion procession in 1854, was in such a partnership with the railroad.

The *War Eagle* had already made five trips and late on the evening of May 14, came up river to dock at the railroad depot at La Crosse where it was scheduled to meet the midnight train from Milwaukee. While the War Eagle waited for the arrival of the train, local people boarded the boat. Among the passengers was Mary Ulrich, an 18-year-old socialite and niece of John Ulrich, the publisher of the German language newspaper of La Crosse. Mary was on her way to a wedding. Ulrich had been concerned about his niece traveling alone and had earlier lunched with Captain Thomas Cushing of the *War Eagle* to discuss Mary's welfare. To look after her during her trip on the *War Eagle*, Cushing had placed Mary under the care of Felix Spiller, the black barber on the boat.

The train from Milwaukee arrived around midnight. Passengers transferred from the train to the boat and workers put the remaining consignment of freight on board. The final items to be put aboard were fifteen wooden barrels filled with "non-explosive petroleum fluid," a substance called "Danforth's Oil" that was intended for use in a new type of lantern. The barrels had been sitting on the La Crosse dock for three months. Soon after they were loaded on the *War Eagle* a deck hand observed that one of the barrels was leaking. This was not unusual and the ship's cooper was called. The cooper held a lighted lantern over his head in one hand while, with the other, he pounded a metal hoop down over the barrel.

Suddenly the barrel exploded in flames spraying blazing liquid in all directions. The startled cooper, his shirt afire, dove into the river. Crewmen raced for the burning barrel and quickly rolled it over the side. Unfortunately the barrel did not land in the river. Instead it became wedged between the boat and the wooden dock where the flaming oil spread over a large area, setting both the boat and the dock on fire. The furiously blazing oil gave off great clouds of black smoke which quickly filled the main stairway leading to the passenger staterooms.

It was between one and two o'clock in the morning so that passengers were asleep in their staterooms. Members of the crew raced to the rooms, waking passengers who had only minutes to make their escape. Six passengers died. Mary Ulrich, whose cabin was directly above the burning barrels of oil, was among them. Rescuers found her body in the river, clasped in the embrace of Felix Spiller. Spiller could easily have saved himself but instead he went to the rescue of his charge. The two of them must have jumped from the upper deck of the boat into the river where they drowned, clinging to each other. Mary is buried in the cemetery at La Crosse under an elaborate marker. The man who almost certainly gave his life trying to save her was buried in a pauper's grave, the location of which is now unknown.

The barrels of "non-explosive petroleum fluid" not only burned the *War Eagle* to the water line, but also burned up the dock, the railroad depot, the train that had just arrived from Milwaukee and a grain elevator. It was a dry period and if it had not been for the slough behind the depot, the entire city of La Crosse might have burned down.

The wreck of the historic *War Eagle* is still in the Mississippi, nosed up to the bank at the spot where she burned, now under 28 feet of water. Low water exposed the wreck in 1914 and again in the 1930's. When the boat's hull appeared above the water people walked onto the wreck and carried off crates of dishes and bottles. Artifacts from the wreck of the *War Eagle* can be seen in the Riverside Museum at La Crosse.

Following the fire the railroad rebuilt its depot uptown, away from the river. No longer was it an advantage for passengers to be able to step off the train onto the deck of a river steamboat. No longer did the railroads look to partner with the *War Eagles* of the Mississippi. A massive retreat from the river was underway. Despite the best efforts of the riverboat captains, there were limitations to riverboat travel that could not be overcome. River traffic was limited to the period between March and the middle of November, depending on the weather. Trains ran year-round. The only way the steamboats could compete with the railroads was in transporting huge volumes of goods.

One entrepreneur who did succeed in competing with the railroads was Joseph Reynolds. His Diamond Jo steamship line began in 1862 when Joseph Reynolds bought a small sternwheeler and put her in the grain trade between Lansing, Iowa, and Prairie du Chien, Wisconsin. Competition from the railroads had taken passengers and most of the freight business away from the steamboats but Reynolds saw an opportunity in the bulk shipment of grain. In 1868 he negotiated an agreement with the Chicago and Northwestern Railroad and began to operate out of Fulton, Illinois, where the railroad elevator was located. Reynolds called his fleet of four boats the Chicago, Fulton and River Line. Within a year he was the leading grain shipper on the Upper Mississippi and his steamers were popularly known as the Diamond Jo Line because of the diamond-shaped logo.

By 1873 Reynolds's fleet consisted of five steamboats and twenty barges. One boat could handle eight barges carrying 100,000 bushels of grain. That was the equivalent of 250 railroad cars, the equal of a train one and a half miles long requiring ten engines to pull it. Reynolds moved the general offices of his Diamond Jo Line from Fulton to Dubuque in 1874. In 1877 McGregor, Iowa, Joe Reynolds's tiny hometown, the town that had begun with a horse ferry across the Mississippi, became the homeport to more barges than St. Paul. The Diamond Jo Line survived until 1890 when it could no longer make money. A final irony: Joseph Reynolds did not allow drinking or gambling on his boats of the Diamond Jo Line. Yet "Diamond Jo" is the name given to the casino boat moored at Dubuque's America's River Park.

Although Joseph Reynolds was able, for a time, to work with the railroads, they eventually put him, and the rest of the boat owners, out of business. In the beginning the railroads had cooperated but as soon as they could they broke with the steamship lines and began to cut rates. The railroads were more intent on eliminating the steamboats than cooperating with them. During the navigation season the railroads carried goods at a loss, only to raise rates in the winter when the boats could not compete. Freight rates were 44.4% higher in winter than in the summer and some captains claimed that when the packet boats were gone the railroads on the Upper Mississippi raised their rates from 50% to 70%.

Residents of the river towns failed to grasp how dependent their economies were on the steamboats and the river. As a result most were unable to respond to the new competitive situation. Few towns had built enough storage facilities to protect river shipments. A typical levee was a dirt bank paved with rocks. For months of the year the levees were seas of mud. Towns built their warehouses back from the river to protect them against floods. The river towns charged high rates for wharfage so it was not profitable for a steamboat to drop off a small amount of freight and only one or two passengers.

Galena merchants had ignored the railroads. When railroad builders pushed two lines from Lake Michigan to the Mississippi —one from Milwaukee to Prairie du Chien and the other from Chicago to Dunleith—they cut off the old line of commercial traffic by way of the Mississippi. The change was fatal to Galena and its steamboat industry. Lead and farm products found their way overland to Chicago and Milwaukee and not down the river.

In 1855 the St. Paul boat landings accommodated 1058 paddlewheel steamboats. Just nineteen years later, in 1874, only 219 steamboats made the trip to St. Paul. By 1889 the railroads had taken over all of the freight business of the Upper Mississippi region and more than 75% of the passenger trade. The conquest of the United States by the railroads was completed in thirty-five years—half the three score and ten of a Biblical life span. The railroad onslaught had been devastating. It overwhelmed the steamboats and the communities they served before they entirely grasped what was happening to them.

Because railroad builders sought the easiest gradient they built their lines along the river. In the towns the rails were laid between the river and Main Street, to be close to the warehouses, lumberyards and grain elevators. This was advantageous to the railroads but it cut off the town connections to the river. Gradually, as river traffic declined, the community attention shifted more and more toward the railroads and away from the waterfront

Though few realized it, the river communities were losing something of major significance—their intimate connection to the great natural force of the river. Multiple rail lines, snaking up the valley, blocked access to the river's banks. Businessmen no longer needed the Mississippi for commerce. The steamboats left and with their departure went the romance and heroics of the river. Towns whose entire reason for being was their site on the great river, turned their backs on the Mississippi to embrace their new love, the railroads. The river, like a rejected lover, faded from the consciousness of the community.

NOTES

Railroad references include William Thompson, *Transportation in Iowa* (1998); William Edward Hayes, *Iron Road to Empire—The History of 100 Years of the Progress and Achievements of the Rock Island Lines* (1953); and Robert Edgar Riegel, *Story of the Western Railroads* (1926). For Lincoln and the railroad bridge see John W. Starr, Jr., *Lincoln and the Railroads* (1927), and B. A. Bodkin, *A Treasury of Mississippi River Folklore* (1955). On James J. Hill, see Albro Martin, *James J. Hill and the Opening of the Northwest* (1976), and Ray Lowry, "Hill's Folly'— the Building of the Stone Arch Bridge," *Hennepin County History* 47: 1 (Winter 1988). Also, Susan E. Williams, "A Wild Hurrah, the Great Northern Celebration of 1893," *Minnesota History* 48: 3 (Fall 1982). The punch bowl given to Hill is a part of the Minnesota Historical Society collections. For narrow gauge tracks information see John Tigges and Jon Jacobson, *Milwaukee Road Narrow Gauge* (1985). See Frederick L. Johnson, *Goodhue County, Minnesota* (2000) for the Colonel Colvill story. Also see Mildred Hartsough, *From Canoe to Steel Barge on the Upper Mississippi* (1934); George Byron Merrick, *Old Times on the Upper Mississippi* (2001, reprint); and William J. Petersen, *Steamboating on the Upper Mississippi* (1968).

CHAPTER 16

The Betrayal

Rolling, rolling from Arkansas, Kansas, Iowa
Rolling from Ohio, Wisconsin, Illinois
Rolling and shouting,
Till, at last, it is Mississippi,
The Father of Waters . . . .

— From "Ode to Walt Whitman" (1935)
by Stephen Vincent Benét

Though the Mississippi River looks like one river, it is actually several streams all running together. Each stream reacts to a combination of forces, constantly changing and reacting to each other. Different levels of water in the river move at different speeds because they are carrying different loads of silt and dirt. Water moves downstream in layers. Clear water, which moves the fastest, flows on the top. Below it, layers of water with different loads of sediment move at different speeds.

Sediment in the water causes it to meander. As the stream meanders it picks up more sediment, drops other particles, changes its character from moment to moment. Water flowing around a river bend flows slowest on the inside curve and fastest on the outside curve—much like the game of "crack the whip" where the child at the end has to run the fastest to keep up. Rivers deposit silt on the inside of bends, narrowing navigation while at the same time scouring the outside edge of the bend, creating new meanders and adding more dirt to the sediment load.

The natural Mississippi, the historic river known to the Indians and French fur traders, was a sprawling watercourse marked by thousands of side channels, islands, sloughs, backwaters, braided channels, sandbars and shallows. Major Long marveled at the clarity and purity of the water. Pike estimated the river to be two miles wide above Prairie du Chien with a bewildering number of islands, courses and broad pools through which the water flowed at a leisurely pace. In late summer and fall, when the water level was low, the river seemed more like a lake, scarcely three feet deep at St. Paul, with a barely discernable flow. The channel, when it could be found, wandered back and forth across the riverbed from one bank to another as if out for a leisurely Sunday stroll.

The spring river, swollen by rains and melting snow, was a far more aggressive stream. It moved with purpose at four miles an hour, overflowing into pools, wild rice fields and sloughs, undercutting banks, toppling trees, spreading into low-lying prairies and bottomland forests, creating and washing away sandbars and flooding the shallows. The hundreds of sandbars in the main channel divided the river into a series of deep pools. The rushing river in spring was far different from the placid stream that, in the fall, held so little water that, at times, steamboat navigation between the Falls of St. Anthony and Lake Pepin became impossible for weeks at a time.

The scarcity of reliable, economical transportation created an untenable situation for the grain farmers of the Upper Midwest. The Midwest's farm population almost doubled between 1860 and 1880 and farmers were producing a prodigious amount of wheat, corn and oats—commodities destined for national and international markets. The lack of reliable and economical transportation for their grain and other products threatened the survival of Upper Midwest farmers. The railroads charged exorbitant rates and often did not have enough rail cars available to move the harvest of grain to markets. Shipping on the river was problematic because of the seasonal variation in water levels and the hazards and obstructions in the river.

Steamboat pilots had long complained about the snags that damaged or sank their boats. "Preachers," "planters" and "sawyers" lurking just below the surface of the water continued to pierce the hulls of the stoutest boats. So long as the Northwest Territory was thinly populated, Congress had been able to ignore the boatmen's complaints. Following the boom in population and after the country had recovered from the Civil War, Congress began to pay more attention to the great waterway down the mid-section of the country.

In 1866 Congress appropriated money to outfit snag boats to remove the hazards that continually threatened the steamboats in the river. Snag boats were specially constructed to approach obstructions such as trees that had toppled into the water from caving banks, grapple for them, drag them to the surface, saw them into short, harmless lengths and dump them back into the water. The snag boats did not remove all of the snags—they were continually being formed—but their work made river travel appreciably safer. Mark Twain thought removing snags was akin to "pulling the river's teeth," making the trip safe but dull.

DREDGING THE
FOUR AND A HALF FOOT CHANNEL

The river itself remained unchanged, natural, and during low water periods in the fall so shallow—at times only 16 inches deep over sandbars at St. Paul—that riverboats found it impossible to navigate. For three hundred miles downstream from St. Paul, during severe dry spells, the water would be only two feet deep over sandbars. The solution, everyone agreed, was to modify the river. Farmers' organizations and business interests launched an aggressive program to lobby Congress for an improved river channel.

They wanted the Army Corps of Engineers to dredge a 4.5 foot deep low-water channel in the Upper Mississippi. Modifying the river, they argued, would free agriculture from the monopolistic rates the railroads charged the farmers, would restore competition to transportation and give farmers realistic alternatives to shipping on the railroads.

The bard of the river, Mark Twain, was skeptical of the campaign to change the river. In a chapter of *Life on the Mississippi* called "Uncle Mumfort Unloads," he wrote, "One who knows the Mississippi will ever promptly aver—not aloud but to himself—that ten thousand River Commissions, with the mines of the world at their back, cannot tame that lawless stream, cannot curb it or confine it, cannot say to it 'Go here,' or 'Go there' and make it obey, cannot save a shore which it has sentenced, cannot bar its path with an obstruction which it will not tear down, dance over, and laugh at." Twain was alone in his skepticism. Under the rubric of "improvement," supporters made plans to alter and control the Mississippi River. Everyone believed it was a capital idea.

In their zeal to lobby Congress for money to dredge and deepen the river, boosters claimed divine foresight and blessing on their project. Discussing the lobbyists and their arguments, John O. Anfinson quoted their plea to Congress: "Direct communication is both natural and necessary and the all-beneficent Creator has graciously anticipated the wants and necessities of unborn millions in having given us exactly such a continuous means of supply and exchange from the Falls of St. Anthony to the Gulf of Mexico." The Mississippi had a "grand destiny" that could never be fulfilled, they wrote, until it had been permanently deepened. Proponents insisted that, "The bounty of Providence has freely provided the river for our commercial convenience. There is no cost of construction but only of improvement."

To resolve agriculture's transportation crisis and in response to pressure from farmers' organizations and states bordering the Upper Mississippi, Congress, on June 18, 1878, authorized the first project that would materially change the river's character. While the Army Corps of Engineers was to continue its work of removing snags and sunken vessels from the river it was also ordered to dredge a four and a half-foot deep low-water channel from St. Paul to Alton, Illinois. The project would entail the construction of wing dams and closing dams.

Wing dams are narrow dams projecting out from the shore into the current of the river. Major Stephen H. Long had constructed the first experimental wing dam on the lower Ohio River to deepen the channel over a sandbar. Even before the dam was completed the deflected water accomplished the desired effect, increasing the channel depth from fifteen inches at low water to thirty-six inches. Wing dams built on the Mississippi were from 500 to 600 feet long and made of willow mattresses sunk to the bottom and covered with piles of rock. Cheap to build, workers constructed them to direct the flow of water into a relatively narrow stream to deepen it and increase the velocity of the water so that the river could scour out its own channel. Although engineers built a few wing dams before 1840, they constructed most of them after 1880.

Engineers built closing dams in the same manner as wing dams but from the shore to an island or from one island to another closing off back channels and sloughs and directing the water into the main channel. The Corps of Engineers built the dams at a furious pace that went on year-round, constructing three hundred wing dams in the thirty miles of river between St. Paul and Prescott and 400 more in the forty miles between Wabasha and Winona. In the twenty-mile stretch from Read's Landing to Minneiska, they built 257 dams.

Eventually more than 1,000 wing dams crowded the 143 miles between the Twin Cities and La Crosse, Wisconsin. Over time the spaces between the wing dams filled up with sediments and plants took root. This process moved the banks of the Mississippi gradually inward and, as the river narrowed the water, velocity increased. Engineers were permanently changing the landscape and ecology of the river.

HENRY BOSSE'S PHOTOGRAPHS

Henry Bosse was an immigrant from Germany who was hired by the Rock Island District of the Corps of Engineers as a draftsman. As part of his duties Bosse took a remarkable series of photographs that depicted the initial assault on the river. Over the years the Corps administrators forgot about Bosse's pictures only to rediscover them decades later in the Washington, D.C., home of Major Alexander Mackenzie, the man who had ordered the taking of the pictures in the first place.

The Corps showed the pictures to curators at Sotheby's, the New York art auction house, who immediately recognized the quality and historic nature of Bosse's pictures and put them on the market in 1990. Bosse's approximately 300 photographs, taken between 1883 and 1892, capture the last views of the river as it once was and document the first steps in the transformation of the Upper Mississippi from a natural river into a commercial water highway.

Bosse's scenes of the river show working snag boats, log rafts and the dredging operation. Other pictures are of the river before it was changed, showing the vegetation, bridges, lost islands, sandbars and the river's banks. Bosse took his photographs on glass negatives and printed them as blue cyanotypes. Henry Bosse, whose work was forgotten for a hundred years, now ranks among America's great nineteenth century photographers and his blue-tinged photographs are worth thousands of dollars. Reproductions of some of the Bosse photographs are on display at the Landmark Center gallery of Ramsey County Historical Society and in the Science Museum of Minnesota's Mississippi River Gallery.

THE DAMS ON THE INDIAN RESERVATIONS

The construction of the wing and closing dams increased the speed of the water flowing downstream but they did nothing to increase the *amount* of water in the river. The lumber industry needed a constant and ample flow of water to carry logs and sawed lumber out of the north woods to markets downriver. Business leaders in Minneapolis, including the lumberman and miller William Washburn, who was a United States

Congressman, Charles Pillsbury, Franklin Steele and John Merriam called on the Corps of Engineers to build dams in the headwaters section of the Mississippi to create reservoirs. When the water level was low, as it often was in late summer and fall, the gates in the dams could be opened to allow the water stored in the reservoirs to flow down to St. Paul. This, they claimed, would improve navigation and provide additional power for the water-driven sawmills and flour mills they had built at the Falls of St. Anthony.

The pressure to modify the river reflected the enormous changes that were taking place in Minneapolis and St. Paul. In 1870 the two towns had been little more than frontier villages with a combined population of 33,000. By 1900, only 30 years later, 365,783 people lived in the Twin Cities, making it the eighth largest metropolitan area in the United States.

Ever since Major Long had explored the headwaters area in 1823, the U.S. Army Corps of Engineers had considered itself the steward of the Upper Mississippi. At the same time, the Corps was the handmaiden of private industry in the Twin Cities. When powerful corporate leaders, such as Washburn, called for dams to be built at the headwaters of the Mississippi, the Corps responded with alacrity to provide them. The fact that the dams would be built on land owned by the Pillager band of the Ojibwe Indians and the reservoirs created by the dams would flood Ojibwe villages, graves and wild rice harvesting areas was considered of little consequence.

In 1874 Congress, reflecting the attitude of the Corps and Twin Cities business leaders toward Indian interests, appropriated funds for a survey of the proposed area of the dams. After intense lobbying by Washburn, Congress, in 1880, included $75,000 in the Rivers and Harbors Act for a dam at Lake Winnibigoshish. The next year Congress appropriated another $150,000 for a dam at Leech Lake. Eventually the Corps constructed six dams, all in the headwaters area of the Mississippi where most of the land belonged to the Indians. To compensate the Indians for their appropriated land, a special commission met and approved a sum of $15,466. The insulted Ojibwe angrily refused the money. "When our lands were given to us by the Great Father we could do something," Flatmouth, chief of the Pillager band of the Ojibwe Indians, explained, "but if these dams are made we will all be destroyed."

Several leading citizens came to the Indians' defense. Episcopal Bishop Henry B. Whipple, who feared that some of the "foolish young men" at Leech Lake might attack the workers at the dam, pointed out that wild rice was a primary source of food for the Indians and, during the long winters, often the only food they had. The rice also had ceremonial significance and the Indians used it for medicinal purposes. The reservoirs that would be formed behind the dams would flood most of the Indian wild rice harvesting areas, as well as many of their village sites.

Whipple urged the Indians to remain calm while he lobbied the Commissioner of Indian Affairs Hiram Price to reopen the subject of compensation. Whipple also asked that work on the dam be stopped until fair payment could be arranged. Major Charles Allen, of the Corps of Engineers, did not agree. Pointing out that any delay in construction would mean a loss to the government, he ordered the work to continue on dams at Winnibigoshish and Leech Lakes. When smallpox broke out among the Leech Lake Indians Flatmouth logically attributed it to the members of the construction crew. Major Allen found this claim "laughable."

Fearing an outbreak of violence similar to the 1862 Dakota Conflict, Henry Sibley and Henry Rice wrote an open letter to Commissioner Price that was published in the *St. Paul Pioneer Press* warning of disaster if the Ojibwe were not treated more fairly. Finally, in 1890, Congress authorized an appropriation of $150,000 to pay the Ojibwe for damages caused by the construction of the federal dams and reservoirs on their property. Much of the money was never paid.

From an engineering standpoint, the reservoirs worked as the Corps had planned. Navigation below St. Paul improved; the mills had additional water for power. The Pillagers, on the other hand, lived in extreme poverty because of the loss of their rice and berry crops. Indian agent T. J. Sheehan of the White Earth Agency reported that "the damage arising to the rice fields, fisheries, hay meadows and cranberry marshes leaves these Indians in a pitiable condition and with small means at their command whereby the necessities of life can be obtained." The Leech Lake agent agreed. "The persistent operation of the upper Mississippi reservoirs at a high level by the War Department is ruining many hay meadows and wild rice fields," he reported.

The Corps continued to operate the reservoirs until the 1930's. Then summer residents from Minneapolis and St. Paul, who had built vacation cottages around Lake Winnibigoshish, complained about the changing levels of the lake and the death of thousands of pike trapped in low water when the dam's gates were left wide open. A final resolution came in 1985 when the Indians received compensation from the federal government for 178,000 acres of reservation land that had been taken by the reservoirs a century before and for the loss of their rice marshes. In addition they were paid 5% interest since 1884. The grand total came to $3,390,288.

DREDGING THE SIX-FOOT CHANNEL

Despite the Corps of Engineers' success in creating a 4.5 foot channel in the Mississippi, river traffic did not increase, as boosters had predicted. Instead traffic continued to decline. Railroads had taken away all of the shipping business and when the timber rafting ended, nothing was left moving on the river. Residents of river towns looked out at a watery landscape devoid of boats, of people, of commerce. The river that only a few years before had been a vibrant, ever-changing scene now flowed by, lifeless and empty. Warehouses closed and Main Streets stood deserted. Residents were shocked even further when James J. Hill in a 1902 speech declared that the epoch of river traffic was over. He called for an end to federal spending on improvements to navigation.

Hill's speech galvanized the leadership of the river towns into action. Representatives from five states met and formed the Upper Mississippi River Improvement Association. The vision for the river held by members of the association was the same as that expressed twenty-five years before—that Divine Providence intended the river to be used for commerce and industry. The only difficulty was that the river's channel was not deep enough. To stimulate shipping, they argued, the channel should be deepened from four and a half to six feet. Washburn, the Minneapolis miller who had earlier lobbied for the dams on Indian lands, proclaimed, "This great river here at our doors should be developed and improved, and it is our part in our day and generation to do what we can to carry out what the Lord has evidently intended should be done."

To do the Lord's work, as the boosters defined it, Congress, on March 2, 1907, authorized the Corps to construct a six-foot low-water channel in the Upper Mississippi. Though the four and a half foot channel had failed to stimulate shipping on the river, members of the Upper Mississippi River Improvement Association assured the public that once the depth was increased to six feet, shipping on the river would absolutely, positively follow.

The Corps of Engineers immediately began dredging and building more wing dams, more closing dams, further speeding up the flow of water down the ever-narrowing river. As the wing and closing dams increased the velocity of the water they also accelerated the erosion of the riverbanks. The imprisoned river tore at its banks like a trapped animal gnawing at its foot. The speeding current, constricted in an ever-narrowing channel, collapsed whole sections of riverbank, toppled trees, and washed tons of soil, rocks and sediment into the river. The Corps responded by dumping thousands of tons of rock along the river's mossy shoreline, cutting down more trees, closing off more sloughs and backwaters to transform the once wild river to the demands of civilization and commerce.

While they were at it, the engineers dredged new channels in the river and removed many of the small islands, sending the water at an ever more furious pace downstream to the Gulf. The cost for construction and maintenance of the six-foot channel from the mouth of the Wisconsin River to Minneapolis between 1878 and 1930 was $15,123,462 or $67,818 per mile. Despite strenuous efforts by the Corps to maintain a clear six-foot-deep channel, commercial traffic on the river failed to increase. Instead it declined every year. The government's own dredging equipment was the single largest presence on the Upper Mississippi.

THE POLLUTION OF THE RIVER

The great river suffered other insults. Following the Civil War sawmills proliferated on the Mississippi and its tributaries. Seventy-five mills operated on the Mississippi from the mouth of the Chippewa to St. Louis. Above the Chippewa and on the river's tributaries, another 200 mills busily manufactured lumber, shingles and lath. By 1890 Minneapolis was the leading lumber market in the world. Of the four largest mills in the U.S. in 1900, Minnesota had three, two of which were in Minneapolis. The Twin Cities mills each produced a prodigious amount—more than 100,000,000 feet of lumber in a year, while eleven other mills in the state each made from 50,000,000 to 100,000,000 feet in a year.

At the turn of the century Minnesota produced 2,314,720,000 feet of rough lumber a year. Every one of the mills dumped its sawdust and lumber refuse into a river, either the Mississippi or a river that flowed into it. By the 1870's steamboat pilots were complaining that refuse in the river was obstructing navigation. In 1880 the sawmills in Minneapolis alone dumped an estimated 1.5 million board feet of sawdust into the river. By the 1990's sawdust accumulated to a depth of twenty feet on some areas of riverbank, according to Rhoda Gilman of the Institute for Minnesota Archaeology.

St. Paul, downriver from the waste stream dumped into the river by its sister city of Minneapolis and unhappy about the pollution, complained in 1879 to the U.S. Secretary of War. The Secretary ordered a survey, carried out by Major Mackenzie of the Corps of Engineers who, indeed, found that "the promiscuous depositing of sawdust in the river is a public evil and liable to injure navigation." Armed with Mackenzie's report, Representative Mark Dunnell introduced a bill in Congress "to protect and promote the navigability of the navigable rivers of the United States and to prevent the deposit of sawdust or other material in said rivers to the injury of navigation." Dunnell's concern was not for the quality of the water, but for ease of navigation. Washburn, a fellow Congressman and leading Minneapolis miller and manufacturer of lumber, opposed the bill. As a result the bill did not go anywhere.

St. Paul's complaints succeeded in arousing some other groups, including members of the Minnesota legislature, the Corps of Engineers (which was concerned solely with the problems of navigation) and steamboat pilots. The pilots complained that they could not tell the difference between natural sandbars and those composed of sawdust and their boats often became stuck in the muck. The Corps reported that the riverbed for several miles south of Minneapolis was "paved with waterlogged slabs and edgings" from the Mill City's mills. Moderating its pro-business stand, the Corps urged passage of a law to curb dumping into the Mississippi River.

The mill owners adamantly opposed any anti-dumping legislation. The newspapers, for the most part, supported the owners' position. One editor wrote, "the rivers are and must forever be the common sewer and dumping ground for everybody." Minneapolis acted on that philosophy by dumping, every day, about 500 tons of garbage into the Mississippi River below the falls. St. Paul, loud with complaints about Minneapolis' polluting, dumped an equal amount of its own refuse into the river. The city contracted with a private trash hauler, The Sanitation Company, which dumped the contents of its barges directly into the river.

In 1888 the Corps of Engineers removed a bar that had formed next to the St. Paul waterfront and found that it was composed entirely of noxious, rotting garbage. The odor of decomposing garbage in the river became so offensive that the city of South St. Paul filed suit against The Sanitation Company. The company agreed to dump the refuse at the lower end of Pig's Eye Slough, south of St. Paul, but most of the time the company just waited until dark and continued dumping into the river. On warm summer nights the odor of rotting garbage in the Mississippi River wafted through open windows into the ornate salons of St. Paul's Summit Avenue.

Sawmills and municipalities were but one class of polluters of the river. At the Twin Cities, breweries, the stockyards and packinghouses dumped their waste into the river. Contamination from the packing industry consisted of "foul, bloody wash water, yard drainage and putrescent scraps of animal matter." The Minnesota Board of Health reported "the river is grossly polluted . . . it would be decidedly dangerous for domestic consumption without purification."

The Corps continued its campaign to pass legislation, motivated not by the problem of water pollution (few were concerned about the quality of the water), but by the problems of navigation faced by the embattled steamboat industry in its losing struggle to compete with the railroads. As a result of the Corps' efforts, the Rivers and Harbors Act included a refuse provision that, if it had been enforced, would have ended the dumping of sawdust and garbage in the river. Unfortunately, the United States Attorney General found loopholes in the law and the act was not enforced.

To its credit, the energized Corps refused to give up. As a result of work by McKenzie and others, the Rivers and Harbors Act contained the "most broad and effective water pollution legislation in existence." Unfortunately, good legislation that is not enforced is useless. Though the laws were on the books, no one had the courage to sue the powerful offenders. The dumping of sawdust and wood waste into the Mississippi and its tributaries continued unopposed for years—stopping only when the sawmills ran out of wood and began to close.

Up until the late 1800's how people disposed of garbage and sewage was considered to be their own affair. Private contractors emptied privies and cesspools. The city of St. Louis sold all of its garbage to a hog farmer in Illinois. St. Paul paid a private contractor to collect garbage and dump it into the river. As the cities grew, it became obvious that a better system was needed and so-called "sanitary sewers" were constructed. There was little that was sanitary about them. By 1884 a network of pipes carried raw sewage directly from homes in the Twin Cities and poured it, untreated, into the waters of the Mississippi.

The river provided a cheap and easy way to get rid of sewage. What went downstream became someone else's problem. As the toxic mass floated down river it not only disappeared from sight, it vanished from the arena of public concern. The cities of Minneapolis and St. Paul were not the only offenders. By 1900 every city and town along the Upper Mississippi had constructed sewers to dump their untreated waste into the river. In the absence of uniform regulation for the region, no city was willing to construct expensive sewage treatment facilities for the benefit of some other town downstream. Residents of the Upper Mississippi now accepted sewage disposal as the principal use for the Mississippi River.

Few people at the time thought there was anything wrong with dumping sewage into rivers. A textbook on "Sewerage" written in 1904 by M.I.T. professor A. Prescott Folwell lamented that "the simplest solution of the problem and the one most frequently employed in this country is to discharge the sewage directly into some flowing stream." He reported that, when inspected in 1907–08, all 35 of the existing sewage treatment plants in the State of Ohio were not in an operating condition. His conclusion that, in the public's view, "the duties of caretaker at a sewage-treatment plant are rather unimportant," was quoted in an Iowa publication on water pollution control.

The 1916 "Report of the Sewerage Commission to the City Council and Mayor, City of Davenport" stated, "There are, of course, aesthetic arguments against turning even small amounts of untreated domestic sewage into streams from which food and water supplies are derived . . . However, the aesthetic side of the question should not be allowed to outweigh the large, practical and financial advantages, which are of very much greater importance in a solution of the Davenport sewage problem." The writer stated that "there is no question but that [dumping raw sewage] in the Mississippi River offers a safe, satisfactory and the most economical solution to all nuisances. It seems unnecessary to provide for treatment at this time." In Dubuque a man put some willow poles in the riverbed in front of a sixteen-foot wide sewer pipe that emptied offal from a packing plant into the river. Every few days he pulled the poles out of the river, stripped off the accumulated grease and sold it. Miles downstream from the packing plant a fish line pulled from the river was greasy, said William Meissner and Robert Wiederaenders of Dubuque.

It took the building of a dam and the subsequent backup of sewage into the residential area of Minneapolis to bring about a change in attitude. Dam building was caught up in the rivalry between St. Paul and Minneapolis and reflected how each city used the river. The Mississippi River drops more than one hundred feet—the height of a ten-story building—between the falls of St. Anthony and downtown St. Paul.

The river's narrow gorge and massive boulders left by the upstream movement of the falls made the river at this point extremely treacherous and few boats ever attempted to go upriver beyond St. Paul. This quirk of geography gave St. Paul the opportunity to become the port, at the head of navigation, while Minneapolis got the waterpower to become a lumber-milling and later flour milling center.

THE RISE AND FALL OF THE MEEKER DAM

This division of commercial roles between the two cities rankled the aggressive businessmen of Minneapolis who saw an opportunity, by building dams, to replace St. Paul as the head of navigation on the Mississippi. The Corps Chief of Engineers Major Mackenzie looked into the matter and agreed that two locks and dams would be sufficient to lift boats over the Falls of St. Anthony, permitting them to steam upriver as far as the Washington Avenue bridge in Minneapolis. Opinion was divided over the project. St. Paul, where 63 steamboats and 180 barges docked at its levees in 1866, was unwilling to relinquish its position as the head of navigation on the Mississippi. The Corps left the decision of where to place the dams up to officials at Minneapolis and St. Paul. Predictably the officials of the two cities debated the issue for years without reaching an agreement.

Impatient after almost two decades of wrangling by the two cities, Congress turned the project over to the Corps of Engineers which, on August 18, 1894, approved the construction of Lock and Dam Number 2 near Meeker Island. Calling this dam "Number 2" indicated that a "Dam Number 1" would also be built as dams were numbered in order, from north to south going downstream. As construction began on the Meeker Island Dam, civic officials of Minneapolis and St. Paul resumed their negotiations over where to put Dam Number 1.

On March 3, 1899, Congress formally authorized the construction of Dam Number 1. Officials of both cities had agreed on a site for the dam, locating it just above the outlet of Minnehaha Creek. After numerous construction delays engineers completed the Meeker Island Dam, with a lift of 13.8 feet, in 1907 and the first steamboat, the *Itura*, passed through its locks. High water and other problems delayed the starting of construction on Dam Number 1 giving officials in both cities time to reconsider the projects. While two dams, each with a lift of a little over thirteen feet, would bring barge traffic into the heart of Minneapolis, the dams would be too low to provide hydroelectric power. At the time the dams were planned that suited Minneapolis just fine. The industrialists of the city intended to maintain their exclusive control over the power source of the falls. They were not promoting the dams to create and share power, especially not with St. Paul.

As Minneapolis civic leaders watched the Meeker dam being constructed (and Meeker Island demolished) and construction begin on Dam Number 1 they began to have second thoughts. It was possible that they had made a mistake. In the technological world that was emerging it was more important to have a reliable source of hydroelectric power than it was to move boats a few miles further upriver. The impressive Niagara Falls hydroelectric plant had opened in 1894 and demonstrated that electric power generated by falling water could travel on wires over long distances.

The two dams under construction at the falls were too low to produce power. Even though the Meeker Island Dam had been completed and Dam Number 1 was twenty percent built, officials in the Twin Cities began to lobby Congress for a change in plans. Build us, they said, one power-generating high dam instead of the two lower ones. Minneapolis industrialists agreed to forgo, for the time being, their dream of replacing St. Paul as the head of navigation. In a rare sign of unity, the two cities agreed to split the cost of raising dam Number 1 thirty feet higher. Minneapolis even offered to advance St. Paul its share in the project.

Because President Theodore Roosevelt favored waterpower, Congressional approvals of the change came quickly. By 1910 the Corps was busy building up Dam Number 1 from thirteen and a half feet to the required thirty feet. Because the water backing-up behind the dam would submerge the five-year-old Meeker Dam the Corps demolished the top five feet of Number 2 to give a ten-foot clearance to boats passing over it. Engineers completed Lock and Dam Number 1 in 1917. Though its official name is Lock and Dam Number 1, it became known as the Twin City Lock and Dam and later as the Ford Dam.

All but one of the sewers in Minneapolis and eleven sewers in the St. Paul system flowed into the five-mile long pool created by the Twin City Lock and Dam. For the first seven years of the dam's operation, the Corps opened the gates in the winter and flushed out the accumulated sewage sludge. Then, in 1924, St. Paul acquired the Ford assembly plant and the Corps contracted to supply electric power from the dam to the plant. To do that, the dam gates had to remain closed year-round.

No longer could the accumulated sewage be flushed downstream every winter. Before many months had passed, scum formed on the water. Gases generated in sludge deposits rose to the surface in giant bubbles that burst, releasing noxious odors. On a hot day no one wanted to go near that section of the river. Minneapolis and St. Paul did not smell like the clean Twin Cities any longer. The pollution of the river suddenly became a public problem.

The situation was far more disastrous than just the pool behind The Twin City Lock and Dam. The entire seventy-five mile section of the Mississippi River below the Twin Cities had become a mammoth sewer. Although Minneapolis and St. Paul had agreed to build a sewage treatment plant they were still looking for ways to pay for it. In May of 1931, Minnesota Representative W. I. Nolan suggested that the War Department help pay for the Twin Cities waste treatment plant on the grounds that the government's new dams made it impossible for the river to carry away the sewage. The Corps' Chief of Engineers quickly rejected that idea. "The cities are the cause of their own trouble," he declared, "and the United States can do anything on the bed of the river that it wants to do for navigation. No other authority than the Almighty having anything to say." God was continually being brought into the discussion.

Pollution came from many sources besides industrial wastes and sewage. Industries dumped oil from shore-based plants into the water, killing fish. The 1924 Oil Pollution Act prohibited only the dumping of oil from boats and said nothing about other offenders. The official policy of the Corps of Engineers, as expressed by Chief of Engineers Harry Taylor, was that pollution of the river was not a problem so long as "the pollution of waters by domestic sewage and industrial wastes does not directly interfere with commerce or commercial navigation." To the Corps and most members of the business community, the river's only value and use was as a canal for shipping and a conduit for sewage. Shipping interests had crowned "commerce" king of the river. No one asked whose river it was or whether any other group, such as outdoorsmen and fishermen, or other species, such as fish, mussels and birds, had any claim on the Upper Mississippi.

Those using the river for the dumping of sewage and for commercial navigation may not have been affected by the pollution, but the sensibilities of residents of Minnesota and Wisconsin were. The legislatures of the two states formed a joint committee to study the problem. The report submitted to the two legislatures presented evidence that sewage from the Twin Cities could be found more than fifty miles downriver. There were no longer any fish in the Mississippi River from below the Twin Cities to the mouth of the St. Croix and the water of the Mississippi was foul for five miles upstream of the dam. It was obvious that until the Twin Cities cleaned up its section of the river—stopped dumping raw sewage and industrial wastes into the water—no downriver community would pay to build its own treatment facilities.

The Izaak Walton League and the U.S. Bureau of Fisheries joined in lobbying for enabling legislation to build a sewage treatment plant downriver from St. Paul. The smell of the polluted river, which could be detected all the way up to Capitol Hill, convinced legislators in 1933 to pass the enabling act for a combined sewage system for the Twin Cities. When the Pig's Eye plant, located downriver from St. Paul, started treating sewage in 1938 it was the first wastewater treatment facility in any major city along the entire length of the Mississippi. Once the Twin Cities signed the contract for its plant, several smaller cities as far downstream as La Crosse began building treatment facilities of their own.

The treatment of sewage before it was dumped into the river greatly improved the quality of the water. No longer was the river what scientist A.H. Wiebe called a "witches' cauldron stirred by gasses generated in the decomposing organic wastes," a place where the vapors lifted "large masses of rotting solids that broke the surface of the river and then sank back into the murky water." Nevertheless the river was still profoundly polluted. As late as 1964 the Twin Cities were dumping over a billion gallons of waste water daily into the river. These wastes included approximately 190 million gallons from municipal sources and at least twenty million gallons of industrial wastes. At the same time the Minnesota River was delivering about twenty-four million gallons of municipal and industrial wastes daily to the Mississippi River.

Pollution disasters occurred. Two major oil spills on the Minnesota River during the winter of 1962–63 polluted the Minnesota and the Mississippi Rivers for 130 miles downstream. An estimated one million gallons of petroleum from the Richards Oil Company at Savage and 2,500,000 gallons of crude soy bean oil from the Honeymead Plant at Mankato spilled into the river and mixed together to coat the surface of the water from Mankato downstream into Lake Pepin. The oil moved south with the ice breakup in late March, its movement coinciding with the migration northward of tens of thousands of ducks which use the Mississippi flyway.

When oil coats the feathers of birds they become water logged, lose the ability to fly and drown. Oil also breaks down the feathers' capacity to insulate the birds and they freeze to death. And when the birds attempt to clean their feathers of the oil, they ingest toxic substances that cause their death. Immediately after the oil spills rescuers found about 3,000 birds either dead or dying. The oil pollution eventually killed approximately 10,000 water birds.

Though the need to treat raw sewage before it was dumped into the river was apparent to officials of the larger cities, the public attitude toward the Mississippi changed little. Citizens who had once been enthralled by the river were now, at best, indifferent. If people considered the river at all, they thought of it as a geographic liability, a barrier to be overcome, crossed over, bypassed, ignored—a nuisance useful only to carry off waste that would flow out of sight and become someone else's problem. Some remarked ruefully that they were glad they lived as far upstream as they did. To commercial interests the river was an imperfect conduit for commerce, a resource that had to be continually "improved," its bottom dredged, its channels straightened, its islands removed, its sloughs cut off and drained, its banks heaped with rock, the trees on its shores cut down. Its human stewards had betrayed the Mississippi River.

NOTES

The lines from Stephen Vincent Benét's "Ode to Walt Whitman" (1935) are found in his *Selected Works* (1942). "A River Dreamed" was the title of an unpublished paper by John O. Anfinson, presented at "The River of Dreams: Humanities and the Upper Mississippi River" conference held at the University of St. Thomas, September 24–26, 1998. Anfinson's book, *The River We Have Wrought* was published in 2003. On Henry Bosse, see John O. Anfinson, "Henry Bosse's Priceless Photographs and the Mississippi's Passage into the Age of Industry," and William Roba, "Who was the Mysterious Henry Bosse?" both in *Ramsey County History* 27: 4 (Winter 1992–1993) and *Views of the Mississippi—the Photographs of Henry Peter Bosse* (2001) by Mark Neuzil.

On the Ojibwe and the headwaters dams, see Jane Lamm Carroll, "Dams and Damages: The Ojibway, the United States and the Mississippi Headwaters Reservoirs," *Minnesota History* 52: 1 (Spring 1990).

Other sources for this chapter include Philip V. Scarpino, *Great River: An Environmental History of the Upper Mississippi 1890–1950* (1985) and Raymond H. Merritt, *Creativity, Conflict and Controversy: A History of the St. Paul District U. S. Army Corps of Engineers* (1979). On Meeker Island Dam and other such structures see John O. Anfinson, "The Secret History of the Mississippi's Earliest Locks and

Dams," *Minnesota History* 54: 6 (Summer 1995). "Iowa's Heritage in Water Pollution Control" was published by Iowa State University in 1974. Interviews with William Meissner and Robert Weideraenders took place in Dubuque (May 2002). On the Minnesota River oil spills, see Stephen J. Lee, "Operation Save a Duck and the Legacy of Minnesota's 1962–1963 Oil Spills," *Minnesota History* 58: 2 (Summer 2002).

CHAPTER 17

The Mussels

The belief that the Mississippi River contained little of value changed dramatically for a few years when one man, an immigrant from Germany, moved to Muscatine, Iowa. John Boepple had been a button-maker in Germany, making buttons from ocean mother-of-pearl shell, when a high protective tariff put him out of business. Boepple was working as a farm laborer in Iowa when he chanced to see a mussel shell from the Mississippi. The Mississippi mussel shell, he realized, would make buttons every bit as fine as those he had carved from ocean shell.

Boepple convinced backers in Muscatine to lend him money to open a button factory. By January 1891, Boepple was in business making pearl buttons. Within a short time he had two hundred workers busily making buttons and the local business community in Muscatine took notice. Boepple's exploit focused attention back on the forgotten river. Perhaps it could be put to some use after all. Here was a foreigner, speaking heavily accented English ("Mein buddons vill make you all rich") making money from what Americans thought were only worthless clams.

For centuries Native Americans had used large quantities of fresh-water mussels for food and had prized the occasional pearl found in the shells. (Although the terms clam and mussel are often used by authors interchangably, only mussels produce pearls.) Hundreds of pearls have been found in Indian burial mounds in Ohio and the French explorers reported seeing Indians wearing necklaces of pearls. In 1857 a shoe-maker near Patterson, New Jersey, gathered some mussels for his dinner from a stream called Notch Creek and, while eating, bit down on a large pearl. A local jeweler told him that, if he had not boiled and bitten the pearl, it would have been worth hundreds of dollars. That started a treasure hunt. When it ended, local people had found $115,000 worth of pearls and every mussel in Notch Creek had been dug up and opened.

Pearl hunting spread to other rivers, including the Upper Mississippi where, by 1891, mussel gatherers had found about $300,000 in pearls. Pearl hunters waded into the river and felt with their bare feet for the mussels which they cut open, inspected for pearls, and discarded—a process that destroyed millions of mussels. At one time twenty-seven pearl buyers from India, France, England and the United States were registered at the Prairie du Chien hotel. When pearl hunting fever combined with the gathering of mussels for buttons the fate of the humble river creatures was as irrevocably sealed as had been that of the white pines of the north.

Button-making became a booming business. Boepple's Muscatine factory was an immediate success and people went to extraordinary lengths to learn his manufacturing techniques. Competitors tried to find out which chemicals he used to polish his buttons. The secretive Boepple, who purchased his supplies at the local Muscatine drug store, bought an assortment of chemicals—ammonia, silver nitrate, muriatic and sulfuric acids—to throw people off the track. To protect himself from any competitors who might break into his plant Boepple often sat in his factory at night with his dog and a gun. With more and more workers employed in Boepple's plant it was impossible to keep the process of button-making a secret. By 1897 eleven button factories operated in Muscatine, employing 1,500 people. A year later there were forty-nine factories in thirteen cities on the Upper Mississippi and a dozen more along tributary rivers. By 1912 the number of factories had grown to two hundred. Thousands of grosses of buttons were sold to underwear mills to fasten long johns to shirts. Factories shipped one or two freight cars full of buttons to New York every week.

In 1903 a designer invented automated machines that could make buttons five times faster than could be done by hand. Boepple did not approve of the quality of the buttons made by the machines and refused to use them. Annoyed with the eccentric old German, his business partners forced him out of the business leaving him with nothing from the industry he had founded. In the fall of 1911, while on a mussel-collecting trip for the Fairport Biological Station, Boepple cut his foot on a mussel shell, developed blood poisoning and died from complications.

Mussel shell was free for the taking from the Mississippi River and at first the mussels were plentiful. One tiny section of the river, an area only one and a half miles long and three hundred yards wide, yielded ten thousand tons of shells—about a hundred million mussels. A shell buyer at LeClaire, Iowa, had a contract to ship one thousand tons of shells to New York. When clammers exhausted the mussels in one location, they moved on to another. Lake Pepin had what were believed to be inexhaustible beds of mussels. In 1914 eight million pounds of shells came from Lake Pepin. Whole families camped out on the river all summer long clamming and buyers came in boats to buy their catch. A family would have from ten to forty tons of shells in a pile. The buyer had to figure out how many of the shells were suitable for buttons. Shell buying became a skilled sub-specialty of the button business.

A good fisherman could gather a ton of shells in a day. The freshwater pearls were even legal tender for drinks in the bars of Winona. One pearl found at Winona weighed 19 grams. A St. Paul pearl agent bought it the next day. Winona had two button cutting factories near the foot of Johnson Street cutting buttons from the mussels dredged out of Straight Slough. At Muscatine people crowded the riverbank where pearls had been found, watching the mussel fishermen. Enterprising clammers sold boatloads of clams, unopened, to people on the beach who were willing to bet that one of the mussels they bought contained a pearl. The town of Prairie du Chien supported two large button factories and several smaller ones. Thousands dug for clams. One clam-digger, a member of the Cardin family, found a perfect 54-grain pearl in 1901 that he sold for $2,000, enough to build the family home.

A protective United States tariff, passed in 1890 on overseas imports, helped support the Mississippi River button industry. Orders poured in. The introduction of automated machinery shot the production of buttons up from 11.4 million gross in 1904 to 21.7 million gross in 1914. Production reached 40 million gross in 1916. By the late 1890's the button industry had taken the place of the timber industry as the most important business in Mississippi River towns—employing at its peak twenty thousand people.

In the spring of 1897 a new device for capturing mussels called a crowfoot appeared. The crowfoot was an iron bar from which dangled an assortment of four-part hooks. Mussels in the river orient themselves facing upstream with their siphons open allowing the free circulation of water from which they receive food and oxygen. If a mussel is touched, it instantly snaps shut and holds fast to anything between its valves. The crowfoot took advantage of this behavior of mussels. Mussel fishermen lowered the crowfoot bars into the water, dragging the hooks along the bottom as the boat floated downstream. When they pulled the crowfoot up, it would be covered with mussels holding tightly to the hooks.

Clam boats were flat scows with a dredge that could be raised or lowered from each side. Rows of crowfoot hooks hung from the bars on the dredge. The dredges moved back and forth over the mussel beds, eventually removing all of the clams. Clammers brought the clams to shore and cooked them in washtubs over open fires on the beaches. It was a smelly, repellent process. By 1914 the crowfoot accounted for 90 percent of the mussels taken from the Mississippi.

Dallas Valley, of Prairie du Chien, is the third generation of Valleys to have earned his living from the river. He fished the Mississippi, full time, for forty-five years, using home-made gill nets for winter ice fishing. Dallas's great-grandfather came from French Canada to work on the railroad but soon turned to hunting, fishing and clamming on the Mississippi—as did his descendants for the next four generations. From the time he was twelve-years-old Dallas Valley helped his family collect mussels, camping all summer with his father and uncle on an island in the river. "The camp was right in front of the clam bed," Dallas remembers. "We would have to row up to the front of it [the clam bed] and drift down. We used a 14-foot bar with crowfoot hooks—pulled the bars up by hand. Then in the afternoon my uncle would go out and clam and I would stay in camp and cook out the ones from the morning. We camped all three months there, every summer. I did that all during high school."

Clam boats showing the crowfoot hooks hanging ready to trap mussels. Real photo postcard, circa 1900, courtesy of Gregory Page.

The Valleys cooked their clams in a massive homemade tank, dumped the boiled clams on a table and opened every one. The meat fell out and they packed it in barrels for fish bait. "We salted it down, put salt in the bottom of the barrel—a layer of clam meats, layer of salt, all the way up. Put a piece of burlap over the top." Dallas' uncle was typical of the men who made their living by clamming. At the end of the season in the fall he rowed his wooden boat down the river from Prairie du Chien to Muscatine, worked in the button factory during the winter, and in the spring rowed back to Prairie du Chien to resume clamming on the island.

At the height of his clamming activity, Dallas Valley built his own clam boat equipped with three twenty-foot bars, from which dangled the crowfoot hooks. Two bars at a time were lowered into the water. "Two bars full of shells were pretty heavy," he explained. "There were hundreds of hooks on there, just as many hooks as we could fit on the bar. Then we would sit there and pick the shells off and after we got the shells off this bar we would drop it down and pull the other bar up from the back. It would be solid full of clams. We would keep switching and run two bars all the time—all day. It was about ten to fifteen minutes between bars. In six hours you could get a lot of shells. My wife, Nancy,

Clam fishermen cooked their haul, then packed the meat for fishbait, while hoping to find pearls in the mussels. Photograph, circa 1904, courtesy of the Minnesota Historical Society.

found a lot of beautiful pearls. We found a lot more pearls in later years because we did such a volume. We did not open all the shells, just the deformed clams. Years ago we looked in all of them. A woman from Stockholm paid pretty good for pearls. You got as much as $2,000 for a pearl. You would get them as big as a marble and you could see yourself in them. "

Wisconsin state regulations at first permitted the taking of shells smaller than four inches but then raised the minimum to four inches. Dallas is in favor of the law. "It was probably a good idea they changed it because we were taking so many clams," he said. "People were coming up from Tennessee and Alabama, bringing their own equipment, and picking every clam off the bottom. One day we were getting a lot of clams on our bars and the next day there were seventy-five divers there. They were so desperate for shells they would dive down right in front of our clam bars and hooks. You'd have to pull up the bar or you would maybe hook them and drown them. They would do anything to get you out of the area where there were some clams."

As the large shells were depleted and before regulations went into effect, mussel fisherman took more and more of the smaller shells to earn the same amount of money. Scarcity drove up the price to $35 a ton, and clammers dredged up every shell, no matter how small. The crowfoot allowed clammers to dredge in deeper waters, destroying areas that might have served to repopulate the depleted mussel beds. In 1898 three species of mussels accounted for more than 99 percent of the shells used to make buttons. Over the next several decades, as shells became scarce, the number of species expanded from three to seventeen.

Aware that a scarcity of mussels could doom the industry, the National Association of Button Manufacturers turned to the federal Bureau of Fisheries and its program of artificial propagation of mussels to be the savior of its business. While the Bureau did research on mussel propagation, the Association lobbied Washington for congressional appropriations to support the Bureau's work. This dependent relationship resulted in a schizophrenic attitude on the part of the Bureau.

Since its mussel conservation activities depended on the pearl button industry's lobbying for financial appropriations, the Bureau had to somehow both encourage mussel fishing while, at the same time, advocate regulation without which the mussels soon would be totally depleted. By 1919 the Bureau had recognized the crowfoot as an infernal device. Nevertheless, an article published that year in the Bureau of

Fisheries bulletin explained exactly how to make a crowfoot, discussed its effectiveness in capturing mussels and then recommended against using it. Twelve years later the Bureau had still not suggested that the crowfoot be declared illegal.

Mussels grow slowly. A mussel takes twenty-five years to develop a four-inch shell and more than a dozen years to reach a minimum size of three inches. The females discharge huge quantities of larvae, called *glochidia,* into the water. Another animal must then adopt the mussel larvae or they will die. After passing through a parasitic phase in which the larvae attach themselves to the gill filaments of certain species of fish, they abandon their hosts, fall to the river bottom, attach themselves to a small pebble and begin to grow. If not buried in silt or poisoned by pollutants in the water, in twenty to twenty-five years the mussels will grow to a commercial size.

The Bureau of Fisheries tried to save the button industry. There were two possible approaches. One was regulatory—by prohibiting the gathering of small shells, restricting how clammers collected them, and establishing license fees and temporarily closing segments of the river to mussel collecting. This route was a political minefield. The second method was to figure out how to propagate the mussels artificially.

The Bureau chose the second, politically safer, route. The fish scientists began by injecting fish with the mussel glochidia and releasing them into the river. This process stocked the water, every year, with one billion glochidia riding on the gills of host fish. It was an elegant solution reflecting nineteenth century attitudes toward nature —which were *propagation* rather than *preservation.* The scientists' efforts failed to produce very many mussels. Then a fish scientist named M. M. Ellis figured out how to stimulate the glochidia to undergo metamorphosis without first riding around on a host fish. Mussels, he believed, could be grown like a farm crop and planted in suitable locations. A memorandum published by the Bureau boasted that "the prodigal waste of nature's seeding could now be avoided, since 'absolute control' of supply had been placed in the hands of fisheries scientists."

Alas, it was not to be that simple. Mussels seeded in the river died. The Bureau commissioned a study that found that for forty-five miles below the Twin Cities the river was seriously polluted. The director of the New York Aquarium pointed out the obvious. "Though we can hatch the fish and place them in the water,"he wrote, "if the water is polluted all the fish culturists in Christendom cannot make it productive."

Besides pollutants, the river was full of silt. The deforestation of the land and poor agricultural practices by farmers led to thousands of tons of silt washing into the river. Sewage, combined with fine silt, flowed further downstream than it would have in clean water. Wing dams caused the current to slow down and pool behind the dams, permitting the sewage-laden silt to settle to the bottom where it decayed and removed oxygen from the water.

While it worked at mussel propagation the Bureau of Fisheries also lobbied the four states involved to regulate mussel collection. By 1919 the Bureau had convinced the states to pass statutes setting size limits on shells, establishing license fees, and to occasionally closing the river to clamming. It was a temporary victory. In the late 1920's the attempt to reproduce mussels in the Upper Mississippi ended. At a conference in Washington, D.C. the Bureau announced that it had ended its efforts at propagation and urged the states that had passed mussel protection laws (Minnesota, Iowa, Wisconsin and Illinois) to rescind them so that the industry could collect the remaining mussels in the river before all were buried by the silt or killed by pollution.

The market for Mississippi River clamshells received a slight boost in the late 1960's as a result of an earlier discovery by Kokichi Mikimoto of Japan. He found that beads from freshwater mussel shells produce the best nucleus for cultured pearls. A demand developed in Japan for high quality Mississippi River shells that could be processed into tiny spheres and implanted into oysters to serve as nuclei for cultured pearls. Like his father Dallas and uncle before him, Mike Valley worked the clam beds full time to supply the Japanese market, often diving with a basket around his neck to hold the clams.

According to Mike, a major die-out of clams took place in the river around Prairie du Chien in the mid-1980's. He is convinced there was a chemical spill up river. "It killed off 70% of the clams in about three months. There were clam meats floating everywhere," he recalls. The Japanese buyers, who would previously purchase only shell from live clams, were now forced by the shortage of shell to accept dead ones. This was a bonanza for shellers like Mike. "We took the dead ones, all full of moss and mud and brought them home. I would clean them up with toilet bowl cleaner or muriatic acid. They washed up just beautiful—like they were fresh dead."

While live clams had grown scarce, the river bottom was covered with dead clams, in some places to a depth of two feet. Mike said he could sit in one spot on the bottom of the river, never move and fill a fifty-five-gallon barrel with dead clams. The DNR of Wisconsin prohibited the taking out of any clam under four inches long—dead or alive. "We had little measuring boards of plastic with metal rings with a hole through it and we had to measure every single clam," Mike says. "If one of them clams could be pushed through that hole, we were going to get a $450 fine. I have no idea why they cared about dead clams. They spent hours and an ungodly amount of money chasing people down to arrest them for a dead clam that today is covered up by two feet of zebra mussels."

The Japanese market for dead clams ended as quickly as it began. According to Mike, a residue of acid on the tiny beads cut from the shells killed the oysters in which they were embedded. "That went on for about a year before they discovered it," Mike reported. The final blow to the men who earned a living from Mississippi River clams was the invasion, in the 1990's, of the zebra mussels.

The freshwater ballast of ocean-going ships carried the larvae of the European zebra mussel into the St. Lawrence-Great Lakes drainage system in 1985 or 1986. The larvae then drifted downstream from Lake Michigan 300 miles through canals into the Illinois River and from there into the Mississippi. It was a link nature never intended. Nineteenth century Chicagoans had engineered the Chicago River to flow backward, away from Lake Michigan, to carry pollution away from their beaches and into a canal that emptied into the Illinois River, a tributary of the Mississippi.

Fishermen found the first zebra mussel in the Upper Mississippi on September 12, 1991. Zebra mussels eat plankton, taking nutrients from the river and leaving behind clear water but nothing for the fish and other mussel larvae to feed on. (Lake Erie, infested with zebra mussels, now has clear water in it and little else.) The bottom of the river at Prairie du Chien is now solidly covered with zebra mussels, in some places to a depth of a foot and a half. It is not uncommon to find 300 to 500 zebra mussels attached to the shell of one native mussel. One washboard mussel, only 3.5 inches in diameter, had approximately 1,000 zebra mussels attached to its shell.

Mike recently took his clam boat down to what had once been the biggest clam bed in that whole area of the Mississippi. "This was the number one bed, where you could drag and always get a boat full of clams," he said. "Now you cannot get one." Mike no longer dives for clams. Because of the zebra mussels a diver now cannot tell if he has "a rock or a clam or a boat anchor in his hand. Everything is encrusted with the zebra mussels." While it took more than a century to capture all of the beaver and forty years to cut all of the white pine, clammers removed the billions of mussels in the river in less than twenty-five years. Another era on the river had ended.

NOTES

References include John Madson, *Up the River* (1985); Philip V. Scarpino, *Great River: An Environmental History of the Upper Mississippi, 1890–1950* (1985); and Dan Kelner, "Mussel Bound in Minnesota," *Minnesota Conservation Volunteer* (July-August 2000). Also, interviews with Dallas and Mike Valley (April 2002).

CHAPTER 18

The Nine-Foot Channel

Two developments far from the Upper Mississippi rekindled interest in the river. The first was the digging of the Panama Canal in Central America. When the canal was completed in 1914 shippers on the East Coast discovered they could ship merchandise to the West Coast cheaper than Midwesterners could ship goods to either coast by railroad. This came as a major shock to farmers in the Midwest whose principal access to world markets was via the railroad. A periodic shortage of railroad cars added to their problems.

The second development was a decision in 1922 by the Interstate Commerce Commission that resulted in a hundred percent increase in railroad shipping rates for Midwest farmers. The Commission ruled in 1909 that rail rates had to be kept lower along the Mississippi River because of competition from boats carrying cargo on the river. Now there were no longer any boats carrying cargo down the river. With the end of commercial shipping on the river, competition with the railroads had ended. The railroad victory was complete.

The new ICC ruling acknowledged that fact when it stated that "Water competition on the Mississippi River north of St. Louis is no longer recognized as a controlling force . . ." and allowed the railroads to raise their rates. The ruling by the ICC recognized that, except for sporadic short hauls, shipping on the river had ended. No commercial boats came down the river as far as St. Louis, let alone as far as the mouth of the river at New Orleans. The Upper Midwest was landlocked—shut off from water-based access to markets. Despite the Corps' success in creating a six-foot channel in the Mississippi, shipping had continued to decline. The railroads and not the river were carrying the grain that was shipped to market.

Twin Cities business interests were shocked by the ICC ruling and decided to put up a fight. It was clear that traffic on the Mississippi River, in the past, had played a critical role in setting railroad freight rates. If a pretense of barge traffic on the river could be considered as competition to the railroads, they would create it. As a first step a group of Minneapolis businessmen organized the Upper Mississippi Barge Line Company in 1925 and negotiated an advantageous deal with the Inland Waterway Corporation, a creation of Congress. The Upper Mississippi Barge Line Company sold stock and with the money built two sternwheeler towboats and eleven barges that they rented to the Inland Waterway Corporation for an annual payment of five percent of the fleet's construction costs. The Company also negotiated an agreement with the IWC to buy all the equipment of the barge line two years after the signing of the initial contract.

The return of barges to the river prompted jubilant headlines in the Twin Cities newspapers. "River Traffic Reopens as Barges Dock Here," cheered the *St. Paul Pioneer Press* on August 25, 1927. The writer of an editorial in the *Minneapolis Journal* on the same date was more forthright in observing that it was the higher railroad freight rates that had prompted the return of barge service to the Mississippi. "It is navigate or be at the mercy of the railroads and an unsympathetic Interstate Commerce Commission," the editor wrote. "[Barge service] means, in time, the wiping out of those rate discriminations endured by the Twin Cities in the years since the powers that rule the rails decreed that water competition, to influence freight car rates, must be actual and not theoretical."

Less than a year after the first barges of the Upper Mississippi Barge Line Company went down the river on their maiden voyages the officers of the company called on the Inland Waterway Corporation to honor its promise to buy them out. When the deal was completed, the IWC owned the towboats and barges and the Minneapolis businessmen had a profit of $95,000.

Five days after the sale the businessmen met at the Minneapolis Club where they resolved to invest their $95,000 kitty in a new project. This would be a campaign to pressure Congress and the Corps of Engineers to agree to a nine-foot low-water channel from St. Paul to St. Louis. The businessmen realized that the six-foot channel was still too shallow for barges to be able to compete with the railroads. As they toasted their new project, they congratulated themselves for having restored traffic on the Upper Mississippi River. Now they would promote a project to transform the river itself. With their help the Mississippi, after several false starts, would at last achieve its true destiny.

Twin Cities industry joined in the lobbying effort. Manufacturers of farm equipment, grain shippers and almost every business, large and small, in the Upper Mississippi valley signed on to support the campaign for the nine-foot channel. The Minneapolis Real Estate Board brought speakers to the Twin Cities to organize popular support for the deeper channel. Agricultural organizations contributed money for lobbying.

With the country sinking into the Great Depression, President Herbert Hoover was, at first, reluctant to back the expensive project, as was the House Rivers and Harbors Committee. Undaunted, boosters turned to the Senate Commerce Committee. The *St. Paul Pioneer Press* editorial writer lamented that," this region is like a giant, tied just beyond reach of a nobler destiny, straining at his chains. We are landlocked, a marooned interior, shut in by the barriers of costly overland carriage, to and from the common highway to the world's markets, the sea." (*St. Paul Pioneer Press*, May 12, 1928.)

MAJOR CHARLES HALL
AND THE CORPS' OPPOSITION

Though support for the nine-foot channel was broadly based, not everyone favored the idea. The project's ardent supporters, who asserted that the nine-foot channel reflected nothing less than the Divine Will for the river, were outraged when Major Charles L. Hall, the Corps District Engineer at Rock Island, who had been assigned the task of examining the feasibility of a nine-foot channel on the Upper Mississippi, reported that the maximum savings of a nine-foot channel were "entirely insufficient to repay the minimum cost of the proposed improvement." Hall, a West Point graduate, knew that the only feasible way to provide a nine-foot channel was through a series of locks and dams that would transform the river from a free-flowing stream into a series of interconnected lakes. Hall's report reflected the skepticism of many in the Corps of Engineers who had seen river traffic continue to decline even after the channel was deepened.

In a speech before the School of Wildlife at McGregor, Iowa, Hall pointed out that the proposed dams would complicate sewage disposal, drastically change the flora and fauna of the river and lead to the extinction of some species of fish and wildlife. "It is certainly impossible to determine by engineering means whether certain advantages to water-borne commerce justify a partial destruction of existing wild-life," he said. "The public can, however, properly demand that the biological effects of a proposed movement be stated before it is adopted."

The editorial writer for the *Minneapolis Journal* could not contain his indignation. He questioned "why Major Hall should worry about flora and fauna at all. His duties are neither floral nor faunal but engineering." Hall's opposition to the project brought forth a torrent of protests to the War Department and Congress from the Midwest boosters of navigation. Shortly after Hall expressed his views at the McGregor School of Wildlife, the Corps transferred him from his position.

Hall was not the only member of the Corps opposing the policy. The Corps' Chief of Engineers, Major General Harry Taylor, under pressure from a House Committee before which he was testifying, refused to state that the new dams would increase the freight traffic on the river. Taylor's successor, Major General Edwin Jadwin, also opposed the project. He shared Hall's environmental concerns and worried about flood control problems.

Jadwin also believed that the Corps projects should not be the product of special interest politics—no matter how powerful the players. The Corps recommended delaying approval of the project until the final survey report and project plan could be completed. Many Corps engineers staunchly opposed authorizing the project until the report could be finished. It was unheard of for waterway projects to be approved by Congress before the report and plan had been completed. For Jadwin, the professionalism of the Corps was at stake.

President Herbert Hoover, an engineer himself, had initially opposed the project—not because he was against dams (he wasn't), but because of the timing. With the country sliding into a depression Hoover was reluctant to commit to a project that would cost almost a hundred million dollars. Supporters urged Hoover to merely approve the authorization of the project. Funding could come later. Gradually Hoover shifted his position. The Army Corps of Engineers replaced Jadwin as Chief Engineer and passed over ten senior officers to name Major General Lytle Brown, who wholeheartedly supported the nine-foot channel project, to the post. Boosters feared the nine-foot channel cause was lost when the House of Representatives failed to put it into the Rivers and Harbors Act. The supporters argued that Congress should have included the nine-foot channel in the Panama Canal project and that the Midwest had "patiently suffered ever since."

In a last ditch effort, lobbyists for Minneapolis business interests succeeded in getting the measure included in the Senate version of the Rivers and Harbors Act. In the resulting conference committee the House was persuaded to add the project to the bill and on July 3, 1930, President Hoover signed the legislation authorizing the nine-foot channel. An initial expenditure of $7,500,000 was approved for the project. It would be another year and a half before the Corps completed its final survey report and project plan.

Passage of the bill assured the Upper Mississippi District of the Corps a secure future. On July 25, 1930, a few weeks after passage of the bill, the Corps hosted the Secretaries of War and Commerce and other dignitaries on an inspection trip down the Mississippi River. When they reached Winona they came upon a tow and a number of barges stuck on a sandbar. The Corps' dredge *General Allen* was busy rescuing the boats from the sandbar. The story received widespread media coverage and it was not learned until later that the barges had been deliberately run onto the sandbar the night before. When Winona residents had rushed out to offer assistance they had been told to go home and mind their own business.

The dredge *Bernie Harris* of the Minneapolis Dredging Company, working near Lock and Dam 3 at Red Wing, Minnesota, September 1936. Courtesy of Frank Harris.

In the end the Corps built 23 lock and dam installations. Engineers eliminated Lock and Dam Number 23 and incorporated three existing dams—the dam at the St. Paul Ford plant, the dam at Hastings and one built in 1913, at Keokuk, Iowa—into the project. The dams converted the Upper Mississippi from a free-flowing river environment to a series of twenty-seven pools separated by short sections of river. The pools descend in a staircase of twenty-six steps from St. Paul, reaching 650 miles to nearly the mouth of the Missouri River.

THE SCHOOL OF
WILDLIFE AT MCGREGOR, IOWA

Major Hall should have known he would get into trouble speaking to the School of Wildlife at McGregor, Iowa. The tiny river community had long been the home of ardent conservationists, concerned about the decreasing catches of fish from the Mississippi. The conservation movement had its beginning in 1871 when Congress created the Office of the U.S. Commissioner of Fish and Fisheries. To help restore the river's fish population the Office raised fish in ponds for release into the river. Under pressure from sport fishermen, the states of Minnesota, Wisconsin and Iowa soon established their own fish commissions.

Iowa's first fish commissioner, B.F. Shaw, looked over the sloughs and backwaters of the Mississippi and realized that the government did not need to raise more fish. Hundreds of millions of naturally hatched fingerlings were dying when they became stranded in pools that dried out or froze during the winter. Rather than artificially raise fish, Shaw thought they should rescue the fish that nature was already providing.

So began an amazing fish rescue operation. Shaw persuaded the Iowa legislature to fund rescue crews and in their first two months of operation they saved over one million Mississippi River fish. In the 1880s Missouri and Illinois began rescuing fish and Wisconsin soon followed. Officials of the U.S. Fish Commission began scooping fingerlings from pools in 1889 and continued as the organization evolved into the Bureau of Fisheries and then into the present U.S. Fish and Wildlife Service. Between 1917 and 1923 the federal government operated 34 fish rescue stations on the Upper Mississippi that saved about 150 million fish a year.

The McGregor School began as a Chautauqua, a summer residential school offering programs and lectures. It was the brainchild of two ministers, the Rev. Stephen R. Ferguson, pastor of the Methodist Church, and George Bennett, a retired Episcopal minister. The two men, with the help of the citizens of McGregor, selected a piece of ground on a high bluff, 300 feet above the Mississippi, for their Chautauqua. They called it the McGregor Assembly. The two were joined by the curator of the Iowa Department of History and Archives, Edgar Harlan, and together they organized the American School of Wild Life Protection and Propagation. Members built cottages on the promontory and Dr. George P. Kay, Professor of Geology and Dean of Liberal Arts at Iowa State University, donated his services as dean of the school.

The McGregor School tapped into a deeply felt concern for conservation of the fish and wildlife surrounding the Upper Mississipi River. Over 1000 people attended the first session in 1919. A distinguished faculty served without pay and the community of McGregor raised the money to pay for their food and lodging. Dr. W.T. Hornaday, of the American Museum of Natural History in New York, was a patron and gave a collection of books to start a library. The teachers at the School were among the most renowned academics in the Midwest. Iowa college professors of botany, zoology and ornithology came to lecture. D.W. Morehouse, an astronomer and president of Drake University, taught at McGregor year after year. Willa Cather and Iowa author Ruth Suckow participated and the governor of Iowa presided over some of the sessions.

For 23 years, until the beginning of World War II, crowds came to the McGregor School to learn about the ecology of the river. One of those who came to a Wild Life School session in 1923 was a Chicago advertising man named Will H. Dilg. Dilg was an avid sportsman who had long fished the Mississippi River. The year before he and fifty-three other men had organized the Izaak Walton League to preserve America's wilderness for future generations of sportsmen.

Dilg was the organization's founder and first president and while sitting on a log tending his fishing line on the Upper Mississippi Dilg had an epiphany. He envisioned a Mississippi River Wildlife and Fish Refuge that would extend along the western shore of the river from Winona, Minnesota, 300 miles to Rock Island, Illinois, preserving 194,000 acres of land for wildlife. The friend who was fishing with Dilg said that, as soon as he announced his idea, Dilg reeled in his fishing line and said it was time to get to work.

Dilg took his idea to the former Secretary of War, General Jacob M. Dickenson, who supplied the legal skills and logic to match Dilg's enthusiasm. The two men drafted legislation and gained as a sponsor Rep.

Harry B. Hawes of Missouri. By 1924 membership in Dilg's Izaak Walton League had reached one million. The organization published a glossy, four-color magazine "Outdoor America." At the bottom of every page, in bold print, was the admonition: "Your conscience should not let you rest until you write your congressmen and senators to vote for the League's bill of a 300 mile Upper Mississippi National Preserve." Secretary of Commerce Herbert Hoover supported the bill and in 1924 Congress passed the Dilg and Dickenson legislation.

Though the passage of the bill was a victory for the growing environmental movement, an amendment to the legislation asserted the primacy of navigation on the Mississippi River. It forbid "any interference with the operations of the War Department in carrying out any project now or hereafter adopted for the improvement of said river."The amendment weakened the bill but it was still a triumph. A headline in the June 26, 1924, issue of the *North Iowa Times* exulted that "Izaak Walton League Wins Battle at Last Minute Session of Congress. Government to Purchase 300 Mile Preserve. Lands Now Worthless for Commercial Use." The refuge, the longest in the lower 48 states, would not exist today if it had not been for Will Dilg. He had the idea, helped write the bill and the Izaak Walton League and the McGregor School of Wildlife provided the constituency to get it passed.

The Upper Mississippi Fish and Wildlife Refuge and the McGregor School of Wildlife immediately joined the debate over the proposed dams needed to create the nine-foot channel. The two organizations were not opposed to river navigation, as such, but tried to get agreements written into the legislation that would protect wildlife. The conservationists' principal concern was with "water draw-down."

During the winter the water level on the Mississippi drops because the water in the tributaries is frozen into ice and snow. To compensate for the low water, the Corps tapped water from "feeder lakes" in northern Minnesota. While this raised the water level in the river, it left animals such as beaver and muskrats stranded because they no longer had a water route into their dwellings. The actions also trapped fish in shallow pools that froze in the winter. The Izaak Walton League agreed to support the nine-foot channel only if the Corps agreed to maintain stable water levels in the upriver lakes.

While Congress had authorized the nine-foot channel in 1930, funds to build it were not appropriated until the administration of Franklin Roosevelt. Roosevelt supported the project as a relief measure for workers unemployed during the Great Depression. Roosevelt's goal was to provide jobs. Because of the nation's economic crisis, the most ambitious river improvement project ever undertaken in the United States was recast as a massive public employment project of the New Deal.

Monies appropriated through the National Industrial Recovery Act and the Emergency Relief Act (names that resonate with the shock of the Great Depression) paid for the employment of over 10,000 men in the Rock Island District alone. Officials geared the project toward maximum employment rather than efficiency. In an ironic outcome, the actions of the businessmen who lobbied for the nine-foot channel (most of whom opposed Roosevelt's New Deal policies) ended up persuading the federal government to finance a massive public works project, not to aid Twin Cities businesses or provide leverage to lower railroad freight rates, but as a relief project for thousands of unemployed workers.

The army took two years to plan the locks and dams. The dam at the Ford plant was named Dam Number 1. The dam at Hastings was Number 2. Dam Number 4, at Alma, was the first to be started. As work progressed on Lock Number 6 at Trempealeau, Wisconsin, about fifteen miles downriver from the town of Winona, Minnesota, the engineers realized that water backing up behind the dam would flood Winona. The solution was to add another lock and dam above Winona. Since locks number 5 and 6 were already under construction and the locks had been assigned numbers, the engineers called the lock and dam above Winona, Number 5A.

Postcard view of the Moline Lock. The sender of the card, postmarked in 1909, tells of a trip by boat, car and ferry along the Mississippi River. Courtesy of Gregory Page.

Locks 5 and 6 have a lift of only six feet, the smallest lift of any locks on the Upper Mississippi River. In 1937 Congress authorized a 4.6 mile extension of the original project at its upstream end. The Corps completed the Lower St. Anthony Lock and Dam in 1956 and the Upper St. Anthony Lock and Dam in 1961. Boats could now reach Minneapolis on the river though St. Paul did not relinquish its claim to being the head of navigation on the Mississippi.

The Corps projected that the dams would be built in three years but it was 1938 before all twenty-six were completed. The result, as Raymond Merritt wrote in a history of the Corps of Engineers, was that "by 1940 the Mississippi between St. Louis and Minneapolis was no longer a part of America's greatest free-flowing river. It had been turned into a canal, an engineered stairway with twenty-six locks and dams. Behind each step was a slack-water pool, a man-made lake with a regulated shoreline. The Upper Mississippi canal is a gigantic public works project."

In 1953 the lock and dam system was again expanded. Lock and Dam No. 27 (known as the Chain of Rocks Dam) and the Chain of Rocks canal at St. Louis were built. The nine-foot channel now has 29 lock and dam complexes extending 669 miles with a fall in the river of approximately 400 feet.

Though the channel is nominally nine feet deep, it is maintained at eleven to thirteen feet as a loaded barge draws almost nine feet. The locks are 600 feet long and 110 feet wide. Towboats are allowed to make two lockages at the 600 foot locks, which limits the maximum number of barges a towboat can tow to 15. One barge is 35 feet wide and 200 feet long. A tow three barges wide and five barges long measures 105 feet wide and 1000 feet long, leaving only two and a half feet of clearance on each side of the tow as it slides into a lock. The combined length of the towboat and string of barges is just a tad longer than a Nimitz-class nuclear-powered aircraft carrier.

Before the construction of the nine-foot channel, commercial shipping on the Mississippi had essentially ended. What shipping there was, was local; the movement of materials across the river rather than down it or for short distances. Almost all of the cargo was sand and gravel dredged from the river channel by the Corps of Engineers. Tonnage dropped as low as 692,000 tons in 1926 and only reached one million tons in 1928, the first full year that the federal government operated the barges (purchased from the Upper Mississippi Barge Line Company).

Old steamboat pilots were scornful of the new boats on the river.

Frank Fugina called them "a motley collection of steam and diesel boats . . . with boxcars for cabins and atop of that small matchboxes for pilot-houses." The veteran captains lamented that no one any longer cared to reproduce the graceful lines of the earlier packet boats. Graceful lines and the beauty of the boats were no longer considerations on the river. Tonnage shipped was what counted and year by year it increased.

Total annual shipments reached two million tons in 1936 and three million tons in 1940. During World War II the total annual commerce on the Upper Mississippi hovered between three and five million tons. By 1950 the total was 11 million tons and it continued to grow until it reached more than 84 million tons in 1983. Barges now transport a total of 151 million tons annually on the Upper Mississippi. Grains comprise sixty million tons of the total; 30 million tons is corn, 12 million is soybeans and the rest other grains. The volume of shipping on the Mississippi River far exceeded the claims made by the supporters of the nine-foot channel as tonnage met and then went far beyond their goals.

According to Lee Nelson, president of Upper River Services, ap-proximately 2,500 to 3,000 barges pushed by 250 towboats are on the Upper River at any one time. (The shipping industry defines the Upper River as being the stretch from St. Paul to the mouth of the Ohio River.) The barges carry corn, soybeans, and potash mined in Canada going downriver and return upriver with salt, fertilizer, coal and a form of mo-lasses that is used for animal feed. Sixty percent of the corn raised in Minnesota is destined for export and sixty percent of that moves down the river to oceangoing ships in New Orleans. Most of the great wheat crops of the Dakotas and Minnesota, which once were shipped down the Mississippi, now move out through the port of Duluth. From 1997 to 2002, tonnage shipped out of St. Paul increased about 6% every year.

Barges take from 15 to 20 days to make the trip to New Orleans, traveling between the middle of March and Thanksgiving. The river at St. Louis is open all year-round. The early freezing of Lake Pepin is as frustrating to modern boat captains as it was to the steamboat pilots. The freezing line moves slowly north with about a week separating the freez-ing up of the river at each of the river towns from Davenport to St. Paul. Officials pay close attention to the weather. In 1985 the tempera-ture dropped unexpectedly. Caught unaware, barges and boats were frozen in and forced to spend the winter in the ice.

Nelson points out the economy of river transportation—one barge load is equivalent to what can be carried by 58 semi-trailer trucks or 15 railroad cars. According to his estimates, one gallon of fuel will move one ton of cargo, in a truck, about 54 miles. On the railroad that gallon will move the freight 212 miles. Using one gallon of fuel, a barge will move one ton 514 miles downriver where locks are involved or, below St. Louis where there are no more locks, up to 1200 miles.

Offsetting these savings is the price of maintaining the Mississippi River channel which must be continuously dredged at an annual cost of about $25 million. A 1996 McKnight Foundation report states that taxpayers nationwide "pay more than 85 percent of the cost of the inland navigation system, placing it among the nation's most heavily subsidized modes of transportation, according to Congressional Budget Office figures."

The locks are busy operations. Dave Haskanson, lockmaster at Lock and Dam Number 3 at Red Wing, estimates that 20,000 pleasure boats and 1000 tows go through his locks in a single season. There is often a two-hour wait to go through the lock. Traversing a lock is a simple procedure for recreational boats. Skippers of pleasure boats, when approaching a lock, pull up to a wall on the lock approach and tug on a dangling signal rope. When the signal light turns green, they move into the lock and hold on to ropes spaced along the lock wall. A green light

Steamboat towing coal barges on the Mississippi River at St. Paul, circa 1918. Courtesy of the Minnesota Historical Society.

is the signal to exit. There is no charge for boats, either pleasure or commercial, to go through the locks.

While the locks make barge traffic possible on the upper river, they are also an impediment to traffic. It takes a 15-barge tow two hours to pass through a lock. The tow has to be taken apart and floated through half at a time. Maneuvering a tow into a lock is a complicated process due to the narrow clearance between the tow and each side of the lock. The pilots of the tows utilize the flag on the bow, called the "jackstaff," with a tiny blue light on the top to help them line up their barges to enter a lock.

Nelson, an avid Minnesota Twins baseball fan, while captaining a tow downriver in 1987 had removed the company flag from the jackstaff and tied a Minnesota Twins baseball pennant in its place. He was about to enter the last lock on the river near St. Louis when the lockmaster came on the radio shouting, "You can't come in this lock." Nelson stopped his towboat and started to back up. "What's the matter?" he called on his radio. "You ain't coming in my lock with that damned Twins jackstaff out there," came back the reply. The Twins were, at that moment, playing the St. Louis Cardinals in the World Series.

ENVIRONMENTAL CONSEQUENCES OF THE NINE-FOOT CHANNEL

The natural environment pays a high price for the commercial use of the river. Dredges must continually scrape the bottom to keep ahead of the natural processes that want to fill the big ditch. Once-fertile wetlands are turned into sandbars. Environmentalists claim that the passage of towboats raises a plume of sediments that stretches back for two miles. Sediment falling back smothers bottom-dwelling creatures.

The healthiest river is a self-regulating river that goes dry in late summer and fall and floods in spring. When the river improves the fingernail clams come back, the mayflies return and the waterfowl reappear. Mussels are indicators of river health. The Mississippi has lost 20 out of 50 species of mussels that once lived in it. The dams between St. Paul and St. Louis destroyed most of the wetlands in Iowa, Illinois and southern Minnesota and created massive collection pools for sediment.

The unnaturally high water levels behind the dams are the cause of the decline in plant diversity and the loss of such marsh plants as wild celery and duckweed that migratory birds depend on. The seeds need exposure to air on the river flats to germinate. Those that do manage to sprout have difficulty in taking root in the soft, loose sediment. While there is now more waterfowl habitat, there is less food because the stable high water levels and increased sedimentation make it difficult for the vegetation birds depend on to grow. The deep holes outside the main channels that are needed by bass to survive the winter are disappearing

Dallas Valley, who fished and trapped full time on the river for 45 years, has observed major changes. "I've seen a lot of the sloughs filled in," he said. "I used to be able to run a boat and motor in places where it is dry land now. The Corps of Engineers raised the water level up and it killed all the vegetation. They should leave the water level real low in the summer, when they've got enough in the channel, so vegetation can grow. Years ago there were all kinds of ox hearts and wild rice growing. Migrating birds and muskrats now have no food. I don't know what their purpose was in doing that because the channel in most places is 30 feet deep just about all over. I set nets out there and I know where the bottom is. There used to be a lot of ducks. Now there aren't near as many ducks coming down this flyway, as they don't have any feed. Muskrats are about gone, too. I was getting 2,000 muskrats a year and now if you got a hundred you would be really lucky. There is no vegetation and the muskrats have no food or place to hide. The hawks and eagles and owls scoop the muskrats up and eat them."

Mike Valley echoed his father's words. "There were a hundred times more birds—ducks and geese—when I was a kid than there are now. Back when I was a kid there was eel-grass, celery grass, cattails, wild rice everywhere. Now you can't find a cattail around here to save your soul. When I was a kid you could go along the bank any place scooping crawdads for bait and there would be moss fifteen feet up from the bank, green beautiful moss. There is just mud there now. Something has killed it."

Valley enjoys the proliferating eagles but believes that the protection of certain species, such as raptors, is upsetting a natural balance—particularly the muskrat population. "Last year, during the winter, there were 300 eagles on the ice every day. When I was a kid to see nine eagles was extraordinary. An eagle eats an awful lot of mushrats [muskrats]—60 to 70 a year. What are we going to do in ten years when there are 5,000 eagles sitting out there? The eagles have to eat, too."

The Izaak Walton League was content with the Corps' management of the river until 1945. World War II was underway and the military engineers broke their agreement with the League (and the Minnesota

Department of Conservation) by drawing down large amounts of water from the reservoir lakes, in the process killing fur bearing animals and fish. Vast numbers of fish smothered under the ice and the aquatic plant life, so necessary for migrating birds, was damaged. The Corps claimed the draw-down was necessary because of wartime navigation over the "chain of rocks" section of the river between Grafton and Cairo, Illinois.

The draw-downs continued after the war. Again the League protested. Finally, on June 19, 1948, Congress amended the Fish and Wildlife Coordination Act to give "full consideration and recognition to the needs of fish and other wildlife resources and their habitat, dependent on such waters . . . within existing facilities (including locks, dams and pools.)" The needs of fish, birds and furry mammals were finally receiving recognition by the law.

Public attitudes on what was an appropriate use of the river changed. Dr. James Curtis, a member of the Upper Mississippi River Task Force, speaking in a hearing before Congress on H.R. 10529 in 1972, expressed the evolving attitude of communities along the river. "I have no quarrel with reasonable navigational use of the river," he said. "But surely this great river is more than a mere highway for hauling freight. Surely it is not too much to ask that the historical, natural, scenic and recreational values of the river, whose worth cannot be estimated in dollars, shall be viewed as equally important to commerce."

Some will never be reconciled to the nine-foot channel in the Mississippi River. A river researcher from the University of Wisconsin wrote, "The nine-foot channel is an artificial imposition on an extraordinary river. It is an imposition born of the parochial self-interest of a group of Twin Cities industrialists who are long dead. . . . Claims that navigation on the upper river bolsters the economic health of the upper Midwest should not be ignored, but they should be considered in the context of a much broader economic framework. . . . We should cherish the pulse of life through this great river valley as an element of our prosperity. . . . A time may come when these locks and dams, these artifacts to the business priorities of another time, should be dismantled and the great river allowed to follow its own course, when the metal gates of the dams should be removed and the concrete walls and monoliths allowed to crumble. Their decay might testify to our ability to recognize abuse of nature's abundance and our desire to heal wounds inflicted by our predecessors."

NOTES

See Richard Hoops, *A River of Grain—The Evolution of Commercial Navigation on the Upper Mississippi River* (1987); Raymond H. Merritt, *Creativity, Conflict and Controversy: A History of the St. Paul District U.S. Army Corps of Engineers* (1979); and William Patrick O'Brien, *Gateways to Commerce* (1992). Author's interviews with Lee Nelson (November 2002), Mike and Dallas Valley (April 2002.) The McKnight Foundation report was entitled *The Mississippi River in the Upper Midwest. Its Economy, Ecology, and Management* (1996). Frank Fugina's comments are in "Old Man River Awakens" (circa 1952), an unpublished manuscript in the Minnesota Historical Society library.

CHAPTER 19

The Floods

In its natural state the Mississippi River flowed about 30,000 square miles of land almost every year. When the ice and snow in the north melt and spring rains fall on the tributaries, the natural river runs over its banks, spreading out into a wide shallow sea and depositing valuable nutrients on thousands of acres of floodplain. When the waters recede, grasses grow on the compacted and dried out flats providing food and habitat for wildlife and the clouds of migrating waterfowl.

A visitor to Prairie du Chien in 1837 described the rising river. "The river is the most singular stream I ever saw. Its bed is from two to six miles wide but so filled with islands as to leave but one channel suitable for steamboats, generally about half a mile wide. . . . The water has been rising at the rate of about two or three inches per day, for three weeks. And though it is now over most of the islands and bottoms and swelling into little lakes, yet the water is not in the least riled or muddy" (*Iowa News Journal*, August 19, 1837).

Every river requires a floodplain. A river overflowing will capture a floodplain wherever one is needed. When a river is allowed to overflow a broad floodplain, its speed is slowed. A narrow river is a faster and more destructive river. The man-made changes in the Mississippi from 1888 to 1968 reduced the surface area of the river by one-third, the island area by one half and the riverbed by nearly one fourth. Dams closed off most of the river's side channels, into which overflowing water once flowed.

With the modification of the river, the word "flood" took on a new meaning. The removal of the northern forests, the draining of marshes and farming practices that allowed water to run off fields rather than be retained, caused the Mississippi to flood more rapidly than in earlier times. The understory of a forest floor absorbs water. In a natural forest the layer of twigs, leaves, needles and moss forms a carpet up to six inches thick that holds water until it can seep into the soil. When loggers cut the trees and left the brush on the ground, fires followed that denuded the land. Water, instead of seeping into the ground, ran off, swelling the streams. The War Department recorded twenty-three Mississippi floods between 1718 and 1859. Following the flood of 1882, floods occurred with greater frequency and were more destructive. Floods causing ever-increasing damage occurred in 1903, 1907, 1912, 1913, 1916, 1920, and 1922 culminating in the catastrophic flood of 1927.

The *Minnesota Pioneer* of February 23, 1853, reported that Little Crow had moved his village to the west bank of the Mississippi because the east bank had flooded. In 1886 A.B. Stickney, president of the Chicago Great Western Railway, who watched as the river rose 19 feet above its normal level, raised the ground level of the South St. Paul stockyards by covering the 260 acres with five feet of fill dirt. His efforts came to naught when the river flooded in 1897 forcing him to herd hundreds of head of cattle up the banks of the west side of the river and into the newly developed residential section of town. The water did not recede for over a week.

Residents of whole neighborhoods, such as the fourth ward of Prairie du Chien, accepted the fact the river would regularly flood. Mike Valley, who grew up near the Villa Louis, recalls that "every year we went through a flood." Three hundred and fifty houses in a town of 5,600 were regularly flooded. "I remember coming back to my bedroom and the water was an inch from the ceiling. Every year we had to tear out stuff, move everything. You couldn't leave. You had no money, where were you going to go? Everything was there, your fish house was there. My grandma had 200 chickens, 200 geese running all over the yard. It was a little community. You knew everybody. When you needed a hand someone was there. It was beautiful. Finally the Corps of Engineers came and made several hundred families move. They knew the river was going to flood every year." The Corps had been involved in flood control since the creation of the Mississippi River Commission in 1879.

As the river continued flooding, towns constructed levees to protect their lowlands. The levees were successful in holding back the water from the floodplains on which they were built but did nothing to protect areas downstream. Instead, levees further constricted the flow of water, making the same volume of water flow faster. For communities downstream, levees upstream only increased the likelihood of a flood by raising the flood stage higher and higher. To protect themselves, down-stream communities also built levees and so they played the game all the way down the river.

While the Corps built levees to constrict the flow of water, it also campaigned to convince communities to restrict building on the river's floodplain. An editorial in the May 4, 1965, edition of the *Chicago Tribune* scolded flood victims for knowingly putting themselves and their businesses in harm's way. "We can sympathize with the victims of this disaster," the editorial explained, "without admiring them for having built their homes and business establishments in the river's floodplain. . . . A flood is one of the oldest natural phenomena known to mankind, nevertheless men keep on building in places where they are likely to be inundated."

That is what happened in La Crosse, Wisconsin. The river, receding from the last ice age, created the terrace on which much of the city is built. But as the town grew and space between the bluffs and the river grew scarce, people began moving onto the floodplain. That area was regulated by the state DNR (Department of Natural Resources) and FEMA (Federal Emergency Management Agency) to the annoyance of La Crosse city officials. "I move we tell the DNR to go to hell in 30 days," said one city councilman in a heated debate about flood regulations. Others saw the floodplain regulations as an infringement on their personal property rights.

Mayor John Medinger, of La Crosse, recognized the political bind he was in. "We had been ignoring federal floodplain regulations but you've got to pay the price later," he said. "In your heart you always know they have good reason. But you're trying to please the local constituency and it's always fun to tell the federal government to go to hell. The DNR and FEMA are not popular agencies, so if you end up defending them, constituents get mad at you." When the river crested at La Crosse in the 1965 flood, the crest was 17.9 feet, nearly six feet above the official 12-foot flood stage. Officials believe the river crested at 7.3 feet above flood stage downriver at Prairie du Chien but no one is certain because the city's gauge was underwater (*La Crosse Tribune*, April 23, 1965).

THE FLOOD OF 1927

The great flood of 1927 demonstrated the fallacy of the Corps' levee-only policy. Within weeks of the Corps pronouncement that the levees would prevent a flood, the levees failed along the Lower Mississippi. Water spread out over 100 miles of flat delta stretching from Cairo, Illinois, to the Gulf. Unusually heavy rains were not the only cause of the flood. The unthinking actions of many people led to the deluge. Loggers had cut over the forests along the tributaries of the Mississippi. Farmers had cleared the land, giving the water no place to go in its headlong rush to the Gulf. For the first time in living memory the tributaries of the Mississippi all filled at once and began pouring their waters into the main channel.

The mass of water rushed to reach sea level and there was no alternative route, no spillway, no reservoir, no sloughs or backwaters. The wing dams and closing dams built by the engineers left no place for the water to escape. Instead the dams directed the water down the central channel and the higher the water in the main channel rose, the more it backed up in the tributaries. For a time the Ohio River reversed itself and flowed backwards. The Arkansas River overflowed as far west as Pueblo, Colorado.

In reclaiming its alluvial plain the Mississippi flooded sixteen and a half million acres in seven states, destroyed 137,000 homes, left 700,000 homeless. To this day no one knows how many died but it was probably in excess of 500. The flood of 1927 was a disaster that changed not only the course of the river, but the history of the United States. It helped put Herbert Hoover in the White House, sealed the fate of New Orleans as a great economic power and began the migration of blacks from the South to the North.

THE FLOOD OF 1993

While the flood of 1927 killed more people, the flood of 1993 caused more property damage ($18 billion), making it the most destructive in U.S. history. The flood began with a wet spring in the north country. In June it rained for eight straight days in South Dakota, Iowa, Minnesota and Wisconsin, saturating the soil and flooding campgrounds and marinas along the river. On June 20 a crest of water eleven feet above flood stage spread across the river at St. Paul and moved down the main channel. The first levee broke at Hatfield, Wisconsin, and the river gauge at Rock Island registered flood stage. By late June only one bridge across the Mississippi remained open between St. Louis and Keokuk, Iowa. The others were closed because their approaches were underwater. Officials closed barge and pleasure boat traffic on the river from St. Paul to St. Louis, stranding 2,000 grain barges and 50 tow boats.

On July 5, officials evacuated 150 families from East Dubuque, Iowa, and 400 families from near St. Charles, Missouri. The flooding on the Mississippi backed water up the Des Moines River, flooding out the public water service. On July 11 five thousand people were evacuated. By July 22, 430 square miles of floodplain and eight million farm acres were underwater. On July 30, flood waters backing up the Missouri River closed all but one bridge between St. Louis and Kansas City, splitting the state in two. On July 31, when the flood crest reached 49 feet at St. Louis, the water plant at Alton, Illinois, washed out and 70,000 customers lost service.

At the flood's peak, more than 1,000,000 cubic feet of water rushed past the Gateway Arch in St. Louis every second. On August 15, the rampaging waters of the Missouri washed out 700 caskets from a cemetery at Hardin, Missouri. "The current would catch [the coffins] and whip them around. And then you'd just watch them glide off into the horizon," reported Don Lam, the postmaster of Hardin.

Weary flood workers and victims were still shoveling the mud from their homes and wringing the water out of their carpets when they read the dispiriting opinion that the floods which had so devastated their homes need not have happened. Worldwatch Institute, an independent research organization in Washington, D.C., declared that the 1993 flood was the result of "ecosystem mismanagement . . . the river was simply attempting to reclaim its floodplain." According to the Institute the billions of dollars spent for flood control had only increased the frequency and severity of floods on the Mississippi. The construction of levees and creation of deep navigation channels, the paving over of urban areas, row crop farming in the floodplain and the draining of wetlands (more than 85% reduction in some states) reduced the ability of the Mississippi floodplain to absorb and slowly release rain and flood water.

The Institute maintained that the 1973, 1982 and 1993 floods were much higher than they would have been if structural flood control had not begun in earnest after the 1927 flood. Measured in constant dollars, economists estimate the damages from the 1927 flood at $236 million while damages from the flood of 1993 were 18 billion dollars.

The flood of 1993 convinced many people that the notion of the "100-year flood" was archaic as the river was flooding with remarkable regularity. Barring droughts they feared that the floods would become even more frequent. The floods demonstrated to thousands of people, firsthand, the destructive power of the river. The hubris of "dominion over the river" shifted to respect for the river's outpouring of energy. The Great Flood of 1993 lasted from late May through mid-September and converted many people to the idea that if they were to live along the Upper Mississippi River, they would have to work *with* the needs of the river rather than *against* them.

David Lanegran, professor of geography at Macalester College, commented, "People think of the river as their enemy. They fight the river, dike the river, pollute the river, ignore the river. Now the river is taking back its old places. You can see the old marshes coming back in the farmer's fields, all the places where the duck ponds used to be. It's almost like a ghost. The river is saying, 'This is where I used to be.'"

Mark Twain may have been right after all when he declared that "ten thousand River Commissions, with the mines of the world at their back, cannot tame that lawless stream, cannot curb it or confine it, cannot say to it, 'Go here,' or 'Go there' and make it obey."

NOTES

Government publications dealing with flood control include *Relation of Forestry to the Control of Floods in the Mississippi Valley* (1929) and "The Protective Forests of the Mississippi River Watershed and Their Part in Flood Prevention," (1982), *U.S.D.A. Circular No. 37*. The South St. Paul stockyards flood is noted in *South St. Paul Centennial 1887–1987*, edited by Lois Glewwe (1987). Floods have been studied by Pete Daniel, *Deep'n as it Come. The 1927 Mississippi River Flood* (1996); in a Natural Disaster Survey Report for the Department of Commerce by D. James Baker and Elbert Friday, Jr., entitled *The Great Flood of 1993* (1994); and by Stanley A. Changnon, *The Great Flood of 1993* (1996).

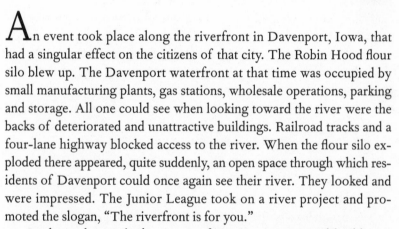

CHAPTER 20

The Return to the River

An event took place along the riverfront in Davenport, Iowa, that had a singular effect on the citizens of that city. The Robin Hood flour silo blew up. The Davenport waterfront at that time was occupied by small manufacturing plants, gas stations, wholesale operations, parking and storage. All one could see when looking toward the river were the backs of deteriorated and unattractive buildings. Railroad tracks and a four-lane highway blocked access to the river. When the flour silo exploded there appeared, quite suddenly, an open space through which residents of Davenport could once again see their river. They looked and were impressed. The Junior League took on a river project and promoted the slogan, "The riverfront is for you."

In the early 1980's the Corps of Engineers proposed building a floodwall on the Davenport riverfront that would extend from Credit Island upstream to the Government Bridge. A citizen's group took a look at the levee plans and, with their newfound appreciation for the river, decided they did not like them. Unlike Rock Island, which is level and flat and when the river floods the whole town is in jeopardy, Davenport is built on hills with only about one-tenth of the town susceptible to flood damage. City Councilman Lloyd Platt led the opposition to the floodwall, pointing out that it would cost seventy million dollars to build plus a million and a half a year for maintenance. "It's best to move further up and let the Mississippi have its say when it is going to make a statement," he said.

The *Quad City Times* (April 1, 1982) joined in the opposition to the levee. "This mound of earth will effectively block any visual appreciation of the Mississippi River unless one moves all the way back up to Third Street," the writer pointed out. "Rock Island is buried behind a levee, never to see the river again. Downtown Moline faces the Sylvan Slough. Forget a river view. Downtown Bettendorf faces a similar plight. The wall of buildings and omnipresent floodwall preclude even a glimpse of the majestic Mississippi. . . . If we could just remove the blinders and take a good look about us, the winning combination is waiting at our river-step. Forget the dike. It will only bury us behind another mound of dirt so commonly hiding towns and cities up and down the river. Don't shut the river out. Open it up. Let the city flow down to the riverfront."

The Corps' floodwall would probably have been built in Davenport, despite Platt's opposition and the impassioned articles in the press, if it had not been for two events. The first was when Kathy Wine, a local English teacher, along with a group of citizens opposed to the dike, organized "River Action." Members of River Action built a plywood wall, twenty-five feet long and seven feet high, the same height as the proposed levee, and placed it on the Davenport riverfront. The wall showed people how their view of the riverfront would be obstructed by a levee and demonstrated that they really would have to go three or four blocks up the hill from downtown before they could catch a glimpse of the river.

The second circumstance that kept Davenport from getting a levee was the Reagan Administration's cutting of funding for public works. This gave Kathy Wine and her supporters time to educate the community on alternative ways to deal with a flooding river. They promoted the use of rain barrels, the planting of native grasses to slow run-off, the removal of industry from the floodplain and the turning of riverfront land into parks that could survive, and even benefit from, the flooding. The floodwall was never built and today Davenport, Iowa, is the largest city on the Mississippi without Federal flood control.

Across the river, Rock Island, in 1991, tore down 230 feet of its floodwall at the downtown levee and replaced it with 22 removable panels (each weighing 4,000 pounds) that can be put into place when a flood threatens. Before the change, to see the river Rock Island residents had to peer over a wall and look down, twenty feet, to the Mississippi. As the result of these approaches to flood control, the Quad Cities now have a forty-mile continuous river front walkway and park connecting public art, galleries, studios and performing art sites along both shores of the Mississippi.

The Quad Cities are not alone in their change of attitude toward the river. A new spirit has energized all of the river towns from the Quad Cities to Minneapolis and St. Paul. Citizens who before seldom gave a thought to the river are newly aware of the extraordinary geographic feature flowing past their doorsteps. They want access to the river—to see it, touch it, wade it in, fish in it, sail a boat on it, or merely have a place to sit and watch as a stick tossed into the water floats downriver, around a bend and out of sight.

As awareness of the river grew, people began to value that ever-flowing fountain of fresh water, not for what it did for one industry or another, but for itself. Like a mountain or an arm of the sea, the river is cherished because it exists, because it is there. Civic officials that once turned their towns' backs to the river, housed its poorest citizens on its banks, used it for a sewer and cursed it for flooding, now regard the river as a basic life force of their communities. The same geographic feature that inspired the birth of their communities contains the inspiration for their renewal

Driven by the rediscovery of their section of the river every town for four hundred miles on each shore is cleaning up its waterfront. Where the backs of dilapidated warehouses once blocked views of the river, parks and public docks now invite citizens down to the shore. Walls have come down, shrubs are replacing rip-rap, sport fishermen are casting for bass and walleyes. Volunteers have planted tens of thousands of trees in the river valley to provide cover and resting places for migrating waterfowl.

Every town and city on the river, from tiny Alma and McGregor to Minneapolis and St. Paul, has made a 180-degree turn, from trying to wall itself off from the river, to embracing it. St. Paul renovated Harriet and Raspberry Islands, moved its Science Museum to the riverfront and routed Shepard Road back away from the river to be replaced by pedestrian and biking trails. Six hundred housing units are going up on riverfront land that was once a junkyard and another 1,300 are planned for the west side of the river. The county jail and offices, once located on the bluff above the river, will be replaced with housing. A seventy-two mile stretch of river through the Twin Cities has been designated as the Mississippi National River and Recreation Area with a Mississippi River Visitor's Center in the Science Museum of Minnesota. The new University of Minnesota Centennial Showboat is docked at Harriet Island and plays to sold-out audiences throughout the summer.

Minneapolis has rehabilitated sixty historic buildings, constructed the Nicollet Island Pavilion and Amphitheater, the West River Parkway and has three thousand housing units under construction near the river.

Over one billion dollars in private funds have been invested. Public monies have developed a substantial portion of Riverfront Regional Park and the 1.8 mile Falls Heritage Trail. The Minnesota Historical Society unearthed the ruins of the historic Washburn A flour mill, destroyed by an explosion on May 2, 1878, and created the Mill City Museum in the heart of Mill Ruins Park. The Guthrie Theater will move to the riverfront where its neighbors are elegant, river-facing condominiums. What had once been the alley of the city, its formerly scorned riverfront, home to old industrial relics, drifters and derelicts has now become its glittering front door.

La Crosse began the reclamation of its riverfront with the development of a park on eleven vacant acres. Called "Harborview," it rose from the ruins of deteriorating structures. City officials offered tax relief to owners of dilapidated historic riverfront building as an incentive to renovate them. The incentive worked. Instead of tearing them down, owners restored and rehabilitated a row of century-old buildings. With improved docking for boats the *Delta Queen* came back, historians established a river museum and La Crosse now has a lively downtown with its old buildings along the riverfront preserved and reused.

Dubuque's opportunity to move back to its riverfront occurred when the venerable Dubuque Boat and Boiler works, where hundreds of river steamers had once been built, went bankrupt and the land lay vacant. It was a discouraging piece of real estate, polluted, littered with old oil tanks and the abandoned detritus of a dying industry. But the site was on the river. Motivated by a gift from Bill Woodward, Dubuque's newspaper publisher, the city embarked on a program to reclaim its river heritage. The place to reclaim the river was exactly where the old Dubuque Boat works had once built the river steamers.

The result is America's River, a complex that includes the National Mississippi River Museum and Aquarium built on a 90 acre peninsula along the river where red brick steps lead down to the water's edge, a casino and the Grand Harbor Resort and Waterpark. Dubuque turned six miles of the levee (built after the 1965 flood) into a river walk with lights, benches and bike trails. A steam dredge boat, the *William Black*, became a Bed and Breakfast.

Hastings transformed a two hundred acre blighted industrial area next to the river into a park and recreational center with restored floodplain habitat, a sculpture garden and band shell. Prairie du Chien, which has five national historic landmark properties on St. Feriole Island—the greatest concentration of such property in the United States—has reconnected itself to the river with passenger boat boarding facilities and an interpretive center. Tiny Trempealeau has done the same, rebuilding its once busy river ramps and docks.

Wabasha plans a new riverside complex for its National Eagle Center and Winona rebuilt the historic Wagon Bridge over which wagons loaded with wood for the steamboats once rumbled. Up and down the river citizens intent on reconnecting their towns to the river have turned abandoned industrial sites into parks, recreational facilities, hiking trails and swimming beaches. Bicycle paths, baseball stadiums and a Mississippi River Education and Conference Center now stand where derelict buildings and polluted industrial sites once despoiled the riverbanks.

WAYNE HAMMER AND "CITIZENS FOR A CLEAN MISSISSIPPI"

Wayne Hammer's father was a member of the Izaak Walton League and Wayne grew up building woodduck houses, planting trees on the banks of eroded trout streams and attending pancake breakfasts to raise money for the League. As an adult he lives on the Sand Prairie, the plug in the river valley created by the delta of the Chippewa River that causes the Mississippi to bulge into Lake Pepin. Sand Prairie, a sparsely populated area next to the river, is about fifteen miles long and a mile or two wide and contains such unusual geologic features as the Weaver Dunes.

In the 1970s Northern States Power (now Xcel Energy), along with a consortium of power companies, proposed building a plant on the Sand Prairie that would burn ten tons of coal an hour—coal that would be hauled to the site by three trains a day. Local residents banded together and, after three years of effort, succeeded in stopping the plant mainly because of a drop in demand for electricity. Hammer had scarcely caught his breath from that campaign when, in 1976, thousands of dead fish began washing up on the shores of Lake Pepin. Depending on which way the wind was blowing, the dead fish either ended up on the Wisconsin shore or on the Minnesota beaches. At the same time Dorothy and Ed Hill on the Wisconsin side of Lake Pepin were puzzling over the green algae bloom in the water and fighting swarms of black midges that befouled their beach.

Concerned citizens from Wabasha and Lake City in Minnesota and Pepin in Wisconsin, including Hammer and the Hills, met in June of

1975 to form an organization called "Citizens for the Preservation of Lake Pepin" to figure out what was killing the fish. They soon discovered that the Pig's Eye Sewage Treatment plant at the Twin Cities was dumping approximately 4.6 billion gallons of untreated, raw sewage into the river every year. The sewage raised the nutrient load of the river to the point where algae bloomed and then died. The toxins from the dying algae killed the fish.

That was not supposed to be happening. The law required sanitary engineers to treat sewage before dumping it into the river. The problem at Pig's Eye was that every time it rained, the storm sewers and sanitary sewers of the Twin Cities, which ran together, overwhelmed the system. The treatment plant could not handle the quantities of water that flowed into the plant after a heavy rain so it dumped the effluent, untreated, into the river. A similar thing happened whenever there were sewage plant maintenance problems or equipment failures. Until they were repaired, plant employees simply poured the untreated sewage into the river. It appeared to the citizens' group that the agencies assigned to monitor Pig's Eye and enforce the law—the Environmental Protection Agency and the Metropolitan Waste Control Commission—did not take the problem of water pollution very seriously.

For a year, members of the organization wrote letters and met with state and federal officials to correct the problem. While they learned a great deal about the complicated process of waste treatment, they realized that their efforts were doing nothing to solve the problem or reduce the quantity of untreated pollutants being dumped into the river. Meanwhile membership in the organization continued to grow. It was obvious that a great many people cared about the quality of the water in the Mississippi. Residents of river towns above and below Lake Pepin joined as did members of county boards in Wisconsin and Minnesota and the city councils from almost every town downriver from the Twin Cities. In May 1976, they changed the name of the organization to "Citizens for a Clean Mississippi." They elected Dorothy Hill president.

A year later, in March 1977, frustrated over continued bureaucratic intransigence the citizens' group that had begun because of dead fish and swarms of black midges, filed suit. They sued the Metropolitan Waste Control Commission, the Metropolitan Council, the Minnesota Pollution Control Agency, the City of St. Paul, the City of Minneapolis and the U.S. Environmental Protection Agency. Outraged residents of the little towns downriver took on the entire official establishment of the

Twin Cities. Their goal was to compel the regulatory agencies to enforce the anti-pollution regulations—laws that were already on the books. They were determined to end the practice of giving the Pig's Eye treatment plant variances that allowed it to dump raw sewage into the river.

The citizens hired an attorney and went door-to-door signing up members. Membership in the organization cost two dollars and people joined from as far away as Florida and California. Eventually they raised $55,000. In 1977 the organization formally protested the dumping of two billion gallons of untreated wastes into the river and actively intervened in seven weeks of contested hearings to set up state and federal permits for the operation of the Pig's Eye plant. Volunteers drove daily to the Twin Cities to testify at the hearings. Slowly they hammered out the terms of the permits.

Unfortunately, the establishment of regulations did not guarantee compliance by the Pig's Eye plant. For the next two years the plant continued to dump pollutants in the river far in excess of the permits. Again the "Citizens for a Clean Mississippi" filed a complaint, explaining to its members, "The terms of those permits were lenient and attainable, but the Metropolitan Waste Control Commission and co-permittee, the Metropolitan Council, were consistently negligent in complying with the permits during the past two years. The Minnesota Pollution Control Agency has the power to enforce compliance but failed to take the proper administrative action."

Other government agencies joined in the suit and just when the "Citizens for a Clean Mississippi" organization was about to run out of money the State of Wisconsin threatened to join in. (Wisconsin, at that time, was in compliance with all of the clean water laws.) That helped tip the balance. The January 1980 newsletter of Citizens for a Clean Mississippi happily informed its members that the U.S. Environmental Protection Agency "has now determined to forcefully address the non-compliance of the Pig's Eye Treatment plant during the past two years. The EPA requested permission to file suit against the Metropolitan Waste Control Commission and the Metropolitan Council for violations of state permits." The little Davids of "Citizens for a Clean Mississippi" won a major victory over the Goliath-size agencies charged with protecting the water quality of the Mississippi River.

As a direct result of the persistence of the "Citizens for a Clean Mississippi," the Twin Cities embarked on a fourteen-year, multi-million dollar project to separate the sewer system from the storm-water drainage system. In a newsletter to members ten years after the organization's founding, Dorothy Hill wrote, "It is a good feeling to know that the Pig's Eye plant is operating well within permit limitations and that excess sludge is no longer dumped into the river. The Lower Beltline Interceptor has also been re-constructed and should no longer bypass raw waste." Hill, a widow who still lives on the shores of Lake Pepin, reports that the black midges, which thrive on pollution, are gone and the mayflies, which can live only in clean water, have returned.

The "Citizens for a Clean Mississippi" campaign energized people up and down the river. When organizers saw that residents as far south as Galena, Illinois, had joined in the effort and that interest in cleaning up the river was broader than just around Lake Pepin they added river cleanups to their activities. As Hammer explained, "We felt that if we showed people downstream that we cared a lot about the river and realized that pollutants we put in the water moved on down to them, we could work together to clean it up." The organization produced a bumper sticker reading, "We can't all live upstream" and plastered it on the cars of their 2,000 members.

The first river cleanup project of "Citizens for a Clean Mississippi" started in Winona. "We got some bands and food from the community to put on a lunch and invited the public and had a good turn-out," Hammer remembers. "That first year we had 60 people turn up and got hundreds of tons of debris out of the river." The cleanup campaigns helped participants develop a wider understanding of the river.

When the group started cleanups in the metropolitan area the participants the first year or two, according to Hammer, "were students and radicals and people concerned about the river." By the third year, however, they had attracted Minnesota governor Rudy Perpich's attention and that of mayors who came to the cleanups. Hammer is convinced that if people will come down to the river and help clean it up, they will develop an ethic of protection and concern for the Mississippi and the lands surrounding it. To Hammer, the condition of the river is a barometer of the psychological health of the residents of the region.

In an early cleanup Hammer and his volunteers were collecting trash on one of the islands below Lock and Dam 5A when they found a pick-up truck buried up to the door panels in the mud. Residents of cottages on the island came to watch the assortment of volunteers, from children to medical doctors, carrying the truck out in parts and loading it into boats to take to disposal areas down the river. When they were about finished one of the onlookers walked over to Hammer and asked, "What about the bus?" "What bus?" Hammer replied. The man led the group through the woods where they found an old school bus that had been taken out on the river for a cottage and abandoned. Hammer and his "cleaner-uppers,"as they called themselves, returned with heavier equipment, a few more boats and cutting torches and removed the bus.

In the early years of cleanup the most common items found were steel 55-gallon drums that had once held chemicals. The drums were popular as flotation devices for boathouses and docks. When they lost their buoyancy owners poked holes in them and sank them. Hammer and his "cleaner-uppers" pulled 750 barrels out of the river in one day as well as junked cars, coin-operated pop machines, bicycles and lawn mowers.

The "Citizens for a Clean Mississippi" eventually morphed into "Mississippi River Revival" which identified another major pollutant in the river, phosphates from laundry detergents. Like the sewage, the phosphates led to a bloom of algae in the water. The organization lobbied the Minnesota legislature and eventually passed legislation that reduced the amount of phosphate permitted in the major brands of laundry detergents that could be sold in Minnesota. For a time, before all makers of detergents took phosphate out of their products, readers of the fine print on boxes of detergent saw the percentage of phosphate listed followed by the line, "except in Minnesota."

The presence of the dams creates numerous problems in the river. Water pooling between the dams makes the river become more of a series of lakes. As Gretchen Benjamin, of the Wisconsin Department of Natural Resources, explains, "Lake-like characteristics develop when the water in a pool above a dam loses current and the islands within that pool become saturated with water, making them more subject to erosion. The sediment from the islands then becomes suspended and begins filling in the deep main channels that are normally present in a large river system."

Keeping the water level high year-round drowns the plants. As the islands erode away, the vegetation disappears, creating a wide, open area without wind breaks. Wind blowing across the river acts like the wind patterns in a desert eventually creating a pool that is shallow and muddy. This is what happened to Pool Number 8 between Dams 7 and 8. A committee consisting of representatives from the DNRs of Wisconsin, Iowa and Minnesota, the Corps of Engineers, the U.S. Fish and Wildlife Service along with other agencies met to devise a solution.

The group decided to draw down the water in Pool Number 8 by eighteen inches—a level that would not interfere with barge traffic. A lowering of the water level by eighteen inches would permit approximately 2,575 acres of muck and shallow water habitat to dry out. This would allow seeds to germinate and, with luck, bring back some of the ecosystem that was present before the locks and dams were built. If successful, according to Benjamin, the emergent aquatic vegetation would help stabilize the river bottom and banks, provide a hospitable environment for aquatic insects and shelter for young fish which feed on the insects in the vegetation. Among the aquatic plants that should respond to a draw-down of water are broadleaf arrowhead, sessile fruit arrowhead, rice cut-grass, cattails, broadfruit burreed, bottle-brush sedge and smartweed.

The draw-down began in 2000 and was immediately successful. Hammer, who watched it closely, strongly supports the experiment of seasonally "drawing down" the water in the pools behind the dams, simulating the normal pulse of the river. "This exposes the mud flats and allows plants to germinate and store energy in their roots. That is what the swans feed on, the mallards and the geese and the diving ducks. The fish population is tied to that system. When the river was no longer allowed to fluctuate these plants died out." Hammer is encouraged by the rapidity with which the river bottoms have recovered when biologists lowered the water level for a few weeks. "Places where these species of plants had disappeared have seen 25 to 30 different species returning and in good counts. As the water receded in the draw-down the variety of shore birds that showed up was incredible. There were 27 different species of shore birds."

The Corps draw-down exposed other unfortunate practices. Boaters, out for a day's recreation on the river, often buried their garbage in plastic bags on the sandbars instead of taking it home with them. When the water level dropped, there were the bags of garbage, sticking out of the sides of the sandbars like hunks of fruit in a piece of cake.

Yet another problem, according to Hammer, is the use of large boats that cause heavy soil erosion on the shores of the river. Where passing tow boats with their 15 barges in tow cause hardly a ripple of water against the shore, the large displacement hulls of the big recreational boats create a massive bow wave that crashes onto the shore and erodes the soil. Hammer believes that large boats, designed for lakes or the ocean, do not belong on the narrow channel of a river.

"Some of these big boats have several engines in them. Their recreational use is simply to drive back and forth. As a result the river has gotten very dangerous," he says. "It used to be safe for a ten-year-old kid to go paddling on the river. You wouldn't dream of it today. A 55 mile-per-hour boat used to be a fast boat but now they go 85 to 90 miles an hour. I hear a lot of stories about people sitting in a backwater or narrow slough quietly fishing in the soft air of a spring day and somebody comes around the corner at 60 miles an hour and swamps them. The old river courtesies have been lost."

A 1994 study by Scot Johnson of the Minnesota Department of Natural Resources bears out Hammer's concern over boat wakes. It is the deep draft boats, moving at a high speed, and not the tows, that create the damaging wave action against the shore. Johnson's report states that "most erosion generally occurred during the recreational boating season . . . erosion was less once the recreational boating season was over and commercial tow traffic was the dominant form of navigation." Johnson's report concludes, "recreational boating on the Mississippi River Main Channel is the contributing influence most responsible for the documented high rate of shoreline erosion."

Commercial fisherman Mike Valley, too, regrets the loss of the etiquette of the river. According to him, recreational use of the river has overwhelmed the fishermen. "Thirty years ago, when I was a kid, there'd be clammers, commercial fishermen, steamboats going by all the time. Anytime you passed anyone fishing you slowed down to no-wake going by him. And they did the same for you. Now there is absolutely no respect. You've got hundreds of jet skiers, people water skiing, cruisers that are ten times too big for the river going by at 100 miles an hour. I commercial fished full time until four years ago. I quit for the simple fact you could not raise nets on weekends. The way people on the river behave, there's no way you can raise nets on the weekend. You just can't do it."

CHAD PREGRACKE AND "LIVING LANDS AND WATERS"

While cities along the river coped with flooding by creating spaces for the river to expand, one consequence of flooding was seldom dealt with—the tons of trash washed into the river by the flooding waters. Tires, refrigerators, tanks filled with chemicals and barrels half-filled with oil washed into the river where the junk piled up on islands or became trapped in the brush and trees along the banks.

The floods were not responsible for all of the trash. Though municipalities on the river curtailed their dumping, many individuals did not. Despite the fact that the river is controlled by a plethora of state and federal agencies it has been individuals like Wayne Hammer and his "cleaner-uppers," acting on their own initiative, who have removed the bulk of the trash from the river. With no government entity responsible for cleaning up the river, a few extraordinary individuals took on the task themselves.

Chad Pregracke grew up a few rods from the Mississippi at East Moline, Illinois. As a boy he swam and fished in the river and when he was fifteen-years-old he and his brother spent three summers earning college money diving for mussels to sell to the Japanese. To save on their expenses, they camped for weeks at a time on the islands in the river. Instead of enjoying a Huck Finn-like camping experience, the boys found themselves pitching their tent amid piles of junk. "We'd come into a nice spot that was supposed to be pristine and there would be a washing machine or a refrigerator and just garbage everywhere," Chad complained. The more time he spent on the river the more he loved it and the angrier he became at the pollution he saw all around him.

The sight that triggered Chad into action was a pile of barrels rusting on the riverbank—junk that had been there for decades. The barrels were next to a marina but no one, not the marina owners, not environmental groups, not boaters on the river, cared enough to do anything about them. Chad called the Illinois Department of Natural Resources and other state agencies asking them to clean up the junk. He received bureaucratic answers. "That's not our responsibility," one said, and "There's no money for that," said another. So Chad decided, on his own, to take action. Home from college in 1997, with nothing more than a 20 foot flat-bottom boat and his own energy, Chad spent the summer dragging junk out of the river and piling it in his parent's yard where he recycled as much of it as he could. By fall he had single-handedly removed 45,000 pounds of refuse from the river.

At the end of the summer Chad realized that if he were going to continue he needed to raise money—for gas for his boat and to pay the landfill where he took the trash he hauled from the river. He decided to ask for corporate sponsorship. When he talked to people about the debris in the river, they would reply, "What junk?" Chad realized people had no idea what was happening to the Mississippi. "They're sitting at their desks, they don't know," he said. So Chad took pictures of the rusting refrigerators, mattresses, water heaters, bathroom sinks and barrels still full of oil that littered the shore.

Starting with the A's in the phone book Yellow Pages he called Alcoa Mills Products at Bettendorf, Iowa. A vice-president heard his story and offered him a small grant—but only as matching funds. Chad promised to be back within a week. For six weeks Chad called almost every business in the Quad Cities and did not get a single donation. Crestfallen, he returned to Alcoa. " I really tried," he said, " and no one is willing to help." Alcoa relented and gave him a small stipend. With that money Chad, again by himself, spent the entire summer amid the mud and mosquitoes of the Mississippi pulling junk from 50 miles of riverbanks.

His efforts did not go unobserved. A story in the *Quad City Times* about Chad's trash-collecting crusade brought supporters. Alcoa stayed with him and the second year the corporation asked Chad to submit a budget. He had never done that but his mother sat down with him at the family kitchen table and together they drew up a budget. Alcoa asked if he were a 501(c) 3—a non-profit charitable organization. Chad had never heard of that legal entity but he promised to become one.

Chad Pregracke now heads a non-profit organization called "Living Lands and Waters" that collects trash from the Mississippi River and its tributaries. For nine months in each of the early years Chad and seven youthful crew members lived on a rickety 42-foot houseboat called *The Miracle* that he had also salvaged from the river. Lashed to the houseboat were two barges that they filled with trash gathered from the islands, backwaters and shores of the river. In two months they removed more than 60 tons of trash from the waterway.

Among the junk Chad and his crew have hauled out of the Mississippi are 294 propane tanks, 287 refrigerators, 35 washing machines, four motorcycles, 8,272 automobile and truck tires, nine bathtubs, 2,199 55-gallon steel drums, 527 plastic drums, a 1930 tractor, 16,067 feet of barge rope, one sunken barge, 675 refrigerators, 75 water heaters, one 1970 Ford truck and enough styrofoam to cover a football field two-feet deep. They have also picked up a quantity of "piss-bottles," named for the towboat captains who urinate in them and then toss them overboard because they can not leave the decks of their crafts.

Chad and his crew work seven days a week. In recognition of his efforts the U.S. Army Corps of Engineers leased him a barge and a sand company gave him a second barge. He bought a towboat and the Caterpillar Company provided him with two free engines. Chad's organization presently has four barges, four trucks, four boats, four trailers, and the towboat. "I'm a realistic environmentalist," says Chad. "I'm not into new laws. I'm into consciousness. This is something I saw that I could do something about. It's 100 years of dumping but we're definitely gaining."

Chad runs sixteen community cleanups each year in towns along the river. In 2002 Chad Pregracke's organization brought six flat-bottom barges to the Twin Cities to participate in a cleanup sponsored by the Minnesota Department of Transportation. More than 1,000 people and 50 organizations spent a week cleaning a 43-mile stretch of the river from St. Anthony Falls to Prescott, Wisconsin. They removed more than 92 tons of trash including a houseboat that had been stuck in a backwater for a decade, 1,634 automobile tires, 24 propane tanks, five bicycles and almost five tons of styrofoam.

Chad's office is now on a barge tucked into a corner of the harbor at Winona. His office on the barge now has a kitchen, bedrooms and a large conference room that serves as a classroom for teacher workshops he began offering in the spring of 2003. Chad's one-day workshops brought 170 teachers together with experts on river shipping and ecology. They met with a clammer, explored the riverbanks, and left with folders full of information about the river. Chad has waiting lists for next year's classes.

Taking her cue from the highway department, Sheila Bosworth of Princeton, Iowa, a member of Chad's organization, has started an "Adopt-a-Mile" program for the river. The entire area around the Quad Cities has been adopted by local residents as well as by devotees of the river from as far away as Chicago and the Twin Cities. Sheila notes that while the four states bordering the Upper Mississippi are responsible for their shorelines, no one is responsible for the islands. "Nobody claims the middle," she says. "The Corps of Engineers manages the river, the Fish and Wildlife Service manages the wildlife refuges but nobody cleans up trash. It is nobody's job. That is what Chad found to be true— it was nobody's job to clean up the trash."

NOTES

Author's interviews included Lloyd Platt (May 2002), Wayne Hammer (October 2002) and Sheila Bosworth (August 2002). Papers of the "Citizens for a Clean

THE RETURN OF THE RIVER ~ 293

Mississippi" were consulted at the home of Dorothy Hill. Gretchen Benjamin's remarks appeared in *Big River,* a monthly newsletter (September 1999). Scot Johnson's DNR report was entitled "Recreational Boating Impacty Investigations, Upper Mississippi River System, Pool 4, Red Wing, Minnesota." Chad Pregracke's work has been described in numerous publications, including *Time* magazine (July 10, 2000); *Harper's* magazine (October 1999); and the *Quad Cities Weekend Magazine* (June 23 and July 15, 2000).

CHAPTER 21

Our River—Our Home

Thames and all the rivers of the kings
Ran into Mississippi and were drowned.

– Stephen Vincent Benet, "Invocation,"
John Brown's Body (1927).

The Mississippi is a river and more than a river. It flows not only through the midsection of the nation, it flows through our history, our literature, our music and our dreams. As children we defined the geography of North America, the division of east from west, by where the land lay in relation to the river. Peoples of the world refer to the Mississippi with the awe reserved for the Nile, the Congo and the Amazon.

One of America's greatest writers, Samuel Clemens or Mark Twain, is forever identified with the Mississippi. Literary critics deem his classic *Huckleberry Finn* to be the Great American Novel. Clemens took his *nom de plume*, Mark Twain, from the terminology of the river. His book, *Life on the Mississippi*, which described his life as a cub pilot on the river, is read as avidly today as when it was published in 1883. Nearly everyone who writes about the river quotes or emulates Mark Twain. No one so captured the essence of the great river as did he.

Other writers on the river both preceeded and followed Twain. Zebulon Pike wrote his *Account of an Expedition to the Sources of the Mississippi* and published it in 1810. Many who took boats down the length of the river wrote about their experience, including Willard Glazier in *Down the Great River*, published in 1888; S.W. McMaster's *60 Years on the Upper Mississippi*, published in 1893; and the artist Henry

Lewis who described his mosquito-ridden canoe voyage from St. Paul to St. Louis. The river inspired novelists Edna Ferber, Frances Parkinson Keyes and Ben Lucien Burman, and poets such as Hart Crane and Stephen Vincent Benét. Captain Bill Bowell, who has long collected books about the Mississippi, will give his collection to the new Mississippi River Museum in Dubuque, where others will be able to appreciate river history and lore. Balladeers and song-writers found inspiration on the river. Who can forget Paul Robeson singing "Old Man River" in *Showboat?*

Rivers and boats are two sides of the same coin and most residents of the Upper Mississippi believe the prime use of the river is for recreation. Where a solitary canoe or fisherman's boat once drifted on the river, now thousands of boats, from fishing boats to sailboats, houseboats to cruisers, crowd the river between Memorial Day and Labor Day. Forty-five-foot long behemoths roar at 90 miles an hour down the channel between the dams. Almost half of the boats on the river are medium-sized powerboats. Large cruisers make up a fourth of the remainder as do fishing boats. Houseboats, though popular, are less than three percent of the total number of boats on the river. Sailboats are dead last comprising less than a quarter of one percent of the river craft.

Mike Fries, who rents houseboats on the river, says people go on the Mississippi to experience the medium of the water. Individuals have a primal need to relate to the river, the same river, much as climbers climb the same mountain. Families or groups of friends take houseboats out for three days at a time, cruising the 35 miles to Red Wing or Winona, going through the locks, anchoring at night on islands in the river. Minnesota State Senator Sandy Pappas and her husband go out on their houseboat several times a week during the season. "Being close to the water mellows us," she says. While boaters go fishing, swimming, exploring, anchoring on sandbars for picnics—what draws them back to the river is the thrill of living on moving water, of having a relationship with the river. The river is a powerful presence and many boaters fall under its spell.

Pleasure boating has become a major activity on the river. The Army Corps of Engineers, which keeps track of such things, calculates that boaters spend 6.9 million boater-days on the Upper Mississippi every year. They dock their boats in 217,364 recreational boat lockages in 18,000 marina slips and take about 2.6 million boat trips a year. The most popular pools with boaters in the river, each accomodating over a half million boaters a year, are river pools number 3 at Hastings, 4 which includes Lake Pepin, 11 at Guttenberg, 12 at Dubuque, 13 at Clinton, 14 at LeClaire and 15 at Davenport. The Corps forecasts a 20% growth in recreational boaters' use of the river by 2050.

The pleasure boaters share the river with tows and barges which, if boaters are not alert, can lead to accidents. While the tows move slowly compared to the boats (5 to 6 miles an hour), they have powerful momentum behind them. A loaded tow with fifteen barges is 27,000 tons of moving mass. Going down river a tow takes a mile and a half to come to a stop. Tows and barges have little ability or room to maneuver. If it collides with a tow and barge, the pleasure boat is always the loser.

A relationship of mutual helpfulness exists among boaters on the river regardless of the boats they are piloting. On numerous occasions tows have rescued pleasure boaters in trouble. One August evening Carolyn Ayers and six friends were cruising south of St. Paul on her houseboat when she ran out of gas in the middle of the channel and began drifting helplessly downriver. Though it was growing dark, Carolyn had turned off the boat's lights for fear of draining her battery—which she would need to start the engine once she found some gas.

Suddenly, around the bend in the river came a towboat towing barges upriver. Carolyn and friends switched on the houseboat's lights and began to shout and wave white towels at the tow. In a few minutes a voice came over the loudspeaker, "Are you out of gas?"

"Yes," they replied.

"We'll pick you up portside. Is your gas 50 to 1?" the voice on the loudspeaker asked.

"Yes."

As the tow pulled up beside the disabled houseboat the tow's crew dropped lines and made the boat fast to the tow. When the two boats were lashed together and moving upriver toward St. Paul, the crew of the tow invited Carolyn and friends aboard to have coffee and cake. "The kitchen of the tow was like a cozy farm kitchen with a warm oven and linoleum on the floor," the grateful Ayers remembers. When it was time to depart, a crew member filled the houseboat's gas tank with the correct mixture of fuel and waved them off.

The mystique of the river attaches to the land bordering it. The "Great River Road" (so designated in 1966) that follows both shores of the Upper Mississippi is misnamed. The roads are not grand parkways, as their name implies, but are quiet asphalt-topped two-laners that commune with the river. Eagles fly overhead. The coulees are dark and inscrutable. Beside the road the great sheet of water glides silently by, its power sensed but invisible. Moving water is a metaphor for the passing of time, for the transient—yet endless course of life. Few people speed on the river roads. Intuitively, drivers slow down, aware that this merging of land and water exudes a profound sense of place

Until it was widened in 2003, Shepard Road, the "river road" of St. Paul, narrowed to two lanes in the downtown area as it squeezed between the limestone bluff on which the town was built and the river. Once past the narrows, the road opens out, revealing tows and barges moored at the Lower Landing. Driving south on Highway 61 toward Hastings the road follows the great sweeping curve of the river as it flows beneath the bluffs of Mounds Park. Except for the barges and tows crowding the shore, the river looks much as it did when the five riverboats of the Grand Excursion, moving abreast, rounded this curve, flags whipping in the breeze, to surprise the residents of St. Paul.

The roadways on both sides of the river offer heart-stopping vistas. The highway meets the river again at Lake City and follows the shore of Lake Pepin to Read's Landing at the end of the lake. The river road on the Wisconsin side, from Hastings to La Crosse and on to Prairie du Chien, lies close to the bank of the river. Only the narrow thread of the single railroad track separates the highway from the water. Motorists drive between the wide expanse of the river on one side and the hills rising from the verge of the road. Few houses cling to the steep hillsides—most are given over to a lush growth of trees, accented by outcrops of rock.

A highway marker notes the site of the battle of Bad Axe. Behind the marker the coulee stretches into the interior, dark, overgrown, forbidding—an ancient setting of tragedy. The road leads on in the narrow space between the water and the abruptly rising hills. Further south, on the west side of the river at Guttenberg and again at Dubuque, the road breaks out at the top of hills to reveal a dramatic stretch of the river valley far below. Can this rugged land be Iowa? Motorists pull off the road to marvel at the scene.

Though from the road the Mississippi appears benign, we would be wise to treat this river gingerly. The great stream only appears to be tamed by man. When swollen by rains the constricted river boils up in geysers miles from its banks. As those who have witnessed the river's floods understand, once aroused, the power of the river is a force beyond human will. If the Mississippi River speaks to us, as some who live by it say that it does, it is warning us to stand aside.

Even the remnants of the pre-historic Mississippi have the power to disrupt our plans. A massive stone and brick warehouse once stood deserted on Shepard Road in downtown St. Paul, Minnesota. Plywood covered the arched-stone doors and first floor windows. In the upper stories birds flew in and out of the windows and made their nests where clerks once monitored the growth of one of America's great fortunes. The warehouse, built in 1887–1888, belonged to the empire builder James J. Hill, a man of no small passions. The first floor walls of Hill's warehouse are three feet thick, constructed of sandstone blocks, each weighing over a ton. The upper stories, whose ceilings are 10 feet high, are built of the finest high-fired brick. Hill's own office with its fireplace was in the south-east corner of the second floor of his warehouse and his desk was placed so he could look out over the multiple tracks of his railroads and beyond them to the great river where his dreams of wealth began.

Hill built his warehouse, like his mansion on Summit Avenue, the Cathedral on the hill to which he gave his money and the Stone Arch Bridge, to last for centuries. A century later his home is a museum and the Stone Arch bridge welcomes pedestrians and bicycle riders, while the Cathedral, newly restored, continues its religious role. Until recently the great warehouse stood vacant, but now it, also, has been restored to new life as the Great Northern Lofts where condominium owners will have Hill's view of the river.

When Captain Bill Bowell, who has spent much of his life on the Mississippi, is asked, "How dangerous is the Mississippi?" he replies, "You better respect it." Bowell exhibits the jaunty attitude of life-long river men. He went to Dubuque in 1951 to get his license from the Coast Guard to run an excursion boat on the river. He found the commander, a man named Smoker, sitting in his office with his feet up on an old 1910 roll top desk. "Come on in, son, and have a chair," Smoker invited. "I hear you want to get a license to haul passengers." "That's right," replied Bowell. "What side is port on?" asked Smoker. "Left side," replied Bowell. "What side is starboard on?" "Right side." "Son," said Smoker, "Congratulations. You just passed your license."

Bowell, an operator of large excursion boats, on an impulse took a 13-foot rowboat with an outboard motor down the river from St. Paul to New Orleans. Packing little more than his toothbrush, Bowell made the trip in eleven days, traveling occasionally at night, though he had no lights. "Off I went, going south," he recalls. "Unfortunately there was a southern wind which ripples the water going downstream. The boat went bang, bang, bang. I had a little cushion with me that saved my seat." Asked why he made the trip he replied, "I did it to escape —to go to a tranquil place—the same reason people go to the mountains." The journey, made in 1978, set a record for the trip down the river in a small boat.

The river reflects the dreams of those who have used it. For the Dakota and Ojibwe the river was an unfailing source of sustenance and its tributaries—the roads connecting them to their trading partners and hunting grounds. In the end the river betrayed them for its waters opened a passage into their ancestral territory—exposing them to the land-hunger of the conquering whites. To the French and British traders, the river was their route to fortunes in furs. To the Yankee explorers and the pioneers who followed them, the river was the high road of the white man's civilization.

To the timber barons, the river was the key to unlocking a king's ransom in logs from the northern forest. For the Minneapolis industrialists, the river provided power for the grain and sawmills and was the club with which to beat back the tariffs charged by the railroads. Every city and village along the river, from St. Louis to St. Paul and Minneapolis, was founded where it was because the river flowed by it.

An industry-based group, supported by a majority of the residents of the Upper Mississippi Valley, created the river we have today and attributed cosmic significance to its actions. As John Anfinson, former historian for the Corps of Engineers, noted of the engineering of the river, "For most of the nineteenth century and throughout the nine-foot channel movement, Midwesterners believed they were fulfilling not only their own dreams but the will of God or Divine Providence."

While commercial navigation continues to dominate the river, other groups insist that their visions be considered. Biologists call for a river restored to a state closer to its original condition where the natural pulse of seasonally high and low water provides the vegetative habitat for fish and birds. They now recognize that without the seasonal drying out of marshes and shorelines below St. Anthony Falls, the natural cycle of vegetation and the life that depends on it cannot survive. Fishermen and hunters want the water level lowered to bring back the ducks and muskrats and to improve the habitat for fish.

When environmentalists look at the river they see a resource that, while improved, still suffers from pollution by more than 100 communities with sewer deficiencies. They point to 129 river locations that have evidence of mercury and polychlorinated biphenyls in the water and note that walleyes taken from below the Pig's Eye Treatment plant in St. Paul have shown sterility and lowered levels of testosterone. Every species of freshwater mussel in the river faces extinction and biologists warn of a total ecosystem collapse.

Recreational boaters want more marinas, more riverside restaurants, expanded docking facilities and additional places to refuel and reprovision their boats. Commercial fisherman long for a return to a slower moving, less crowded, more courteous river.

Owners of barges and shippers of grain call for further modification of the river. They point to the need for a still deeper channel and the lengthening of the five most congested lower locks from 600 to 1200 feet to speed the passage of tows. The river, to them, is first and foremost an industrial canal, a transportation system for industry. They point to the increased costs to shippers and farmers as barges wait, sometimes for hours, to go through the locks.

The question of who owns the river, how to use it, how to share it, whose needs should take precedence, has never been satisfactorily answered. It is as if Mary Gibbs were still standing with her hand on the sluice gate lever and the foreman was threatening to shoot it off. Barge companies, farmers shipping grain to international markets, recreational boaters, sportsmen, hunters, commercial fishermen, environmentalists, urban planners—all have legitimate claims on the river. How those claims are negotiated, how the river is shared and protected, how the needs of clams, fish and waterfowl are reconciled with those of jet skiers, fishermen and growers of corn will determine how this century of life is experienced in the valley of the Upper Mississippi.

The Mississippi River remains an enormous force of nature, constant in its presence. It is a national historic and ecological treasure that has served, over the centuries, as the pulsing artery of the continent, the subject of song and of story, the source of life and the bearer of destruction. Its watershed is one million square miles, 41 percent of the continental United States. The Mississippi River valley is twenty percent larger than that of China's Yellow River, twice that of Africa's Nile and fifteen times that of the Rhine. Measured from the headwaters of the Missouri, its greatest tributary, the Mississippi is the longest river in the world.

The river flows through ten states, most of it along state borders which means that no state considers protection of the river system as its exclusive problem. Besides the states, a host of government agencies share management of the river including four regions of the U.S. Environmental Protection Agency (EPA), two regions of the U.S. Fish and Wildlife Service, two divisions and six districts of the U.S. Army Corps of Engineers, the National Park Service, the U.S. Coast Guard, the Department of Agriculture and the Upper Mississippi River Basin Association (UMRBA).

The river is crucial habitat for many fish and wildlife species. It is home to 241 species of fish, 300 bird species, 50 species of mammals, 45 species of reptiles and amphibians and 37 species of mussels. The river corridor is a major flyway for migratory birds including 40% of North America's ducks, geese, swans and wading birds. Three-quarters of the nation's entire canvasback duck population spend time on the Mississippi. About 60% of all of the bird species of the United States (excepting Alaska and Hawaii) travel on the Mississippi flyway. Tens of thousands of birds depend on a stopover on the Upper Mississippi for rest and refueling during their annual migration.

It may be only through music and story that we can grasp the ineffable nature of rivers as mighty as the Mississippi. The waterfowl of the world follow its bounty into the northlands. Life forms beyond counting live in its flow. Great cities spring up and are nourished on its bosom. Artists and poets find their inspiration on the river; fishermen and hunters live off its gifts. Midwest grain farmers depend on the river for their life-link to global markets. The breadbasket of the world floats down the waters of the Mississippi.

> *A single drop of water falls*
> *Into the tumult of a rushing chasm.*
>
> *Through air, onto rocks,*
> *Roots and pebbles, mosses and grasses.*
>
> *From the highest point, in all directions*
> *Seaward.*
>
> *Simple beginning for an avalanche*
> *That will divide a continent*
> *In two.*
>
> —Steven Cole DeCoster

NOTES

John Brown's Body by Stephen Vincent Benét appears in the poet's *Selected Works* (1942). Statistics on pleasure boating are based on a recent report by Dan Wilcox for the U.S. Army Corps of Engineers, "Effects of Recreational Boating on the Upper Mississippi River System." Remarks by Captain William Bowell were quoted from interviews held in August, 2002. Comments on fish and wildlife totals come from a report for the National Resource Defense Council and the Izaak Walton League, "Restoring the Big River. A Clean Water Act Blueprint for the Mississippi" (1994) by Ann Robinson and Robbin Marks. For the James J. Hill warehouse see *St. Paul Pioneer Press,* November 16, 2003. Steven Cole De-Coster's poem appears in his *Water's Edge* (2002) and it is quoted with his permission.

LIST OF ILLUSTRATIONS AND MAPS

INDEX